The Freedom Not to Speak

The Freedom
Not to Speak

Haig Bosmajian

NEW YORK UNIVERSITY PRESS
New York and London

NEW YORK UNIVERSITY PRESS
New York and London

Library of Congress Cataloging-in-Publication Data
Bosmajian, Haig A.
The Freedom not to speak / Haig Bosmajian.
p.   cm.
Includes bibliographical references and index.
ISBN 0-8147-1297-5 (cloth : alk paper)
1. Freedom of speech—United States—History.   2. Silence (Law)—
United States—History.   3. Confession (Law)—United States—
History.   4. Self-incrimination—United States—History.
I. Title.
KF4772.B67   1999
342.73'0853—dc21   98-33383
                              CIP

New York University Press books are printed on acid-free paper,
and their binding materials are chosen for strength and durability.

Manufactured in the United States of America

10 9 8 7 6 5 4 3 2 1

Contents

Introduction

Through the centuries, men and women have been coerced by church and state to "sacrifice to the gods," to recant, to sign loyalty oaths, to disclose their associational ties, to reveal their political and religious beliefs, to name names, to become informers. Declare whether you believe the king is supreme; deny papal supremacy! Declare whether you believe the earth to be the center of the universe! Do you believe in Marxism? State whether you believe in God! Supply us with the names of your political acquaintances! Declare or be punished!

For over two decades in the middle of the twentieth century, the United States was a land where local, state, and federal governments were sending to prison their "heretical" citizens who refused to speak when asked to disclose their political beliefs and associations. Those who were not jailed were blacklisted, lost their jobs, or left the country as self-exiles.

On February 13, 1946, Dr. Edward Barsky appeared before the House Committee on Un-American Activities (HUAC), refused to produce for the committee "all books, ledger sheets, documents and writings evidencing the receipt of money by the Joint Anti-Fascist Refugee Committee," and as a consequence was tried, convicted, and sentenced to jail for willful failure to produce the records. When in *Barsky v. United States* (1948) the United States Court of Appeals decided against Barsky, Judge Henry Edgerton dissented, arguing that HUAC's investigation "restricts freedom of speech by forcing people to express views. Freedom of speech is freedom in respect to speech and includes freedom not to speak. 'To force an American citizen publicly to profess any statement of belief' is to violate the First Amendment."[1] The United States Supreme Court refused to consider the case.[2] The June 15, 1948, *New York Times* reported: "Eleven leaders of the Joint Anti-Fascist Refugee Committee today were denied a Supreme Court review of their convictions of contempt of Congress. . . . Dr. Edward K. Barsky, a surgeon and chairman of the Joint Anti-Fascist Refugee Committee, was sentenced to six months imprisonment. His ten associates received three months each."[3]

In 1947, a HUAC subcommittee, chaired by newly elected representative Richard Nixon and conducting an investigation into "un-American Propaganda Activities in the United States," was confronted by Leon Josephson, who refused to be sworn in to testify. The following colloquy took place between Nixon and the subpoenaed Josephson:

> *Nixon:* Will you stand and be sworn at this time?
>
> *Josephson:* I will not.
>
> *Nixon:* You refuse to be sworn?
>
> *Josephson:* I contest the right, the legality of this committee to examine me.
>
> *Nixon:* You contest the legality of this committee, and on that ground you refuse to be sworn?
>
> *Josephson:* That is correct.
>
> *Nixon:* On the ground that you question the legality of this committee?
>
> *Josephson:* That is correct.[4]

As a result of his refusal to testify before the committee, Josephson was cited for contempt of Congress and jailed. As reported in the October 16, 1947, *New York Times:* "Leon Josephson, who as a Communist was part of the pre-war underground seeking the elimination of Hitler, was jailed yesterday afternoon to begin a one-year sentence for his refusal to testify on March 5 before a subcommittee of the House Committee on Un-American Activities."[5]

When the United States Court of Appeals decided against Josephson, Judge Charles Clark dissented in *United States v. Josephson* (1948), beginning his dissenting opinion by emphasizing at the outset the importance of the issue being considered by the court, "whether this defendant was properly deprived of his liberty" after he refused to appear before HUAC: "I find it neither easy nor pleasant to disagree on this issue, one of the more momentous which has come before us."[6] Judge Clark reiterated the significance and gravity of the issue in this case: "[T]he necessity of decision becomes all the more pressing when, as I think it obvious, no more extensive search into the hearts and minds of private citizens can be thought of or expected than that we have before us. If this is legally possible, it can be asserted dogmatically that investigation of private opinion is not really protected under the Bill of Rights. In other words, there will then have been discovered a blank spot in the protection covering that venerated document."[7]

The views of Judges Edgerton and Clark did not prevail, and that "blank spot" in the Bill of Rights remained. Expressing concern about the punishment of the Hollywood writers and directors who refused to answer questions put to them by HUAC in 1947, Charles Curtis, special assistant to the Undersecretary of State during World War II, wrote in 1948: "We have a right to be secure in our persons, houses, papers, and effects against unreasonable searches and seizures. This is the Fourth Amendment. I do not believe this goes far enough to make our political opinions secure against interrogation. . . . We have the right to speak. Have we equally a right to choose when to speak? Perhaps we should have. Constitutionally we have not got it yet."[8]

In 1955, legal scholar Leo Pfeffer also noted the absence of any clearly defined freedom not to speak: "To what extent Congress may infringe upon a private citizen's right to silence in order to carry out its 'informing function' remains yet to be definitely decided by the Supreme Court."[9] The freedom not to speak was especially emphasized by constitutional authority Milton Konvitz in 1957: "The freedom *not* to speak, not to profess beliefs, may be more important than the freedom *to* speak, since the *profession* of beliefs that one does not maintain may do more violence to the conscience than the *failure* to express the beliefs that one does maintain."[10]

In *American Communications Assn. v. Douds* (1950), a case dealing with the requirement that union officials sign a non-Communist affidavit, United States Supreme Court Justice Robert Jackson warned: "[I]f power to forbid acts includes power to forbid contemplating them, then the power of government over beliefs is as unlimited as its power over conduct and the way is open to force disclosures of attitudes on all manner of social, economic, moral and political issues." To those who might think that he was exaggerating, Jackson declared: "These suggestions may be discounted as fanciful and far fetched. But we must not forget that in our country are evangelists and zealots of many different political, economic and religious persuasions whose fanatical conviction is that all thought is divinely classified into two kinds—that which is their own and that which is false and dangerous. . . . It is not to be supposed that the age-old readiness to convert minds by pressure or suppression, instead of reason and persuasion, is extinct."[11]

The "evangelists and zealots" remain, and that "age-old readiness" to convert minds by pressure is not extinct. There remain in society individuals and institutions that would, given an opportunity, reinstate their coerced oaths and pledges, the investigations to identify the "enemy," the "godless," the "heretics." There is little reason to believe, on the basis of historical precedence, that we will not again be confronted with state, perhaps church, demands for public expressions and confessions of beliefs and associations. Present-day authoritarians replace seventeenth-century monarchs. Present-day fundamentalists replace fifteenth-century inquisitors. Intolerant majorities replace eighteenth-century parliamentarians who enacted oath after oath.

Attempts to coerce religious and nationalistic orthodoxy have continued through the centuries: the obligatory rituals, the compelled recantations, the mandatory loyalty oaths, the forced revelations of one's religious and political beliefs and associations. While in the first and second centuries Christians who refused to "sacrifice" to the Roman gods were burnt at the stake or beheaded, in the twentieth century American students of the Jehovah's Witness faith who refused to salute the flag were expelled from school and threatened with incarceration in reformatories maintained for criminally inclined juveniles.

While during the un-Catholic investigating committees of the fourteenth and fifteenth centuries "heretics" who refused to utter recantations were tortured or burned at the stake, in the twentieth century American citizens who appeared before the un-American activities committees and refused to take the posture of subordination and to name names were blacklisted and found themselves unemployable or jailed for contempt.

While during the sixteenth and seventeenth centuries men like Giordano Bruno and Galileo Galilei were ordered by the church to recant, to deny the truth of their beliefs, in the twentieth century scientists such as Linus Pauling and Albert Einstein who attacked the un-American activities committees and the compulsory loyalty oaths were denounced as un-Americans and traitors.

While in the seventeenth century Sir Thomas More was beheaded for refusing to take the oath demanded by Henry VIII, in the twentieth century professors, students, attorneys, and others who refused to sign the oaths demanded by local, state, and federal officials were denied employment or dismissed from their jobs.

The names of the "heretics" change; the ideologies of the inquisitors change; the wordings of the loyalty oaths change; the pledges and rituals change; the punishments change. But the oaths and inquisitors always remain, demanding that the citizen participate in the rituals, reveal religious and political beliefs, inform on other "heretics." Almost all who have refused these demands found, unfortunately, that there was no freedom not to speak to protect them.

There is more than sufficient historical evidence to demonstrate that church- and state-coerced speech for the past twenty centuries has led to ostracism, degradation, jailing, and death. As the decades and centuries pass, we look with dismay and regret on the forced recantations, the requirements to sign loyalty oaths, the demands to name names, to become informers.

We now condemn the church's demands that the fifteenth-century church reformer John Hus recant, right up to the time he was readied at the stake to be burned. We now condemn the church's burning of Giordano Bruno, who refused to recant, who was jailed for seven years, and who declared before his death that he "did not want to, nor did he wish to retract." We now condemn the forced recantation imposed by the church on Galileo. We now condemn the beheading of Sir Thomas More.

In his 1969 article titled "The Long and Unhappy History of Loyalty Testing in Maryland," Lewis Asper observed that in the aftermath of the eighteenth-century federal and state loyalty oaths imposed on Americans, "the whole process left the nation feeling a little embarrassed and a little ashamed."[12] Asper's article, appearing just as the two decades of anti-Communist loyalty oaths and investigations were coming to an end, concluded: "Perhaps such a feeling [of shame and embarrassment] is emerging again."[13]

A half-century after Hollywood's blacklisted screenwriters were denied screen credits for their contributions to such films as *The Brave One, Roman Holiday, The Defiant Ones, Bridge on the River Kwai, Lawrence of Arabia, Born Free, Broken Arrow, Friendly Persuasion,* and *Cry, the Beloved Country,* the nation finally recognized the shameful treatment of the blacklisted artists who refused to name names, who refused to reveal their political beliefs and associations. Films by screenwriters labeled "Communists" or "Communist sympathizers" and denied screen credits for their work in the middle of the twentieth century were finally being revised, at the end of the twentieth century, to include correct screen credits. On October 5, 1997, Bernard Weinraub wrote in his *New York Times* article titled "The Blacklist Era Won't Fade to

Black": "The blacklist still torments Hollywood. Even now, 50 years after many of the victims and accusers of the Hollywood blacklist have died, the movie industry is struggling to make amends for the McCarthy era, when it seems, almost everyone crumbled before the House Committee on Un-American Activities and its investigations of Communist influence." Condemning the blacklist today "is a safe cause," wrote Weinraub. "Yet the blacklist, in which friend betrayed friend, remains one of the darkest episodes in Hollywood's history. . . ."[14]

The feelings of shame and regret, our sense of the sordidness of church-and state-coerced speech, derive from the recognition that such compelled expression constitutes an insensitivity to human dignity. In his discussion of the church's order that Galileo speak "the truth," that is, deny "that the sun is the centre of the world and does not move," that he abjure, Sherwood Taylor has written: "From the modern point of view there is little need to comment on those proceedings, for who can but feel them to have been shameful, cruel, and useless? But even from the point of view of the seventeenth-century Catholic their legality is doubtful."[15]

In his discussion and condemnation of the "compulsory affirmation of belief," especially in the context of the required flag salute involved in *West Virginia State Bd. of Education v. Barnette* (1943), legal scholar Thomas I. Emerson has declared: "The full protection extended to the right of belief in the *Barnette* case is essential to an effective system of freedom of expression. Forcing public expression of a belief is an affront to personal dignity."[16]

The humiliations and degradations that came with the coerced naming of names and signing of loyalty oaths in mid-twentieth-century America were recognized in the 1950s by journalist Alan Barth, who asserted that "the protestations extorted by loyalty oaths and inquiries are humiliating—senselessly humiliating" and that insisting that a person become an informer was "a kind of degradation which any sensitive man might understandably desire to escape."[17]

When actor Larry Parks testified before HUAC on March 21, 1951, he expressed in an opening statement his dismay at being coerced into answering questions about his political associations and into revealing to the committee names of other actors about whom it was inquiring. He pleaded with the committee not to force him to "crawl through the mud": "I don't think I would be here today if I weren't a star, because you know as well as I, even better, that I know nothing that I believe would be of great service to this country. I think my career has been ruined because of this, and I would appreciate not having to—don't present me with the choice of either being in contempt of this committee and going to jail or forcing me to really crawl through the mud to be an informer, for what purpose?"[18]

Later that same day, Parks again pleaded with the committee not to force him to become an informer: "And I have told you I think to force me to do something like this is not befitting this committee. I don't think this is American justice to make me choose one or the other or be in contempt of this committee, which is a committee of my government, or crawl through the mud for no purpose, because you know who these people are. This is what I beg you not to do."[19] Parks's "begging" was of no avail; HUAC demanded he name names, and Parks eventually identified several acquaintances as being Communists.

Playwright Arthur Miller, who had refused to answer questions put to him by HUAC, upon being asked, "Was Arnaud d'Usseau chairman at this meeting of Communist writers which took place in 1947 at which you were in attendance?" responded: "[M]y conscience will not permit me to use the name of another person."[20] Miller was cited for contempt of Congress and was convicted; in 1958 the conviction was overturned on a "technicality."[21]

In 1948, Washington state's own un-American activities committee, the Canwell Committee, conducted hearings focusing at one point on suspected heretical professors at the University of Washington. Several professors were subpoenaed, including philosophy professor Herbert J. Phillips, who refused to answer the all-important committee question:

> *Mr. Houston [committee investigator]:* Mr. Phillips, I will ask you if you are, or have you ever been a member of the Communist Party.
> *Professor Phillips:* For conscience—for conscience sake, and political sake, I refuse to answer the question.
> *Chairman Canwell:* Put the question to Mr. Phillips again. I wish to advise you, too, Mr. Phillips that your failure to respond, to this question, will be considered by the Committee a refusal to testify, and will be the termination of your testimony.
>
> *Mr. Houston:* Mr. Phillips, I will ask you if you are, or have you ever been, a member of the Communist Party.
> *Professor Phillips:* I must say that in light of the testimony that has

> previously been given, that I would regard it a violation of my
> principles, a violation of what I regard to be the most sacred—
>
> *Mr. Houston:* Mr. Chairman . . . [Phillips] is attempting to make a
> speech, and not responsive, and that he be instructed to answer the
> question "yes" or "no."[22]

Professor Phillips was cited for contempt, acquitted, and subsequently
dismissed from the University of Washington faculty, his conscience and
principles notwithstanding.

The Canwell Committee also subpoenaed University of Washington
English professor Joseph Butterworth, who, like Phillips, would not an-
swer the committee's question about his membership in the Communist
Party "because of conscience":

> *Mr. Houston:* Mr. Butterworth, are you, or have you ever been a
> member of the Communist Party?
>
> *Mr. Hatten [Butterworth's attorney]:* I object to that question, Your
> Honor.
>
> *Chairman Canwell:* You will make no further vocal objection, Mr.
> Hatten. If you do you will be removed. Now, Mr. Butterworth may
> answer the question.
>
> *Mr. Hatten:* I advise you not to answer the question.
>
> *Professor Butterworth:* Mr. Chairman, because of conscience and be-
> cause I should not be required to testify against myself, I will de-
> cline to answer that question.[23]

Professor Butterworth was cited for contempt, convicted, and dismissed
from the University of Washington faculty, his conscience notwithstanding.

Comedian and actor Zero Mostel's refusal to become an informer was
based partly on ethical-religious grounds; as Victor Navasky has reported: "When the comic actor Zero Mostel was called in by the producer of a play in which he was appearing and told he had to clear his
name [Mostel had refused to answer HUAC questions and was black-
listed], Mostel, the son of a rabbi, explained that he couldn't inform,
because 'as a Jew if I inform, I can't be buried on sacred ground.' "[24]

Albert Einstein argued in 1953 that the refusal to testify before the
un-American activities committees should not be based on the Fifth
Amendment, "but on the assertion that it is shameful for a blameless

citizen to submit to such an inquisition and that this kind of inquisition violates the Constitution."[25]

On May 10, 1954, professor of mathematics at the University of Michigan Horace Chandler Davis appeared before HUAC and did not rely on the Fifth Amendment when he refused to answer the committee's questions related to his beliefs and associations; instead, he relied on the First Amendment:

> *Mr. Tavenner [HUAC counsel]:* During the period of time that you were at Harvard as an undergraduate, say between 1942 and 1945, were you aware of the existence on the campus or in Cambridge of an organized group of the Communist Party made up chiefly of members of the student body of Harvard?
>
> *Mr. Davis:* This a question concerning my political associations, I believe, and I will refuse to answer all such questions before this committee.
>
> *Mr. Tavenner:* I suggest that the witness be directed to answer the question.
>
> *Mr. Clardy [Representative]:* The witness is so directed.
>
> *Mr. Davis:* I don't believe I am under any legal compulsion to answer that question. I believe that when you direct me to answer a question concerning my political beliefs or my political affiliations, that it entirely without force. You are a congressional committee, and you can take no action which will infringe freedom of speech or freedom of assembly, and I maintain that questions concerning my politics under these circumstances do infringe my rights in that respect.
>
> *Mr. Scherer [Representative]:* Do you consider the Communist Party to be a political party, as we hold political parties in the United States, Doctor?
>
> *Mr. Davis:* Mr. Scherer, that is again a political question. You are asking my evaluation of a political subject, and I am not going to answer that either.[26]

In explaining further his reliance on the First Amendment in refusing to answer the above question, Dr. Davis told the committee: "It seems to me that such a question infringes my freedom of speech. It infringes my freedom of speech because it seeks to oblige me to discuss my political activities and my political opinions under highly abnormal circumstances. . . . I would claim . . . it also infringes the freedom of speech of people who are not on the stand. It infringes the freedom of speech of everyone in that it acts as a threat—it implies a threat that if their opinions are not such as meet with the favor of this committee, they may be subjected to the same sort of treatment that the witnesses today are being subjected to, and in that respect it opens the way to stigmatization of political views which would lead the citizens to make political choice on the basis of fear rather than on the basis of reason."[27] Professor Davis was cited for contempt of Congress and was convicted by a United States district court.[28] The First Amendment did not save him.

"The HUAC hearings were degradation ceremonies," observes Navasky in his *Naming Names*: "Their job was not to legislate or even to discover subversives (that had already been done by intelligence agencies and their informants) so much as it was to stigmatize."[29]

The degradation ceremonies, the coerced speech, constituted an affront to human dignity. For a quarter of a century the power of the state was used to intrude into the citizen's inner, intimate, personal beliefs and thoughts. For a quarter of a century the power of the state was used to do violence to the citizen's conscience, to force participation in humiliating rituals. As philosopher Avishai Margalit has argued in *The Decent Society*, the decent society is "one whose institutions do not humiliate people" and "cause people to compromise their integrity."[30]

However, when the courts in the United States have decided cases involving individuals who refused publicly to divulge their political beliefs and associations when commanded to do so by the state, the courts' arguments have not been based on premises dealing with dignity, integrity, degradation, humiliation, or stigmatizing. If the courts did give any constitutional protection to those who refused to sign the loyalty oaths and disclaimer affidavits and to those who refused to answer HUAC questions, this protection was based on arguments dealing with academic freedom, the vagueness of the oaths, or the "pertinence" of the inquisitors' inquiries. But the lack of "pertinence," academic freedom, or specificity of oaths did not save the heretics in *Uphaus v. Wyman* (1959), *Barenblatt v. United States* (1959), *Braden v. United States* (1961), *Wilkinson v. United States* (1961), *Konigsberg v. State Bar* (1961), or *In re Anastaplo* (1961). Nor did these lacks save the Hollywood Ten, who were sent to prison.

By the end of the twentieth century, those labelled un-Americans a half century earlier were having their reputations reestablished and were being recognized for their principled behavior in refusing to answer HUAC inquiries, to name names, to sign loyalty oaths and disclaimer affidavits. The quarter-century of blacklisting and jailing "unfriendly" HUAC witnesses, of requiring compulsory oaths and affidavits as a condition of employment, came to be recognized for what it was, a time of state-imposed humiliation, degradation, and intrusion on human dignity. What the heretics at the time recognized as unconscionable was acknowledged later by the nation as outrageous, contemptible, and damaging to both the individuals involved and the nation.

In 1994, the New York Public Library for the Performing Arts at Lincoln Center arranged an exhibit about the blacklisting and the un-American activities committees. It held a symposium, "Remembering the Blacklist," at which various actors, writers, and others spoke of their experiences, including Ring Lardner, Jr.; Kim Hunter; Madeline Lee Gilford; and Francis Chaney. Merle Debuskey, a theatrical publicist acquainted with some of the blacklisted artists, spoke of rights that were diminished or destroyed:

> There was absolutely nothing that came out of this except exploitation. No plot was unfolded. It was a hollow drum that was being beat, and beat loudly, which gave rise to headlines. Nothing happened. And the First Amendment, which had been in existence since the creation of this Government and was one of the great documents in the history of man, was diminished. And the right of people to have their political convictions and not have to reveal them if they didn't want to do so was destroyed.[31]

In 1995, the *New York Times* editorialized about the "victims of past injustices," including those blacklisted a half-century earlier:

> From the Communist world to South Africa, the collapse of old regimes has brought attempts to satisfy the victims of past injustices. In a quieter vein, some in Hollywood have been trying for years to redress grievances from the old era of blacklisting. That effort led last week to an honor to the blacklisted screenwriter Michael Wilson; he was awarded credit as co-writer of "Lawrence of Arabia." Mr. Wilson died 17 years ago, but the Writer's Guild is asking Columbia Pictures to change the credit for all future laser disks, cassettes or new prints of one of the most literate movies ever made.[32]

In 1995, a former member of the Reed College Board of Trustees apologized for the firing of philosophy professor Stanley Moore, who in 1954 had refused to answer questions about his political affiliations. In

1954, an HUAC ex-Communist witness identified Moore as a former member of the Communist Party. Moore was subpoenaed to appear before an executive session of HUAC in June 1954, and he refused to answer questions related to the charge that he had been a Communist in California in 1947 and to his current membership in the party. He argued that these questions "infringed upon (1) his freedom of speech as protected by the First Amendment and (2) his right to testify against himself as protected by the Fifth Amendment."[33] Within three months, Professor Moore, a tenured professor, was fired by the Reed College Board of Trustees. Four decades later, in 1995, one of the two surviving members of the trustees who had fired Moore issued the following statement of apology: "As the only surviving member [sic] of the 1954 board of trustees, I regret that body's action in dismissing Stanley Moore. I and others had reservations at the time and the passing of the years has erased any doubt in my mind: we were wrong in what we did and I apologize, albeit only for myself. In retrospect I just wish the board had possessed the fortitude to tell the McCarthyites, Congressman Velde [HUAC chair] and others of that ilk: 'Go jump in the lake.' "[34]

The Abraham Lincoln Brigade, one of the "un-American" organizations listed by HUAC and the United States attorney general a half-century earlier, was recognized in 1997 for its important and honorable role in the fight against fascism. The headline in the May 9, 1997, *Chronicle of Higher Education* read: "Honoring Those Who Took Up Arms Against Fascism." The article was an announcement of a New York art gallery exhibition titled "The Aura of the Cause: A Photo Album for North American Volunteers in the Spanish Civil War." What had been an "un-American" organization in 1950 became in 1997 an organization composed of "[e]arnest, serious, hopeful, and often very young" men and women. The exhibition catalogue stated: "Based on what we know now, it is not possible to overstate the danger we faced as fascism began to sweep across Europe. So hindsight should lead us to give special honor to the insight these men and women of the International Brigades possessed. . . ."[35]

In February 1998, a week-long commemoration was held at the University of Washington as a reminder of the 1948 Canwell Committee hearings, at which several professors refused to answer inquiries into political beliefs and associations and were subsequently dismissed from their tenured teaching positions at the University of Washington. Writing in a 1998 afterword to *False Witness*—a work authored by philosophy professor Melvin Rader that recounts his battle with the Canwell Committee, which had falsely accused him of Communist affiliations—attorney Leonard Schroeter wrote: "The McCarthy era gave its name to a form of political lawlessness characterized by the reckless destruction of individual rights, by vulgar demogoguery and overt reliance on exaggerated falsehoods. Its synonyms are still witch hunt and Inquisition, apt historic references to out-of-control abuse of power."[36] Eventually the nation recognized the impropriety of the use of state power to coerce speech.

However, we are left with the fact that the courts, especially the United States Supreme Court, upheld the convictions of many who refused to divulge their political beliefs and associations. The High Court has never admitted that it decided wrongly in *Uphaus, Barenblatt, Braden, Konigsberg, In re Anastaplo, Wilkinson*, and other cases in which punishment was inflicted on citizens who refused to reveal their political beliefs and associations to state authorities. Until the highest court in the land clearly indicates that American citizens have the freedom not to speak when the state inquires into political and religious beliefs and associations, until the High Court repudiates its earlier decisions penalizing and punishing Uphaus, Barenblatt, Wilkinson, *et al.*, we cannot be assured that the inquisitional inquiries and punishments will not come back another day.

I am not reassured by the predictions that all this is not likely to happen again. In 1965, Senator Charles E. Porter wrote: "The McCarthy episode was, short of war, one of the most dramatic and provocative events in this century, if not in all American history. It is unlikely that fate will ever again assemble a similar cast or write a comparable script."[37] Yet the history of church and state inquisitions indicates that it is more than likely, not unlikely, that a "similar cast" will assemble and "write a comparable script."

Richard M. Fried concludes his *Nightmare in Red: The McCarthy Era in Perspective* (1991) with guarded optimism: "Most Americans are now less gullible about the Red menace and slightly more attuned to civil liberties than in the past. This is not the firmest stay against a new time of troubles, but it may have to do."[38] "But it may have to do" is far from reassuring.

Blacklisted film director Martin Ritt (*Hud, Sounder, Norma Rae, The Front*), when asked whether the blacklist could happen again, replied by referring to those who refused to cooperate with HUAC and who refused to name names: "Sure, it's possible, but it's less likely because there was that core of people who did the right thing at that time."[39] "Sure, it's possible, but it's less likely" is, at best, a tenuous hope.

Writing about the dismissal of Jean Schuddakopf, a public-schools counselor in Tacoma, Washington, who refused to answer HUAC's inquiries about her Communist affiliations, Ron Magden concluded: "The Schuddakopf case demonstrates the weakness of educators in preserving academic freedom in the classroom. . . . The air of suspicion generated by the superpatriots destroyed morale among educators from the kindergarten level through high school. Intimidated instructors worried about what they said and to whom they said it. No one knew who the FBI informers might be." At the end of his article, "The Schuddakopf Case, 1954–1958," Magden asks: "Could the Schuddakopf case happen again?" His answer: "Certainly . . . All it will take is another issue."[40] If history is any indication, "certainly" is most accurate.

Over the centuries, the issues have changed, but the demand to speak has not. Roman authorities demanded that Christians "revile Christ"; Henry VIII demanded that Thomas More take the loyalty oath; the church demanded that Galileo recant; colonial authorities demanded that colonists baptize their children and disavow transubstantiation; state and federal governments compelled Reconstruction-period attorneys and teachers to sign loyalty oaths; state officials required students to salute the flag; a variety of un-American activities committees coerced citizens to reveal political and religious beliefs and affiliations. Always the demand to speak, to utter what church and state demanded. Speak or suffer beheading; speak or be sent to the stake; speak or lose your job; speak or be blacklisted; speak or go to prison.

At the outset of this work, I have traced some of the continuing history of coerced speech over the centuries. Having established that the inquisitions—the demands by church and state that one recant, reveal religious and political beliefs and associations, sign oaths, name names—keep reoccurring century after century, I come to the conclusion that when another inquisition occurs we may not be in a significantly better position to protect the rights and freedoms of the future "heretics": We have yet to establish a clearly defined freedom not to speak and to apply this freedom consistently to control the state's power to penalize and punish those "heretics" who resist state-coerced political expression.

1

Heresy, the Inquisition, and Coerced Speech

What becomes clear as one reviews church and state coercions to speak in past centuries is that the procedures and ceremonies imposed by the authorities have remained much the same into modern times: the identification of the heretic; the opportunity, the demand to recant; the ritualistic "trial"; the public humiliation and degradation of the heretic; the punishment. Heretics of the thirteenth century were interrogated about their thoughts, opinions, and beliefs; they were required to divulge the identities of other suspected heretics; they were exhorted to recant and repent. The heretic who refused to utter what church and state demanded was subjected to some form of degradation before actual punishment was imposed.

Among the earliest to be punished for not speaking what the state demanded were the Christians who refused to "sacrifice" to the Roman gods and emperors. When the Christians themselves became dominant and acquired power, they instituted their own inquisitions and searches for heretics, demanding they recant or face various degrees of punishment. While these early coercions to speak what the authorities demanded involved a religiously oriented vocabulary—repent, sacrifice, Christian, gods, penance—the "trials" and rituals were as much political as religious. Century after century, secular authorities, along with the ecclesiastical courts, humiliated, tortured, and executed heretics who refused to utter what was commanded. What appeared as a religiously based refusal to speak became an act of disobedience to the secular authorities, a political act affecting both ecclesiastical and secular governments.

The "contagious disease" of heresy was seen as a threat to both church and state. As historian John A. O'Brien has indicated: "Conscious of the threat to social and political stability posed by the heretics, the emperors of the thirteenth century had enacted severe measures against them. The motivation was civil rather than religious or from any special attachment to the Holy See."[1] Theologian Harold O. J. Brown has said of this nexus between the religious and political treatment of heretics: "In establishing the Inquisition, the Christian church in the West called on the power of the secular state to help enforce its claim to spiritual dominion. Theology had become a political theory, or at least a theory with immediate and direct political consequences. . . . Christians began to cite theological doctrines as the authority for them to overthrow rulers and transform political structures—a thirteenth-century 'theology of revolution.' Heresy became a political event."[2] Henry Charles Lea writes in his classic work, *A History of the Inquisition of the Middle Ages*, that the story of Joan of Arc affords "another illustration of the ease with which the inquisitional process was employed for political ends."[3]

Christians refusing to "sacrifice" to the emperors; the Theodosian Code providing for a state religion; John Hus's refusal to recant resulting in his burning at the stake; Joan of Arc's disavowal of her recantation leading to her being sent to the stake as a relapsed heretic; Thomas More's refusal to take King Henry VIII's loyalty oath resulting in the beheading of More; Giordano Bruno's refusal to recant and his burning at the stake—such sacrifices, oaths, codes, and demands to recant were of consequence to both the political and ecclesiastical systems of the times.

In 112, Pliny wrote to Roman Emperor Trajan, asking for advice on what to do with the "atheist" Christians who rejected the gods of the Roman state: "I have never been present at an examination of Christians. Consequently, I do not know the nature or the extent of the punishments usually meted out to them, nor the grounds for starting an investigation and how far it should be pressed. Nor am I at all sure whether any distinction should be made between them on the grounds of age, or if young people and adults should be treated alike; whether a pardon ought to be granted to anyone retracting his beliefs, or if he has once professed Christianity, he shall gain nothing by renouncing it. . . ."[4]

Pliny reports in his letter what measures he has already taken: "I have asked them in person if they are Christians, and if they admit it, I repeat the question a second and third time, with a warning of punishment awaiting them. If they persist, I order them to be led away for execution; for, whatever the nature of their admission, I am convinced that their stubbornness and unshakeable obstinacy ought to not go unpunished. There have been others similarly fanatical who are Roman citizens. I have entered them on the list of persons to be sent to Rome for trial."[5]

Pliny describes how he dealt with persons identified as Christians in "an anonymous pamphlet": "Among these I considered that I should dismiss any who denied that they were or ever had been Christians when they repeated after me a formula of invocation to the gods and had made offering of wine and incense to your statue (which I had ordered to be brought into court for this purpose along with the images of the gods), and furthermore had reviled the name of Christ: none of which things, I understand, any genuine Christian can be induced to do."[6]

Trajan's reply to Pliny may have answered some of his inquiries, but not others. Trajan asserted that repentant Christians who offered prayers "to our gods were to be pardoned"; in his reply to Pliny, Trajan wrote: "You have followed the right course of procedure, my dear Pliny, in your examination of the cases of persons charged with being Christians, for it is impossible to lay down a general rule to a fixed formula. These people must not be hunted out; if they are brought before you and the charge against them is proved, they must be punished, but in the case of anyone who denies that he is a Christian, and makes it clear that he is not by offering prayers to our gods, he is to be pardoned as a result of his repentance however suspect his past conduct may be. But pamphlets circulated anonymously must play no part in any accusation. They create the worst sort of precedent and are quite out of keeping with the spirit of our age."[7]

At least it can be said for Emperor Trajan that he advised that the Christians "not be hunted out" and that anonymous accusations were "quite out of keeping with the spirit of our age." Later inquisitors were more receptive to hunting out heretics anonymously accused. What is clear is that punishment awaited the Christians who did not repent, who did not offer prayers to the Roman gods, who did not "sacrifice" when ordered to do so by the state.

One of the first who refused to speak what the Roman authorities demanded was Bishop Polycarp of Smyrna, who was burned at the stake in 156 after the Proconsul unsuccessfully attempted to persuade him to deny his faith. Polycarp was told to "Swear by the genius of Caesar" and to say, "Away with the Athiests"—that is, the Christians. He was then told again, "Swear, and I release you; curse Christ," which he refused to do. Finally, the proconsul declared: "Unless you change your mind, I shall have you burnt." Polycarp was bound, placed on the pyre, and burned.[8]

Ten years later, in 165, several Christians, including Justin, were "brought before the prefect of Rome, by name of Rusticus." After they were questioned regarding their beliefs, the prefect Rusticus said to Justin, "First of all obey the gods, and make submission to the Princes. . . . If you do not obey, you shall be punished without mercy." Justin and his companions responded: "Do what you will. For we are Christians and offer no sacrifice to idols," whereupon they were sentenced: "Let those who will not sacrifice to the gods and yield to the command of the Emperor be scourged and led away to be beheaded in accordance with the laws."[9]

From 249 to 251, under the rule of the Roman emperor Decius, it was ordered that all inhabitants of the empire "participate in sacrifice to the gods by pouring a libation, burning incense, or tasting sacrificial meat. Commissions were set up throughout the state to supervise the sacrifices and to grant certificates of participation to those who complied."[10] While Christians were not required to renounce their religion, they, along with others, were coerced into participating in the sacrifice to the gods. The thousands who refused to pour the libation, burn the incense, or taste the sacrificial meat were executed.

When Cyprian, the bishop of Carthage, was put on trial in 257, the proconsul Aspasius Paternus informed him: "The most sacred Emperors Valerian and Gallienus have honoured me with letters, wherein they enjoin that all those who do not observe the religion of Rome, shall make profession of their return to Roman rites; I have made accordingly inquiry as to how you call yourself; what answer do make of me?" Cyprian answered: "I am a Christian, and bishop; I know no other gods beside the one and true God, who make heaven and earth, the sea, and all things therein." Refusing to profess his "return to Roman rites," Cyprian was ordered into exile, but was also commanded to become an informer; the proconsul, directing his remarks to Cyprian, said: "The letters, wherewith I have been honoured by the Emperors, speak of presbyters as well as of bishops; I would know you, therefore, who be they, who are presbyters in this city?" Cyprian replied: "By an excellent and beneficial provision of your laws you have forbidden any to be informers; therefore they cannot be discovered and denounced by me; but they will be found in their own cities." Cyprian spent a year in exile and was recalled and again was questioned. When told that "the most sacred Emperors have commanded you to conform to the Roman rites," he answered by declaring, "I refuse." Whereupon the sentence of the court was read: "It is the sentence of this court that Thascius Cyprianus be executed with the sword."[11]

In 303, the Emperor Diocletian issued edicts requiring Christian clergy to sacrifice to the Roman gods. Having sacrificed, they would be freed: "[T]he order was given that the presidents of the churches should all, in every place, be first committed to prison, and then afterwards compelled by every kind of device to sacrifice."[12] One year later, the order was made applicable to all Christians: "[T]he command was given that in the several cities all the people in a body should sacrifice and offer libations to the idols."[13]

But the demand that Christians sacrifice and offer libations to Roman emperors and gods was rejected by Emperor Constantine, who had converted to Christianity. His Edict of Milan in 313 declared at the outset that "we should . . . give to Christians and to all others free facility to follow the religion which each may desire, so that by this means whatever divinity is enthroned in heaven may be gracious and favourable to us and to all who have been placed under our authority." The edict then provided that "no one who has given his mental assent to the Christian persuasion or to any other which he feels to be suitable to him should be compelled to deny his conviction, so that the Supreme Godhead ('Summa Divinitas'), whose worship we freely observe, can assist us in all things with his wonted favour and benevolence."[14] No longer were Christians who refused to sacrifice or deny their Christian beliefs to be punished.

With the Christianization of the Roman Empire came the persecution of heretics whose beliefs differed from those of the established church and state. As Edward Peters has indicated, "A final legacy of western Christianity from the Roman Empire was the practice of coercing heretics back to the orthodox faith. Although, in principle, membership in the Christian community had to be purely voluntary, from the fourth century on coercion became one of the possibilities in Christian life, backed by the civil authority of the Roman Empire."[15]

In 390, the Theodosian Code, instituted by the Roman state, provided for a state religion to which all were to subscribe; those who did not subscribe were identified and labeled as "demented and insane" with "depraved desires and beliefs": "It is Our will that all the peoples who are ruled by the administration of Our Clemency shall practice that religion which he introduced makes clear even unto this day. . . . We command that those persons who follow this rule [belief in 'the single Deity of the Father, the Son, and the Holy Spirit, under concept of equal majesty and of the Holy Trinity'] shall embrace the name of Catholic Christians. The rest, however, whom we adjudge demented and insane, shall sustain the infamy of heretical dogmas, their meeting places shall not receive the name of churches, and they shall be smitten first by divine vengeance and secondly, by the retribution of Our own initiative which We shall assume in accordance with the divine judgment."[16]

The Theodosian Code further provided that heretics could avoid punishment through repentence and confession: "Although it is customary for crimes to be expiated by punishment, it is Our will, nevertheless, to correct the depraved desires of men by an admonition of repentence. Therefore, if any heretics, whether they are Donatists or Manichaeans or of any other depraved belief and sect who have congregated to profane rites, should embrace, by a simple confession, the Catholic faith and rites, which We wish to be observed by all men, even though such heretics have nourished a deep-rooted evil by long and continued meditation, to such an extent that they also seem to be subject to the laws formerly issued, nevertheless, as soon as they have confessed God by a simple expression of belief, We decree that they shall be absolved from all guilt."[17]

In 386, the first person condemned to death for what the church considered heresy was Priscillian, the bishop of Avila, who was first imprisoned and tortured and then finally executed along with six of his followers, all having been charged with heresy, immorality, and magic. Priscillian refused to plead guilty to the charges, but after being tortured he did not deny that he studied "obscene doctrines, held nocturnal gatherings even of disgraceful women, and prayed naked," the latter probably meaning praying with naked feet.[18] While one source has Priscillian "executed on charges of sorcery and Manichaeanism,"[19] another source has him "suffer[ing] death for heresy,"[20] and still another asserts that he was charged with "heresy . . . augmented with accusations of sorcery and sexual immorality."[21] Whatever the specific charges may have been, Priscillian was beheaded, along with his six followers, the first "heretical" victims of the church. The charges against Priscillian were further elaborated after his death, writes Virginia Burrus, "at least partly in an effort to justify his brutal execution. Severus and other fifth-century sources depict the Spanish teacher [Priscillian] as a gnostic seducer, a Manichaean astrologer, a Sabellian, a Samosatene, and the founder of a new heresy of 'Priscillianism.' ''[22]

By the beginning of the fifth century, in 425, it was commanded that "the Manicheans, heretics, schismatics, astrologers, and every sect inimical to the Catholics shall be banished from the very sight of the City of Rome, in order that it may not be contaminated by the contagious presence of the criminals." A "truce of twenty days" was offered, but "unless they return within that time to the unity of communion, they shall be expelled from the City as far as the hundredth milestone and shall be tormented by the solitude of their own choice." Within a month, the banishment penalty was extended to other cities: "We command the Manichaeans, heretics, schismatics, and every sect from the very sight of the various cities, in order that such cities may not be contaminated by the contagious presence of the criminals. We therefore order that all adherents of this unholy false doctrine shall be excluded unless a speedy reform should come to their aid."[23]

The heretics' power "to contaminate by their contagious presence" was a disease metaphor that was supplemented with other dreaded metaphors inviting punishment, exile, and death. In 1163, Englishman William of Newburgh wrote: "[H]eretics spread the poison of their wickedness through many lands. Indeed so many are said to have been infected by this plague throughout France, Spain and Germany, that they seem, as the prophet says, to have 'multiplied beyond number.' " Further, "[W]hen the fire of God kindles the zeal of the faithful against them they slink [like treacherous foxes] back into their holes and do less harm, though even then they continue to speak their poison secretly. Foolish and unsophisticated men whose power or reason are limited become so thoroughly imbued with this disease once they have contracted it that they are stubborn towards all discipline, and it is very rare for any of them to return to the faith after they have been discovered and dragged from their hiding place."[24]

The heretic was identified not only as a "contagious criminal," a plague, and poison, but also as a "pest," a "cancer," a "leper," and a "germ"; William of Newburgh declared: "To prevent the germ of heresy from spreading more widely the bishops had them publicly denounced as heretics, and handed them over to the king to be subjected to fleshly discipline. He commanded the mark of their heretical infamy to be branded on their foreheads, and ordered them to be driven out with rods and expelled from the city in view of the people, strictly forbidding anybody to give them hospitality or any comfort."[25]

Eckbert of Schonau composed several sermons in the 1160s directed against the heretic Cathars. In "Sermon 1," Eckbert attacks the Cathars with a series of denigrating, dehumanizing metaphors: "They have secretly corrupted the Christian faith of many foolish and simple men, so that they have multiplied in every land and the Church is now greatly endangered by the foul poison which flows against it on every side. Their message crawls like the crab, runs far and wide like infectious leprosy, infecting the limbs of Christ as it goes."[26] The Cathars, he wrote, "are extremely dangerous to the Catholic faith, which they crawl through cunningly, undermining and corrupting it like grubs."[27]

Such denigrating and dehumanizing metaphors carried with them the necessity for strong remedies and antidotes with which to defend the community. The heretic who refused to recant, who refused to recite the appropriate pledges and oaths, was seen as the most dangerous "disease" and hence the community's health called for his detection and eradication. In 1022, the French knight Arèfast, "with the help of God, and his own admirable native cunning," wrote Paul of St. Père de Chartres, "detected a wicked heresy which was active in the city of Orlèans and was spreading its vicious and deadly poison through the provinces of Gaul, and had it thoroughly crushed." Having posed as a "Simple disciple," Arèfast learned of the heretical clerics' "wickedness." The heretics had told him: "Christ was not born of the Virgin Mary, he did not suffer for men, he was really buried in the sepulchre and did not rise from the dead [and] there is no cleansing of sin in baptism, nor in the sacrament of the body and blood of Christ administered by a priest. Nothing is to be gained from praying to the Holy martyrs and confessors."[28]

Attempts were made to have these heretics "renounce their errors," but "they resisted with the obstinacy of iron." Whereupon they were "all commanded to put on the holy vestment of their order, and immediately stripped of them again with full ceremony by the bishops." With this humiliation ceremony completed, they "were taken outside the walls of the city, a large fire was lit in a certain cottage, and they were all burned, with the evil dust of which I have spoken above, except for one clerk and a nun, who had repented by the will of God."[29]

Six years later, in 1028, Archbishop Aribert discovered heretics in Monforte, Italy, near Milan, who professed: "We value virginity above everything. We have wives, and while those who are virgins preserve their virginity, those who are already corrupt are given permission by our elder . . . to retain their chastity perpetually. We do not sleep with our wives, we love them as we would mothers and sisters. We never eat meat. We keep up continuous fasts and unceasing prayer. . . . We hold all our possession in common with all men. . . . We accept the Old and New Testaments and the holy canons, and read them daily."[30]

An attempt was made to convert the heretics to the Catholic faith because Aribert "was greatly concerned that the people of Italy might become contaminated by their heresy. For, whatever part of the world these wretches had come from, they behaved as though they were good priests, and daily spread false teachings Wrenched from the scriptures among the peasants who came to the town to see them." If the heretics "wanted to embrace the cross, abjure their wickedness, and confess the faith which the whole world holds, they would be saved. If not, they must enter the flames, and be burned alive. So it was done: some of them sent to the holy cross, confessed the Catholic faith, and were saved. Many others leapt into the flames, holding their hands in front of their faces, and dying wretchedly were reduced to wretched ashes."[31]

By the end of the twelfth century, the church began its efforts to wipe out the Waldenses, heretics who refused obedience to the pope, believed that lay men and women had a right to preach, denied purgatory, denied the cult of saints, and refused to take oaths because Biblical text declared, "Swear not at all." Over the next four centuries, thousands of Waldenses were required to abjure or face imprisonment or death. Lea has written: "The sincerity with which the Waldenses adhered to their beliefs is shown by the thousands who cheerfully endured the horrors of the prison, the torture-chamber, and the stake, rather than return to a faith which they believed to be corrupt. I have met with a case in 1320, in which a poor old woman at Pamiers submitted to the dreadful sentence of heresy simply because she would not take an oath. She answered all interrogations on points of faith in orthodox fashion, but though offered her life if she would swear on the Gospels, she refused to burden her soul with the sin, and for this she was condemned as a heretic."[32]

In the thirteenth century, a series of edicts, laws, and pronouncements defined the heretics and the punishments to be imposed on those who refused to abjure. Those who refused to speak as commanded were not simply imprisoned or sent to their deaths; the ritual included public degradation and humiliation. In 1231, the *Liber Augustalis* of Frederick II heaped one denigrating metaphor upon another in describing and condemning the heretic being led to his or her public burning. Heretics, it was declared, "inside were violent wolves, but they pretend the tameness of sheep until they can get inside the sheepfold of the Lord. They are the most evil angels. They are the sons of depravity from the father of wickedness and the author of evil, who are resolved to deceive simple souls. They are snakes who deceive doves. They are serpents who seem to creep in secretly and, under the sweetness of honey, spew out poison. While they pretend to administer the food of life, they strike from their tails. They mix up a potion of death as a certain very deadly poison." These heretics, who were "unwilling to relinquish the insidious darkness of the Devil and to recognize the God of Light," it was concluded, "should be condemned to suffer the death for which they strive. Committed to the judgment of the flames, they should be burned alive in the sight of the people."[33]

In 1229, the Council of Toulouse promulgated a decree which, after providing that heretics had to be hunted down and publicly identified, stated: "A *haereticus vestitus* who of his own free will abjures heresy is not to remain living in the same place if the area is believed to harbour other heretics. He must be moved to a staunch Catholic district, of good repute. Such converts are to wear two crosses on their outer garment, one on the right and the other on the left side, and of a different color from the garment itself. . . . They shall be ineligible for public office or any legal function till their rehabilitation (after suitable penance) by the Pope or his Legate."[34]

While the church had issued decrees before the thirteenth century providing that secular authorities were to prosecute heretics who refused to recant and stipulating various punishments, "the repression of heresy . . . remained unorganized."[35] As Jean Plaidy indicates in her classic work *The Spanish Inquisition*, "When in the twelfth century Pope Innocent III commanded members of the Church to persecute suspected heretics, he heralded the birth of the Inquisition, although this was not firmly established as such until the reign of Pope Gregory IX."[36] In 1233, Gregory issued the bull *Ille humani generis* designating the Dominicans as the inquisitors to detect the heretics and sentence them; thus "for the first time there now existed a body of law that, under the initiative of the papacy, placed the punishment of the enemies of the faith under exempt jurisdiction. This marked the birth of the Inquisition. . . ."[37]

G. G. Coulton also sees Pope Gregory IX's bull as the beginning of "the full blown Inquisition."[38] Similarly, Malcolm Lambert, after reviewing previous anti-heretical legislation, concludes that with Gregory's decrees issued between 1231 and 1233, "the papal inquisition of the Middle Ages was born."[39]

Recantation was what the inquisitors were primarily interested in; the goal was to have the heretic utter, through coercion if necessary, a rejection of the heretical beliefs and an acceptance of Church orthodoxy. As Lea has observed: "The duty of the inquisitor . . . was distinguished from that of the ordinary judge by the fact that the task assigned to him was the impossible one of ascertaining the secret thoughts and opinions of the prisoner. External acts were to him only of value as indications of belief. . . . The crime he sought to suppress by punishment was purely a mental one—acts, however criminal, were beyond his jurisdiction."[40]

It was the inquisitor's purpose to lead the heretic into submission, to require the heretic to publicly recant, to utter what was demanded by church and state. As Gordon Leff has explained: "The heretic was one who persisted in his mistake, refusing correction after his fault had been shown to him. It was for obduracy that he was finally punished after all efforts to make him abjure had failed. Consequently the test of heresy was a moral and practical one—willingness to submit; and conviction for it was an admission of defeat. It meant failure to save a soul form damnation: in consigning a man to the flames he was being consigned to the devil."[41]

Various manuals for use by inquisitors searching out "heretical depravity" were issued immediately preceding and following the formal establishment of the Inquisition. The manuals described the procedures to be used in interrogating and punishing heretics. In 1325, the Dominican Friar and Bishop Bernard Gui completed his *Practica officii inquisitionis pravitatis*, "an elaborate work which summed up three quarters of a century of inquisitorial experience."[42] Gui warned the inquisitor of the deviousness of the heretic under examination and presents a dialogue to illustrate the heretic's tricky use of language. After the inquisitor tells the heretic that he "may be a heretic in not believing . . . matters which are to be believed," the heretic replies: "I believe all things that a Christian should believe." Whereupon the following interrogation takes place:

> *I.* [inquisitor] I know your tricks. What members of your sect believe you hold to be that which a Christian should believe. But we waste time in this fencing. Say simply, Do you believe in one God, the Father, and the Son, and the Holy Ghost?

A. [heretic] I believe.

I. Do you believe the bread and wine in the mass performed by the priests to be changed into the body and blood of Christ by divine virtue?

A. Ought I not believe this?

I. I don't ask you ought to believe, but if you do believe.

A. I believe whatever you and other good doctors order me to believe.

I. Will you then swear that you have never learned anything contrary to the faith which we hold to be true?

A. (growing pale) If I ought to swear, I will willingly swear.

I. I don't ask whether you ought, but whether you will swear.

A. If you order me to swear, I will swear.

I. I don't force you to swear, because as you believe oaths to be unlawful, you will transfer the sin to me who forced you; but if you will swear, I will hear it.

A. Why should I swear if you do not order me to?

I. So that you may remove the suspicion of being a heretic.

A. Sir, I do not know how unless you teach me.

Gui advises the "vigorous inquisitor" not to be taken in by the heretic's evasiveness, but to "proceed firmly till he makes these people confess their error, or at least publicly abjure heresy, so that if they are subsequently found to have sworn falsely, he can, without further hearing, abandon them to the secular arm."[43]

One of the best known manuals for inquisitors was Nicolau Eymeric's 1376 *Directorium Inquisitorum*, in which the following is said about treatment of the obstinate heretic: "Such a man . . . shall be shut up in prison, strictly confined and in chains. None except the warders shall enter his cell. . . . The bishop and Inquisitor . . . shall frequently summon him and instruct him in the truth of the Catholic faith and the falsity of those articles to which, in the obstinacy of his mind, he still clings. . . . But if he shows no willingness to be converted, there is no need for haste . . . ; for the pains and privations of imprisonment often bring about a change in mind. . . . And . . . the bishop and Inquisitor . . . shall try to bring him back by certain alleviations, placing him in a less unpleasant prison . . . and shall promise that mercy awaits him if he be converted from his errors."[44]

In 1401, the English Parliament enacted the statute "De Haeretico

Comburendo," noting that there were "divers false and perverse persons of a certain new sect [notably the Lollards], thinking in a damnable way of the said faith [the Catholic faith]." The statute provided punishment for heretics who refused to abjure: "If any person within the realm and dominions, upon these wicked preachings, doctrines, schools, etc. be convicted by sentence before the diocesan of the same place or his commissaries and do refuse duly to abjure the same wicked preachings, etc., or . . . after abjuration be pronounced relapsed . . . then the sheriff of the county of the same place . . . or mayor and bailiffs of the city . . . shall be personally present at the passing of such sentences by the diocesan . . . against such persons . . . and after such a sentence is promulgated, they shall receive such persons . . . and cause them to be burnt before the people in a conspicuous place; that such punishment may strike fear into the minds of others, so that no such wicked doctrines . . . or their supporters . . . may be in any way tolerated. . . ."[45]

In 1401, chaplain William Sawtre became the first Lollard to be burned after he had been "condemned for heresy, and who aforetime abjured, in form of law, and has now relapsed into the aforesaid heresy." The royal writ for the burning of Sawtre decreed that he "should be degraded" and be left to the secular court; the royal writ commanded the mayor and sheriffs of London to commit Sawtre "to the fire in any public and open place, within the liberty of the city aforesaid," and "cause him to be actually burnt in the same fire, in detestation of such crime, and to the manifest example of other Christians."[46]

But before Sawtre was sent to the stake, he was required to take part in the "degradation" ritual: "And in the sign of thy degradation and actual deposition, for thine incorrigibility we take from thee the paten and chalice, and do deprive thee of all power of celebrating the mass, and also we pull from thy back the casule, and take from thee the priestly vestment, and deprive thee of all manner of priestly honor." Further: "And in sign of this thy degradation and actual deposition, we take from thee the book of exorcisms, and do deprive thee of all and all manner of honour of an exorcist"; also, "in sign of thy actual degradation and deposition, we have caused thy crown and clerical tonsure in our presence to be rased away, and utterly to be abolished, like unto the form of a secular lay man. . . ."[47]

Another Lollard, John Badby, went to his death by burning in 1410, after he refused to assert that the sacrament of the body of Christ, consecrated by the priest upon the altar, is the true body of Christ by virtue of the words of the sacrament. As he was being prepared for the stake, Badby was admonished to "speedily withdraw himself out of these dangerous labyrinths of opinions." He was shown the sacrament and then it was "demanded of him how he believed in it" and he answered that "he knew well it was hallowed bread, and not God's body." Whereupon "the tun was put over him and fire put unto him." But as he cried out, "Mercy!" it was ordered that the tun be taken away and the fire quenched: "This commandment being done, he [the king's eldest son] asked him if he would forsake heresy, to take him to the faith of holy church? which thing, if he would do, he should have goods enough. . . ."[48] Again, Badby refused to utter what was demanded and finally succumbed in the fire.

In 1415, John Hus of Bohemia was burned at the stake after he refused to abjure. As Malcolm Lambert observes, Hus "refused because of his utter unwillingness to abjure articles extracted from his works that he did believe and to recant articles that he claimed were not his own."[49] In summarizing Hus's beliefs, David Christie-Murray has written that Hus was opposed to papal supremacy, "fulminated against worldly and corrupt clergy from the parish priest to the Pope, asserting that many popes had been heretics. Christ, not Peter (and, by implication, his successors), was the rock upon which the Church was built. . . . He allowed private interpretation of the Scriptures and preached that it was lawful for men to resist authority for conscience's sake. . . ."[50]

Before being sent to his death at the stake, Hus was required to appear before the Council of Constance, which decreed that "he be deposed and degraded from the priestly order." Matthew Spinka describes the degradation ritual in his biography of Hus:

> The seven high dignitaries order Hus to put on the vestments required for the celebration of mass. Thereupon, after exhorting him once more to recant, he was bidden to mount the table and from there spoke to the assembly, protesting his innocence. He declared mournfully that he fear to abjure "lest I be a liar in the sight of God." He then descended and the bishops proceeded with the ritual. First they took the cup from his hands with the formula of deprivation. . . . They disrobed him, pronouncing in each instance an appropriate curse. He responded that he was willing to suffer the shame for the name of the Lord. When it came to obliterating his tonsure, the bishops fell into a dispute among themselves as to the proper procedure: was it to be shaved with a razor or merely cut with scissors? Finally, they agreed on the latter method, pronouncing at the

same time the formula wherewith they turned him over to the secular arm. Nevertheless, before they actually did so, they placed on his head a tall paper crown on which were painted three devils fighting for the possession of a soul. The inscription on it read: "This is a heresiarch."[51]

Hus was bound to the stake and again exhorted to recant. Again he refused. The pyre was lit, but his body was not completely burned, whereupon more wood was added; his clothes were thrown into the fire to avoid their becoming venerated relics to his followers. The ashes were gathered up and thrown into the Rhine River.

In 1431, Joan of Arc was condemned by the church, which concluded that the visions she experienced and the voices she heard were "false and diabolical." She was declared a heretic and turned over to the secular authorities to be burned at the stake if she refused to recant. But first she was shown the instruments of torture in an effort to coerce her to abandon her claims of having visions of angels and saints, her refusal to "obey the mandate of the Church if contrary to the pretended command of God," and her refusal to give up wearing men's clothing. Being told that she faced burning at the stake, Joan agreed to sign a retraction, whereupon she was sentenced to perpetual imprisonment. However, within a few days she was again claiming that "God had told her, through St. Catherine and St. Margaret, of the great pity of this signal treason to which she, Joan, had consented in making the abjuration and recantation in order to save her life." Further, she again put on the male clothing that had been condemned by her accusers. On May 29, 1431, Joan was declared a lapsed heretic, and on May 30 she was taken to the scaffold with a paper crown on her head reading: "Heretic, Relapse, Apostate, Idolator." The pyre was lit. Her ashes were thrown into the Seine River.

In the 1500s, there was an increase in the number of Britons who refused to recant and to take the oaths demanded of them. In 1531, Thomas Bilney was burned at the stake after he refused, again and again, to renounce his heretical Lutheran views. Protestant John Frith, a follower of William Tyndale, critical of transubstantiation, refused to recant and was burned at the stake in 1533. In 1535, Bishop John Fisher refused to take the entire oath demanded by the Act of Succession; while he was willing to take the oath to the succession to the throne, he was unwilling to answer, "Would he 'approve the marriage of the king with the most noble queen Anne to be good and lawful'" and would he "affirm the marriage with the lady Catherine to have been unjust and unlawful?" Fisher was beheaded on June 22, 1535. Two weeks later, Thomas More, after a year's imprisonment in the Tower of London, was beheaded for refusing to take the oath repudiating papal supremacy.

In 1538, friar John Forest, who preached against King Henry's divorce, was charged with heresy, declared a relapsed and obstinate heretic, and burned at the stake. That same year, Protestant John Lambert, who denounced the worship of saints and refused to believe that the "Sacrament of the Altar is the Body of Christ," was also burned at the stake. Anne Askew died in 1546 at the age of twenty-five, burned at the stake because she refused to recant her anti-Sacrament views, even after being placed on the rack. In 1550, Joan Bocher refused to recant her Anabaptist views and was sent to the stake. Protestant John Rogers, a one-time Catholic, was burned at the stake in 1555 when he refused to recant, right up to the time he was led to the stake and offered a pardon if he recanted. Bishop Nicholas Ridley was declared a heretic and excommunicated, refused to recant, was degraded from the priesthood, and was burned at the stake in 1555. Bishop John Hooper also was sent to the stake in 1555 for refusing to recant after he was excommunicated, imprisoned, and degraded from his clerical orders.

In 1556, Archbishop Thomas Cranmer of Canterbury, rejecting transubstantiation and the Pope, was imprisoned, recanted, recanted his recantations, and was burned at the stake. Before being set afire, Canmer was compelled to participate in the degradation ritual conducted by church officials. He was "dressed in priest's vestments and degraded from the priesthood, his hair being shaved to remove the tonsure which he had worn for nearly forty years, and his fingers scraped to remove the unction from the hands that had been anointed to celebrate the Sacrament of the Altar. . . . After being successively degraded from the five minor ecclesiastical orders, Cranmer was dressed in a townsman's cloak and cap and delivered to the secular power."[52]

As he was led to the stake in his final hour, Cranmer publicly repudiated his recantations when told to declare that he believed in the true Catholic faith. Instead, he declared: "As things written with my hand contrary to the truth which I thought in my heart, and written for fear of death, and to save my life if it might be; and that is all such bills which I have written or signed with mine own hand since my degradation; wherein I have written many things untrue. And forasmuch as my hand offended in writing contrary to my heart, it shall be first burned.

And as for the Pope, I refuse him as Christ's enemy, and Antichrist, with all his false doctrine. . . ."[53]

In 1600, Giordano Bruno was burned at the stake after being imprisoned for seven years because he refused to recant his heretical views. Some of the charges against him were of a religious nature: "denial of Christ's divinity; mythical character of the Holy Writ; belief in universal salvation at the end of time, and particularly salvation of the fallen angels." Other charges concerned "the philosophical and scientific opinions set forth in the Latin and the vernacular cosmological treatises, especially in the *Cena de le Ceneri*, in the treatise *De l'Infinito Universo et Mondi*, and in *De Immenso*: eternity of the universe, plurality of the worlds, rejection of geocentrism, etc."[54] After the heretical propositions were read to him, Bruno was given several days to recant, but he declared that "he did not want to, nor did he wish to retract." [55] Bruno was excommunicated, and his books were burned and then listed in the *Index*. On February 16, 1600, Bruno was burned at the stake in Rome as an obstinate heretic refusing to recant.

Thirty years later, Galileo Galilei was brought before the Inquisition to be tried for heresy, for "having believed and held the doctrine—which is false and contrary to the sacred and divine Scriptures—that the sun is the centre of the world and does not move from east to west, and that the earth moves and is not the centre of the world; and that an opinion may be held and defended as probable after it has been declared and defined to be contrary to Holy Scripture; and consequently you have incurred all the censures and penalties imposed and promulgated in the sacred canons and other constitutions, general and particular, against such delinquents. From which we are content that you be absolved, provided that first, with a sincere heart, and unfeigned faith, you abjure, curse, and detest the aforesaid errors and heresies, and every other error and heresy contrary to the Catholic and Apostolic Roman Church in the form to be proscribed by us."[56]

After being threatened with torture, Galileo, on his knees before the assembled inquisitors, recanted:

I, Galileo Galilei, son of the late Vincenzo Galilei, Florentine, aged seventy years, arraigned personally before this tribunal, and kneeling before you, most Eminent and Reverend Lord Cardinals, Inquisitors general against heretical depravity throughout the whole Christian Republic, having before my eyes and touching with my hands, the holy Gospels—swear that

I have always believed, do now believe, and by God's help will for the future believe, all that is held, preached, and taught by the Holy Catholic and Apostolic Roman Church. . . .

Therefore, desiring to remove from the minds of your Eminences, and of all faithful Christians, this strong suspicion, reasonably conceived against me, with sincere heart and unfeigned faith I abjure, curse, and detest the aforesaid errors and heresies and generally every other error and sect whatsoever contrary to the said Holy Church; and I swear that in future I will never again say or assert, verbally or in writing, anything that might furnish occasion for a similar suspicion regarding me; but that should I know any heretic, or person suspected of heresy, I will denounce him to this Holy Office. . . . [57]

Having abjured, Galileo was placed under house arrest at his home in Arcetri, near Florence, and remained there until his death in 1642.

In the sixteenth and seventeenth centuries, a different group of people increasingly was required to participate in coerced speech, confessions, and recantations—witches, especially female witches. Witchcraft, Henry S. Lucas has written, "was a striking phenomenon of the sixteenth century. More people were burned for alleged relations with the devil and his minions than for heresy."[58] Prior to this time, while there had been demands made that witches recant or be punished, the "holy Inquisition, which in the thirteenth century came to the aid of the Holy Church against her intellectual foes, could find no time to deal with sorcery. . . . The penalty of sorcery was seldom death, and, when it was, could usually be escaped by abjuration."[59]

As Walter Wakefield and Austin Evans have pointed out, "though the Church censured the belief in man's ability to invoke demons, such belief was not initially considered heresy. Only slowly did the Church come to emphasize that communing with demons might involve veneration of them, which is heresy."[60] In his decretal of 1258, Pope Alexander IV declared: "The Inquisitors, deputed to investigate heresy, must not intrude into investigations of divination of sorcery without knowledge of manifest heresy involved. It is reasonable that those charged with the affairs of faith, which is the greatest of privileges, ought not thereby to intervene in other matters. The Inquisitors of pestilential heresy, commissioned by the apostolic see, ought not intervene in cases of divination or sorcery unless these *clearly savour* of manifest heresy."[61]

The debate as to whether sorcery was a heretical matter continued through the fourteenth and fifteenth centuries. As Lea has observed, "Evidently the difficulty of subjecting sorcery to the Inquisition was due to its having cognizance not of acts but of beliefs—or of acts only as evidence of beliefs—and this may explain why John XXII finally withdrew the black arts from its jurisdiction."[62] The debate as to when witchcraft and sorcery became heresy was taken up by a fourteenth-century lawyer, Oldrado da Ponte, who argued that "heresy, being a very serious crime, demanded both sure proof and initial careful definition. Simple sorcery, including love magic and abortion magic, is not heresy. The invocation of demons may be. If one calls up demons to *use* them, it is not heresy; if one adores them or offers them sacrifices, it is."[63]

Pope Innocent VIII's 1484 bull, *Summis desiderantes*, advised ecclesiastical authorities to search out and punish witchcraft; he stated that it had been brought to his attention that in Germany "many persons of both sexes, heedless of their own salvation and forsaking the catholic faith, give themselves over to devils male and female, and by their incantations, charms, and conjurings, and by other abominable superstitions and sortileges, offences, crimes, and misdeeds, ruin and cause to perish the offspring of women, the foal of animals, the products of the earth, the grapes of vines, and the fruits of trees . . . ; that they afflict and torture with dire pains and anguish, both internal and external, these men, women, cattle, flocks, herds, and animals, and hinder men from begetting and women from conceiving, and prevent all consummation of marriage. . . ." The papal bull concluded that "it shall be permitted to the said inquisitors in these regions to exercise their office of inquisition and to proceed to the correction, imprisonment, and punishment of the aforesaid persons for their said offences and crimes. . . ."[64]

In 1486, the influential encyclopedia of witchcraft and demonology, *Malleus Maleficarum*, was published by two Dominican inquisitors, Heinrich Istitor (Kramer) and Jakob Sprenger. The *Malleus*, Jeffrey Russell has argued, "defined witchcraft as the most abominable of all heresies, its four essential characteristics being the renunciation of the Christian faith, the sacrifice of unbaptized infants to Satan, the devotion of body and soul to evil, and sexual relationships with incubi. Witches have become servants of the Devil by making a pact with him and engaging in ritual copulation with Satan."[65] The *Malleus* went so far as to argue that disbelief in witchcraft was itself heresy.

Further, this influential work explained why there were more female than male witches, why "a greater number of witches is found in the fragile feminine sex than among men."[66] Their inquiry, they said, "will first be general, as to the general conditions of women; secondly, particular, as to which sort of women are found to be given to superstition and witchcraft; and thirdly, specifically with regard to midwives, who surpass all others in wickedness."[67]

Among the reasons "why there are more superstitious women found than men" are the following, according to *Malleus*:

> [Women] are more credulous; and since the chief aim of the devil is to corrupt faith, therefore he rather attacks them. See *Ecclesiasticus* xix: He that is quick to believe is light-minded, and shall be diminished. The second reason is, that women are naturally more impressionable, and more ready to receive the influence of a disembodied spirit; and that when they use this quality well they are very good, but when they use it ill they are very evil.
>
> The third reason is that they have slippery tongues, and are unable to conceal from their fellow-women those things which by evil arts they know; and, since they are weak, they find an easy and secret manner of vindicating themselves by witchcraft. See *Ecclesiasticus* as quoted above: I had rather dwell with a lion and a dragon than to keep house with a wicked woman. And to this may be added that, as they are very impressionable, they act accordingly.
>
> But because in these times this perfidy is more often found in women than in men, as we learn by actual experience, if anyone is curious as to the reason, we may add to what has already been said the following: that since they are feebler both in mind and body, it is not surprising that they should come under the spell of witchcraft.[68]

Further examples from Scriptures reveal that in regards to intellect and the understanding of spiritual things, women "seem to be of a different nature from men. . . . Women are intellectually like children. . . . No woman understood philosophy. . . ."[69]

"But the most natural reason" that woman, not man, is involved in witchcraft "is that she is more carnal than a man, as is clear from her many carnal abominations. And it should be noted that there was a defect in the formation of the first woman, since she was formed from a bent rib, that is, a rib of the breast, which is bent as it were in a contrary direction to man. And since through this defect she is an imperfect animal, she always deceives."[70] The wicked woman "is by her nature quicker to waver in her faith and consequently quicker to abjure the faith, which is the root of witchcraft. . . . And indeed, just as through the first defect in their intelligence they are more prone to abjure the faith;

so through their second defect of inordinate affections and passions they search for, brood over, and inflict various vengeances, either by witchcraft, or by some other means. Wherefore it is no wonder that so great a number of witches exist in this sex."[71]

Two centuries after *Malleus*, Ignatius Lupo da Bergama presented in his work on the Inquisition similar reasons why women were more prone than men to become witches: "They are talkative and tell whatever they know, so that a single one will corrupt a whole district. They are cowardly and cannot shake off sadness, giving the demon opportunity to tempt them. . . . They are credulous and ignorant and the demon can deceive them, often under the appearance of righteousness. . . . They are by nature fragile, so that the demon ensnared the first woman as the weakest vessel."[72]

Joseph Klaits has written that "everywhere, witchcraft was a woman's crime": "Evidence from about 7,500 witch trials in diverse regions of Europe and North America during the sixteenth and seventeenth centuries shows that nearly 80 percent of accused witches were female, and, in parts of England, Switzerland, and what is now Belgium, women accounted for over nine out of ten victims."[73] John Demos agrees that the evidence demonstrates that women were the accused witches, not the men: "The rule in early New England was that witches were women. Significantly, it has also been the rule elsewhere. Recent studies in European witchcraft, while uncovering much regional and period variation, agree on this one point—the primacy of women as suspects. . . . The great mass of the evidence, from whatever quarter, declares a profound connection between witchcraft and womanhood."[74]

The power of witches was portrayed as formidable, and their actions destructive: children were devoured; men had intercourse with succubi and women with incubi; infants were strangled; witches caused plagues of locusts, and poisoned cattle. According to *Malleus*, witches "send hail and lightning and evil winds; they procure sterility in men and beasts; the infants whom they do not devour they offer to the demon. . . . ; they cause horses to go mad under their riders . . . ; they make men impotent and women barren; with a touch they can kill the unborn child, with a look they can bewitch and kill . . . ; they have carnal congress with demons."[75]

The debate about whether witches were heretics was ongoing, whether witchcraft was punishable by ecclesiastical or secular authorities. As Wakefield and Evans have indicated in their study of heresy during the eleventh, twelfth, and thirteenth centuries, "Though the Church censured the belief in man's ability to invoke demons, such belief was not initially considered heresy. Only slowly did the Church come to emphasize the danger that communing with demons might involve veneration of them, which is heresy."[76]

Writing in 1981, Charles A. Hoyt asserts that "the development from heresy persecution to witchcraft persecution is not as simple and straightforward as it has heretofore appeared. The witch trials probably *were* developed from earlier heresy trials, but not in the smooth, self-assured manner which some historians have ascribed to the Church. . . . Witchcraft, like all the fine arts, passed at a certain point in its development from the clergy to the laity. . . . Following the Church's lead, the nations passed laws against witchcraft which eventually led to its being considered a state crime as well as heresy."[77]

From 1450 to 1750, Brian Levack has observed, "thousands of persons, most of them women, were tried for the crime of witchcraft. About half of these individuals were executed, usually by burning. Some witchcraft trials took place in the various ecclesiastical courts of Europe, institutions which played an important role in regulating the moral and religious life of Europeans during the Middle Ages and the early modern period. More commonly, especially after 1550, the trials were held in the secular courts—the courts of kingdoms, states, principalities, duchies, counties and towns."[78]

Malleus directed that "as with heretics, witches who have abjured the faith and wish to return to the Church are to be received as penitents without abandoning them to the secular arm, but are in every way to be restored to the bosom of the Church if they ask it. If they do not wish to return to the Church, they are to be left to the secular arm on account of the temporal crimes committed. . . ."[79]

A century after *Malleus* was first published, another treatise on witchcraft, *Tractatus de Sorilegiis* (1592), recognized the problem of distinguishing between witchcraft and heresy; for example, "Use of the Sacrament in amatory sorcery, if it is to ascertain whether a person loves another, it seems not to savor of heresy, because the help of the Sacrament is involved for that which belongs to the divine power—the knowledge of the secrets of the heart; but it is heretical if the knowledge is expected from the demon himself, and many now fall into this species of heresy. . . . To invoke the aid of the demon *per modum imperii* to tempt women to sin is not heretical; to learn the future savors manifestly of heresy. To invoke the aid of the demon *per modum adorationis* is always heretical." Further examples are provided to clarify what constitutes witchcraft and what is heresy: "The abuse of sacramentals—baptismal oil, chrism, holy water, blessed candles, palms, agnus Dei, etc.—is not heretical, as appears from the punishments decreed for this, which are not those of heresy—provided what is asked is within the demon's power and the invocation is not supplicatory. All this is sacrilege, not heresy. . . . Rebaptizing a boy in sorcery is heresy."[80]

While heresy and witchcraft both involved coerced speech, confessions, and recantations, the differences between the two were especially important in determining whether the trial was to be ecclesiastical or secular. In his 1622 commentary on witchcraft, after asserting that a "demon may throw the sufferer into a profound sleep and then insert articles [pieces of wood, knives, nails, etc.] through a cut [in the body] which he then closes" and that "plagues of locusts, snails, mice, and other vermin are frequently caused by witches," German bishop Peter Binsfeld declared that "witchcraft is worse than ordinary heresy, which is a simple sin, for it involves that and much more, because it leads to evil deeds, which heresy does not necessarily do. When there has been no evil wrought upon others, witchcraft is subject to ecclesiastical courts alone."[81]

In 1631, another tract on witchcraft, written by an official of the Roman Inquisition, Caesar Carena, distinguished between heretical sorcery and nonheretical sorcery, deviating somewhat from what had been defined as nonheretical a century and half earlier in *Malleus*. Carena stated: "Heretical sorcery is that which is exercised with any heretical speech or act or with abuse of the sacraments or of what the theologians call Sacramentalia, such as blessed oil and candles, Agnus Dei, etc., or when any sacred texts are used or the Symbol or Pater Noster or prayers, especially when a mortal sin is to be effected. Also when anything is asked of the demon which is reserved to God, as the resurrection of the dead, etc. Or in baptizing a child or a figurine or a corpse."[82]

What becomes evident is that while heresy was an intellectual crime, witchcraft was a demonic crime involving physical injury of some kind. Witches, wrote French judge Henry Boguet in 1590, "afflict people with all kinds of ills of the stomach and the head and the feet, with cholic, paralysis, apoplexy, leprosy, epilepsy, dropsy, strangury, etc. All this they do easily with the help of Satan, who secretly causes persons to swallow certain poisons and drugs. . . ." As usual in tracts dealing with witches and their powers, Boguet's *An Examen of Witches* warned of the sexual ills witches afflicted: "They also cause a man's virile member to disappear and be concealed, and then reappear at their own pleasure. ... At times also they prevent carnal copulation between a man and woman by relaxing the nerves and depriving the member of rigidity: at other times they prevent procreation by turning aside or blocking up the seminal ducts so that the semen does not reach the generative cells."[83]

In contrast, heretics were interrogated on matters related to beliefs, teachings, opinions, faith. Those who held heretical beliefs and opinions were required to recant, and upon refusing to recant, they were jailed, tortured, and/or burned at the stake. Deny that God is not a trinity! Deny that fornication is not a sin! Do you deny the papal power to release souls from purgatory? Acknowledge transubstantiation! In 1428, William White, a follower of John Wickliff, was forced to recant on the following points: "That men should seek for the forgiveness of their sins only at the hands of God. That the wicked living of the pope and his holiness, is nothing else but a devilish estate and heavy yoke of Antichrist, and therefore he is an enemy unto Christ's truth. That men ought not to worship the holy men who are dead. That the Romish church is the fig-tree which the Lord Christ hath accursed, because it hath brought forth no fruit of the true belief. . . ."[84]

While both males and females were tried and sentenced to death as heretics and witches, the fact remains that women were almost exclusively tried as witches and men as heretics. Carol F. Karlsen reports: "The single most salient characteristic of witches was their sex. At least 344 persons were accused of witchcraft in New England between 1620 and 1725. Of the 342 who can be identified by sex, 267 (78 percent) were female."[85] During the Salem witch trials in 1692, seventeen "witches" were hanged, twelve of them women.

The practice of hanging witches, not burning them, was followed in England and the colonies. On continental Europe both witches and heretics were burned at the stake. In England heretics were burned, witches hanged. While Agnes Waterhouse at Chelmsford was hanged as a witch in 1566, Bishop John Hooper was burned at the stake as a heretic in Gloucester in 1555. While Joan Byden was hanged in Kent in 1565 as a witch, Reverend Lawrence was burned as a heretic in Coventry in 1555. While Ellen Smythe was hanged as a witch in Essex in 1579, Thomas Bilney was burned at the stake as a heretic in 1531.

Heretics or witches, they had to be defined in such a manner as to invite persecution and extermination. To varying degrees, they were associated with Lucifer and said to behave like "apes," "corrupting like grubs." Their "message crawls like the crab, runs far and wide like infectious leprosy, infecting the limbs of Christ as it goes." The "diseased" heretics were "infected by this plague" and spread their "vicious and deadly poison through the provinces of Gaul."[86] Church and state searches for heretics and witches led to proceedings in which the authorities demanded that other witches and heretics be named and identified so that they, too, could be brought to "trial" to repent or be punished. Through the use of certain metaphors—"apes," "infectious leprosy," "disease," "grubs," "poison"—human beings were dehumanized, un-Christianized, and demonized, all of which invited repentance, punishment, confessions, degradation, imprisonment, or death by hanging or burning at the stake.

2

Coerced Speech in Early America

When the colonists left Europe in the seventeenth and eighteenth centuries to claim for themselves the lands in the "new world," they brought with them some of the compulsory rituals and oaths imposed by church and state. While they left Europe to find religious freedom, they did not hesitate to impose their own restrictions on freedom by demanding that colonists publicly declare their beliefs and faith. Compulsory oaths, punishment for church nonattendance and for refusing to recant heretical doctrines and beliefs—"These practices of the old world," wrote Supreme Court Justice Hugo Black in *Everson v. Board of Education* (1947), "were transplanted to and began to thrive in the soil of the new America. The very charters granted by the English Crown to the individuals and companies designated to make the laws which would control the destinies of the colonials authorized these individuals and companies to erect religious establishments which all, whether believers or non-believers, would be required to support and attend."[1]

The result was that "Catholics found themselves hounded and proscribed because of their faith; Quakers who followed their conscience went to jail; Baptists were peculiarly obnoxious to certain dominant Protestant sects; men and women of varied faiths who happened to be in a minority in a particular locality were persecuted because they steadfastly persisted in worshipping God only as their own consciences dictated."[2]

Delivering the opinion of the Court in *Torcaso v. Watkins* (1961) Black again referred to the coerced speech imposed on the colonists: "Indeed, it was largely to escape religious test oaths and declarations that a great many of the early colonists left Europe and came here hoping to worship in their own way. It soon developed, however, that many of those who had fled to escape religious test oaths turned out to be perfectly willing, when they had the power to do so, to force dissenters from their faith to take test oaths in conformity with that faith."[3]

The imposition of oaths was widespread in the colonies, and the person who refused to take the required oath lost various privileges and rights. As Leonard Levy states at the outset of *The Establishment Clause: Religion and the First Amendment*, "dissenters were excluded from universities and disqualified for office, whether civil, religious or military. Their religious institutions (churches, schools, orphanages) had no legal capacity to bring suits, hold or transmit property, receive or bequeath trust funds. Test oaths usually discriminated against dissenters. Every establishment employed such oaths, although some governments, such as those of the middle Atlantic colonies that had no establishments, also imposed religious tests on officeholders to make certain that only believers in the gospel would be entrusted with an official capacity."[4]

Punishments for dissension could also include fines, excommunication, jailing, banishment, and exile. In seventeenth-century Massachusetts, unless one professed the beliefs of the established authorities, one could be subject to banishment, as Sanford H. Cobb reports: "In 1646 the Act against Heresy ordained that any person denying the immortality of the soul, or the resurrection, or sin in the regenerate, or the need for repentance, or the redemption by Christ, or justification through Christ, or the morality of the fourth commandment, or the baptism of infants or 'who shall purposely depart the congregation at the administration of that ordinance,' or shall endeavor to seduce others to any of these heresies, should be banished."[5]

In Virginia, "Dale's Laws" were introduced in 1611 ordering punishment of those who did not participate in church services. The "laws" commanded "all Captaines and Officers . . . to have a care that the Almighty God bee duly and daily served, and that they call upon their people to heare Sermons, as that also they diligently frequent Morning and Evening praier themselves by their owne exemplar and daily life, and dutie herein, encouraging others thereunto, and that such, who shall often and wilfully absent themselves, be duly punished according to the martiall law in that case provided."[6] According to the law, missing church three times would be fatal: "[E]very man and woman shall repaire in the morning to the divine service, and Sermons preached upon the Saboth day, and in the afternoon to divine service, and Catechising, upon paine of the first fault to lose their provision, and allowance for the whole weeke following, for the second to lose the said allowance, and also to be whipt, and for the third to suffer death."[7]

In April 1699, Virginia law ordered punishment of persons Christian faith who expressed "denial of the being of a god or the Holy Trinity; asserted there were more gods than one; declined to recognize the truth of the Christian religion; and refused to acknowledge the Divine authority of the Old and New Testaments." The person persisting in holding the heretical beliefs faced three years in prison; however, as Gustavus Meyers points out, "the same law obligingly proffered a way of escape. If, within six months, the convicted person renounced his opinions, he was to be relieved of all penalties."[8]

While any heretic who recanted or repented could avoid punishment, the obstinate heretic faced severe penalties. As Meyers reports: "Any person more than sixteen years old, professing the Christian religion, who by word or writing denied any of the books of the Old and New Testament 'to be the written and infallible word of God' should be arrested. Then he was to be committed, without fail, to prison, and held for trial. Unless he publicly recanted after conviction, he was to pay a fine not exceeding 50 pounds or 'be openly and severely whipt by the executioner, not more than forty strokes.' And if, after recantation, he persisted in 'maintaining his wicked opinions he was to be banished or put to death, as the court should judge.' "[9]

Before Roger Williams was banished from Massachusetts, he was told to recant, but he refused. As Thomas Wertenbaker has indicated, Williams was charged in Salem with " 'diverse dangerous opinions' which were adjudged by all, Magistrates and ministers alike, 'to be erroneous and very dangerous.' But before pronouncing sentence they gave him time to meditate over his 'error' so that he could recant."[10] In 1635, Williams was sent into exile.

Anne Hutchinson, referred to by colonial governor John Winthrop as the "American Jezebel" of the seventeenth century, was also banished from Massachusetts when she refused to recant "two dangerous errors": "1. that the person of the Holy Ghost dwells in a justified person. 2. that no sanctification can help to evidence to us our justification."[11] As recorded in *Winthrop's Journal* in 1638, when Hutchinson appeared before the magistrates, "errors were read to her. The first was, that the souls of men are mortal by generation, but, after, made immortal by Christ's purchase. Then they proceeded to three other errors: 1. That there was no resurrection of these bodies, and that these bodies were not united to Christ, but every person united hath a new body, etc. These were also clearly confuted, but yet she held her own; so as the church (all but two of her sons) agreed she should be admonished, and because her sons would not agree to it, they were admonished also."[12]

The warnings, the "admonitions," were unsuccessful, though "she had given hope of her repentance." Winthrop records on March 22 that Hutchinson "impudently persisted in her affirmation, to the astonishment of all the assembly. So that, after much time and many arguments had been spent to bring her to see her sin, but all in vain, the church, with one consent, cast her out."[13] Hutchinson was excommunicated, moved to Rhode Island, and finally moved to New York, where she and her children were killed in an Indian raid.

"Recusant convicts"—Catholics who had refused to attend Church of England services—were denied suffrage in Virginia in 1699 by a law that read, in part: "[I]t is the true intent of this act that no woman sole or covert, infants under the age of twenty-one years, or recusant convict being freeholders shall be entitled to give a vote or have a voice in the election of burgeses." As Albert E. McKinley has observed, "this clause, by excluding 'recusant convicts,' deprived Catholics of the right to vote, an exclusion which was continued until the Revolution. . . ."[14]

Freemen in Massachusetts were required in 1643 to take the "Oath of a Freeman," which provided not only that the oath-taker would submit himself "to the wholesome lawes & orders made and established by the same [commonweale]," but also provided the following: "[A]nd furthr, that I will not plott nor practice any evill against it, nor consent to any that shall soe doe, but will timely discover & reveale the same to lawfull authority, nowe here established, for the speedy preventing thereof. . . . Soe helpe mee God, in the Lord Jesus Christ."[15]

Maryland's 1716 "An Act for the better Security of the Peace and Safety of his lordship's Government and the Protestant Interest within this province" required "all persons admitted to positions of trust in the province to take the oaths of allegiance, of abhorrency, of abjuration, and the disavowal of the belief in transubstantiation in the forms prescribed in the English statutes."[16]

Quakers especially were persecuted for their "radical" beliefs, including their belief that biblical authority required that they refuse to take oaths. William Berkeley, Virginia's governor in the 1660s, is reported by Harold Hyman to have "turned his fierce attention upon the 'turbulent' Quakers, whose meetings he felt were seditious and whose refusal to swear loyalty was self-convicting treason. Shrewdly, he let it be known that Quaker women were proselytizing among Negro slaves, which deprived the Friends of popular support. Berkeley's sheriffs raided Quaker meetings and dragged men and women worshipers to prison for their nonjuring."[17]

Quakers who entered Massachusetts in 1656 were confronted with laws that grew "more and more severe and culminating, two years after, in the doom of death on persistent return after banishment."[18] Massachusetts law provided that Quakers who persisted in returning to Massachusetts after being banished were subject to various punishments: "[E]very such male Quaker shall for the first offence have one of his ears cut off and be kept at work of correction till he can be sent away at his own charge, and for the second offence shall have his other ear cut off . . . and every woman Quaker . . . shall be severely whipt and kept at the house of correction at work till she shall be sent away . . . and for every Quaker, he or she, that shall a third time herein again offend, they shall have their tongues bored through with a hot iron."[19] Quakers who returned to New Haven, Connecticut, for a second time were to be "branded on the hand with the letter H, be committed to prison and kept to work till he can be sent away at his own charge. . . ." Quakers who returned to New Haven for the fourth time "shall have their tongues bored through with a hot iron."[20]

The requirement that colonists take test oaths as a precondition for holding office and voting was another instance of coerced speech, and one that was also widely demanded in sixteenth- and seventeenth-century England. So widespread was the use of loyalty oaths in England that in the middle of the seventeenth century, British politician and legal writer John Selden commented on the plethora of oaths: "Now oaths are so frequent they should bee taken like pills, swallow'd whole, if you chew them, you find them bitter, if you think what you sweare, twill hardly goe downe."[21]

The 1559 Act of Supremacy, "restoring to the crown the ancient jurisdiction over the state ecclesiastical and spiritual and abolishing all foreign power repugnant to the same," required "all and every archbishop, bishop, and all and every other ecclesiastical person . . . and all and every temporal judge, justicer, mayor, and other lay or temporal officer and minister, and every other person having your highness's fee or wages within this realm or any your highness's dominions" to "take, and receive a corporal oath upon the Evangelist," the oath reading: "I, A. B., do utterly testify and declare in my conscience that the queen's highness is the only supreme governor of this realm and of all other her highness's dominions and countries, as well in all spiritual or ecclesiastical things or causes as temporal. . . . therefore, I do utterly renounce and forsake all foreign jurisdictions, powers, superiorities, and authorities, and do promise that from henceforth I shall bear faith and true allegiance to the queen's highness, her heirs, and lawful successors. . . ."[22] All persons refusing to take the oath were ineligible to hold church and state offices.

In 1606, Parliament passed "An Act for the better discovering and repressing of Popish Recusants," which provided that "it shall be lawful for any bishop in his diocese, or any two justices of the peace . . . to require any person of the age of 18 years or above, which shall be convict or indicted for any recusancy (other than noblemen or noblewomen) for not repairing to divine service according to the laws of this realm, or which shall not have received the said sacrament twice within the year then next past . . . to take the oath hereafter following upon the Holy Evangelists. . . ." Any such person who refused "to answer upon oath to such bishop or justices of peace" or refused "to take the said oath so duly tendered" was to be punished by being committed "to the common gaol . . . until the next assizes or general or quarter sessions, . . . where the said oath shall be again . . . required of such person . . . ; and if the said person . . . shall refuse to take the said oath . . . every person so refusing shall incur the penalty of praemunire. . . ."[23]

In 1661, Parliament passed "An Act for preventing dangers which may happen from popish recusants," which required every person, peer as well as commoner, "that shall bear any office or offices civil or military" to take the "several oaths of supremacy and allegiance . . . by law established. . . ." The Act required still another oath: "And be it further enacted by the authority aforesaid, That at the same time when the persons concerned in this act shall take the aforesaid oaths of supremacy and allegiance, they shall make and subscribe this declaration following, under the same penalties and forfeitures as by this act is appointed. 'I, A. B., do declare, That I do believe that there is not any transubstantiation in the sacrament of the Lord's supper, or in the elements of bread and wine, at or after the consecration thereof by any person whatsoever."[24] Those who refused to take the oaths "shall be *ipso facto* adjudged uncapable and disabled in law, to all intents and purposes whatsoever, to have, occupy or enjoy the said office or offices. . . ."[25]

In 1662, the Act of Uniformity became law in England, and over a thousand English clergy refused to take its oath and suffered the penalties. The act applied not only to the clergy, but also to "every public professor elsewhere, and every parson, vicar, curate, lecturer, and every other person in holy orders, and every schoolmaster keeping any public or private school, and every person instructing or teaching any youth in any house or private family as a tutor or schoolmaster." The required oath read: "I, A. B., do declare that it is not lawful, upon any pretence whatsoever, to take arms against the king, and that I do abhor that traitorous position of taking arms by his authority against his person or against those that are commissioned by him, and that I will conform to the liturgy of the Church of England as it is now by law established; and I do declare that I do hold there lies no obligation upon me or any other person, from the oath commonly called the Solemn League and Convenant, to endeavour any change or alteration of government either in church or state."[26]

The refusal of Quakers to take the oaths imposed by English authorities led Parliament to enact in 1661 a statute "for preventing the mischiefs and dangers that may arise by certain persons called quakers and others, refusing to take lawful oaths." The act provided the following penalties: "That if any person or persons, who maintain that the taking of an oath in any case whatsoever . . . is altogether unlawful, and contrary to the world of God . . . [and] shall willfully and obstinately refuse to taken an oath . . . or shall endeavour to persuade any other person to whom any such oath shall in like manner be duly and lawfully tendered, to refuse and forebear the take of the same. . . ."—such persons upon conviction "shall lose and forfeit to the King's majesty, his heirs and successors, for the first offense, such as shall be imposed upon him or her, not exceeding five pounds."

Upon conviction a second time for this same offense, a fine of not more than ten pounds was imposed. The Quaker who persisted and was convicted a third time faced the following punishment: "[I]f any person after he, in form aforesaid, hath been twice convict of any of the said offenses, shall offend a third time, and be thereof, in form aforesaid, lawfully convict, that then every person so offending and convict shall for his or her third offense abjure the realm: or otherwise it shall and may be lawful to and for his Majesty, his heirs and successors, to give order, and to cause him, her or them to be transported in any ship or ships, to any of his Majesty's plantations beyond the seas."[27]

The Test Act of 1678, "An Act for the more effectual preserving the

King's person and government by disabling papists from sitting in either house of parliament," provided that "no person that now is or hereafter shall be a peer of this realm, or member of the house of peers, shall vote, or make his proxy in the house of peers, or sit there during any debate in the house of peers" and that no "person that is, or hereafter shall be a member of the house of commons, shall vote in the house of commons, or sit there during any debate in the said house of commons after their speaker is chosen" unless they had subscribed to and audibly repeated the following declaration: "I, A. B. do solemnly and sincerely in the presence of God profess, testify and declare, That I do believe that in the sacrament of the Lord's supper there is not any transubstantiation of the elements of bread and wine into the body and blood of Christ, at or after the consecration thereof by any person whatsoever: (2) and that the invocation or adoration of the virgin Mary or any other saint, and the sacrifice of the mass, as they are now used in the church of Rome, are superstitious and idolatrous. . . ."[28]

The widespread use of these loyalty oaths, which Quakers refused to take, led William Penn and Richard Richardson to write *A Treatise on Oaths* (1675), which they addressed "To the King and great Council of England, assembled in Parliament." They explained why "we cannot for pure Conscience take any oath at all: we dare not Swear because we dare not Lye, and that it may appear to the World, that we can speak the Truth upon easier Terms then an Oath: For us then to be forc'd to swear, is to make us do a needless thing, or to suspect our own Honesty. The first we dare not, because, as we have said, it is to take God's Name in vain; and we have no Reason to distrust our selves, being no wayes conscious of fraudulent Purposes. Why then should we swear? But much rather, why should we be imposed upon? It is a Saying ascribed to *Solon*, That *a good man should have that Repute as not to need an Oath; that it is a Diminution to his Credit to be put to Swear*. It becomes not an Evangelical Man to Swear, was a primitive *Axiom*."[29]

Penn and Richardson then provide pages of "*Memorable,* TESTIMONIES against Swearing, *collected out of the Writings of Gentiles, Jews & Christians; some of which were deliver'd to the World several Ages before* Swear not at all *was writ by* Matthew, *or spoken by Christ which makes* Swearing, *but especially* Punishing for not Swearing, *among* Christians, *so much the more* Disallowable."[30]

Socrates, Plato, Meander, Plutarch, Hesiod, Quintilian, Isocrates, and M. Aurelius Antoninus, among others, are cited in the section devoted to "the Sayings of Gentiles or Heathens, in Dislike of Oaths." Solon, "the famous Law giver of Athens, and one of those Seven Sages, exhorted the People to '*observe honesty more strictly then an Oath*. As if he had said, Honesty is to be preferred before Swearing, as another Saying of his imports, '*A good Man should have that Repute, as not to need an Oath; it is a Diminution to his Credit to be put to Swear. . . .*"[31]

In reference to Quintilian, Penn and Richardson write: "*Quintilian* saith, that 'in Time past it was a kind of *Infamy for Grave and Approved Men to Swear*, as if their Authority should suffice for Credit: Therefore the Priests or *Elamins* were not compelled to it; for then *to compel a Noble Man to Swear, were like putting him upon the Rack, etc.* Which shows an Oath to be an Unnatural and Extorting Way of Evidence, and that they preferred Virtue and Truth before an Oath."[32]

The "rack" simile appears again when Penn and Richardson cite Plutarch: "*Plutarch* . . . put the Question, '*Why is it not Lawful for* Jupiter's *Priest to Swear?* Is it because an Oath ministred unto Freemen is as it were the *Rack & Torture tendered unto them?* For, certain it is, that the Soul, as well as the Body of the Priest ought to continue free, and not be forced by any Torture whatsoever. . . ."[33]

After citing twenty-five of the "Gentiles or heathens in dislike of oaths," Penn and Richardson offer "Testimonies from the *Jews* in Dislike *of all Swearing*": "*Maimonides*, out of the most ancient of the *Jewish Rabbies* extracts this memorable Axiom, 'IT IS BEST FOR A MAN NOT TO SWEAR AT ALL."[34] "*Raimundus* quotes him thus, '*Maimonides* in tract. de juramentis; IT IS A GREAT GOOD FOR A MAN NOT TO SWEAR AT ALL; *The ancient and lawful Doctrine of the Synagogue.*"[35]

Having cited the "Gentile, heathens, and Jews," Penn and Richardson write: "These Testimonies, though they are of Weight with us, and we hope they will have a due Impress upon the Minds of many of our Readers; yet because nothing produced out of *Jews* and *Gentiles*, may advance our Cause with some, or render it ever the more acceptable, We shall next betake our selves to the more *Christian* Ages of the World, for Approbation of our Judgment, who we are sure will kindly entertain us, their Liberality being Extraordinary to our Cause; and from whom we shall never want *Votes* for SWEAR NOT AT ALL, while their Works are in the World. . . ."[36]

Penn and Richardson then proceed to present almost one hundred

"Christian" sources to support their rejection of oathtaking. They begin with Polycarp: "The first Testimony recorded against Swearing, after the Apostles Times, was that *Polycarpus*, who had lived with the Apostles, and was said to have been Disciple to *John*, not the least of the Apostles; for at his Death, when the Governor bid him Swear, *Defie Christ, etc.*, he said, '*Fourscore and Six Years have I served him, yet hath he never offended me in any thing.* The *Proconsul* still urged and said, *Swear by the Fortune of* Caesar; to whom *Polycarpus* answered, '*If thou requirest this Vain-glory, that I protest the Fortune of* Caesar, *as thou sayest, feigning thou knowest not who I am, hear freely*, I AM A CHRISTIAN. This Good man began his Fourscore and Six Years, which was about Twenty Years after *James* wrote *Above all things, my Brethren, Swear Not. . . .*"[37]

In citing Justin Martyr, Penn and Richardson write: "It was some time before his Suffering that *Justin Martyr*, who is the first we find writing of it, publisht an *Apology* for the *Christians* in the year 150, as himself saith, and a second after that, wherein he tells us, after the Doctrine of his Master, '*That we should* NOT SWEAR AT ALL, but always speak the Truth. He, that is, Christ, hath thus commanded, SWEAR NOT AT ALL, *but let your* YEA be YEA, and your NAY, NAY; and what is more then these is of Evil. . . ."[38]

In entry thirty-nine in *A Treatise on Oaths*, referring to Cyprian, Penn and Richardson declare: "Again, Writing of Pastors and Teachers, he [Cyprian] biddeth them, 'Remember what the Lord taught, and said, *Let your saying be* Yea, Yea, and Nay, Nay. In another Place, he saith, 'It is unlawful for any man to compel another to take an Oath.' "[39] Other citations expressing opposition to oath-taking come from, among others, Erasmus, Ambrosius Anseertus, Jacobus Faber, Chrysostom, and Chaucer.

A Treatise on Oaths was published in 1675; seven years later, William Penn published *Reasons Why the Oaths Should not be made a Part of the Test to Protestant Dissenters*. Penn argued that the oaths, instituted as protection against the "Papists," should not be required of "Protestant dissenters": "We, who are no *Papists*, but by our Faith and Doctrine *Repugnant* to all Popery; And We, who have never shown the least *Disallegiance* or *Unfaithfulness*, but on the Contrary have been patient and peaceable under all that Excess of Severity, that in several parts of this Nation hath been inflicted upon us, ought not to be brought under the same *Jealousies* with the *Papists*: It is suspecting an Integrity, that was never *Tainted*. For with submission, what is it but to say, the *Papists* have plotted against the King, Government and Protestant Religion; *therefore the* Quakers *and such like Dissenters that have not plotted, shall take the Oaths, to try and bind* them, *as if they had plotted?* This makes no Distinction, where really there is a great one."[40]

The pressure on Quakers to participate in the loyalty-oath ritual increased during the American Revolution. As Harold Hyman has observed, "Each state had, by 1778, created a loyalty test for all its residents to swear. . . . Nonjurors faced patterns of coercion different in each state, but basically similar in purpose and techniques. Those who refused state oath tests came under suspicion as potential disloyalists. If persistent in nonjuring, they faced imprisonment, fines, attainder proceedings and possible exile into British lines after state authorities confiscated their property. Less officially, nonjurors faced the bitterness and almost unchecked vengeance of their neighbors."[41] In June 1778, New York law, writes Arthur Mekeel in *The Relation of the Quakers to the American Revolution*, "empowered the Commissioners for Detecting and Defeating Conspiracies to tender the oath or affirmation of allegiance to anyone believed 'to have influence sufficient to do mischief.' Those who declined to comply with this requirement were to be sent within the enemy's lines."[42]

Hyman refers to the widespread use of loyalty oaths during this period of American history as "the addiction of the times."[43] He provides several examples of the fate of those who refused to take the loyalty oaths. In 1776, Peter van Schaack of Kinderhood, New York, "simply wished to remain neutral, especially after the Declaration of Independence demanded separation from the mother country. But the state loyalty commission decided otherwise. Late in 1776 it proffered him the loyalty test. Schaack refused it."[44] He was sentenced to exile, but appealed to higher New York authorities, asserting that "his nonjuring to Whig oaths was a matter of principle, but a matter on which no sacrifice would make him compromise." He was given a stay of sentence, but in 1778 the commission again ordered him to swear the state loyalty, and he again refused. He was sentenced to perpetual exile. Before embarking for England he wrote to his friend John Jay: "I think it is manifestly improper to tender it [the oath of allegiance] to persons of opposite principles, because it is a temptation to perjury . . . because, if taken, it adds no obligation in point of morality, . . . because . . . it gives no security to the public; and I think this measure most cruel, because it is carried on at a time when no *state necessity* . . . can be made to justify it."[45]

Before, during, and after the Revolutionary War, Quakers endured a variety of punishments. Margaret Bacon reports: "When American troops regained Philadelphia after the British occupation, anti-Quaker sentiment was very strong. The homes of many of the Quakers were stoned, and some individuals were hooted through the streets. An oath of allegiance was demanded of all school teachers, and a number of Quakers who refused to swear lost their jobs."[46] The neutrality of many Quakers during the Revolutionary War led to job losses and jailings of those who refused to take the loyalty oaths. As Rufus M. Jones has observed, after the war, in addition to suffering increased personal unpopularity, Quakers were subjected to jailings: "Six Friends were kept in Lancaster jail for months, because they would not take a test of allegiance to the new government. . . . School teachers were required to take the test. There were then a number of Friends' schools and teachers. Some closed the schools, and some took the consequences. As is always the case with this class they had no money, and so jailing was the only satisfaction the State got."[47]

The debate over state-imposed oath-taking continued after the war, when ratification of the Constitution was being considered. The question was whether the Constitution should include the provision that "no religious test shall ever be required as a qualification to any office or public trust under the United States." During the debate, Mr. Isaac Backus argued against requiring a religious test: "Let the history of all nations be searched from that day (Constantine's) to this, and it will appear that the imposing of religious tests hath been the greatest engine of tyranny in the world. . . . Some serious minds discover a concern lest if all religious tests be excluded, the Congress would hereafter establish Popery or some other tyrannical way of worship. But it is most certain that no such way of worship can be established without any religious test."[48]

In arguing that he could see no "conceivable advantage . . . that would result to the whole from such a test," Reverend Mr. Shute declared: "Unprincipled and dishonest men will not hesitate to subscribe to anything, that may open the way for their advancement, and put them into a situation the better to execute their base and iniquitous designs. Honest men alone, therefore, however well qualified to serve the public, would be excluded by it, and their country be deprived of the benefit of their abilities." After observing that "[i]n this great and extensive empire, there is and will be a great variety of sentiments in religion among its inhabitants," Reverend Shute said: "Far from limiting my charity and confidence to men of my own denomination in religion, I suppose, and I believe, sir, that there are worthy characters among men of every denomination—among the Quakers—the Baptists—the Church of England—the Papists—and even among those who have no other guide, in the way to virtue and heaven, than the dictates of natural religion."[49]

The following excerpts are from Oliver Ellsworth's 1787 newspaper article attacking the test oath; Ellsworth, who later became chief justice of the United States Supreme Court, wrote that test oaths were demeaning, tyrannical, and useless:

> A religious test is an act to be done, or profession to be made relating to religion (such as partaking of the sacrament according to certain rites and forms, or declaring one's belief of certain doctrines) for the purpose of determining whether his religious opinions are such, that he is admissible to a public office. A test in favor of any one denomination of Christians would be to the last degree absurd in the United States. If it were in favor of either Congregationalists, Presbyterians, Episcopalians, Baptists, or Quakers, it would incapacitate more than three-fourths of the American citizens for any public office; and thus degrade them from the rank of freemen. There need be no argument to prove that the majority of our citizens would never submit to this indignity.
>
> But to come, to the true principle by which this question ought to be determined; the business of civil government is to protect the citizen in his rights, to defend the community from hostile powers, and to promote the general welfare. Civil government has no business to meddle with the private opinions of the people.
>
> [I]n this state [Connecticut], we have never thought it expedient to adopt a test-law; and yet I sincerely believe we have as great a proportion of religion and morality, as they have in England, where every person who holds a public office, must either be a saint by law, or a hypocrite by practice. A test-law is the parent of hypocrisy, and the off-spring of error and the spirit of persecution. Legislatures have no right to set up an inquisition, and examine into the private opinions of men. Test-laws are useless and ineffectual, unjust and tyrannical; therefore the Convention have done wisely in excluding this engine of persecution, and providing that no religious test shall ever be required.[50]

During the 1787 Constitutional Convention debates, Mr. Pinckney proposed that the Constitution include, among other things, "No religious test or qualification . . . annexed to any oath of office, under the authority of the United States."[51] When the proposed Constitution's Article 20 was taken up (requiring that "members of the legislatures, and the executive and judicial officers of the United States, and of the several states, shall be bound by oath to support this Constitution"), Mr. Pickney moved to add to the article, "but no religious test shall ever be required as a qualification to any office or public trust under authority of the United States."[52] When the Constitution was finally ratified, with the ninth state vote coming from New Hampshire in 1788, Article Six read in part: "but no religious test shall ever be required as a qualification to any office or public trust under the United States."

While Selden asserted in the seventeenth century that "oaths are so frequent they should be taken like pills," and while Hyman describes the eighteenth-century loyalty oaths of the Revolutionary War period as "the addiction of the times," and while future United States Supreme Court Chief Justice Ellsworth declared that "legislatures have no right to set up an inquisition, and examine into the private opinions of men," the nineteenth-century Civil War and "the subsequent Reconstruction, richly deserve the title 'Era of the Oath,' " writes Hyman; he chose this as the title of his work on oaths during the Civil War and Reconstruction.[53] The middle of the nineteenth century brought with it loyalty oaths required of, among others, teachers, attorneys, ministers, government officials, and jurors.

After pointing out that the "whole experience" of loyalty testing during the Revolutionary War "testified to the fragility of coerced expressions of loyalty," Lewis Asper writes in "The Long and Unhappy History of Loyalty Testing in Maryland": "By mid-nineteenth century the lessons of the revolutionary period were forgotten. The War between the States prompted a burst of reckless loyalty testing illustrating the evils of which test-oaths and loyalty investigations are capable."[54]

In 1862, federal legislation was passed that provided that before anyone could serve as a grand or petit juror in a United States court, the following oath had to be administered:

> You do solemnly swear (or affirm, as the case may be) that you will support the Constitution of the United States of America; that you have not, without duress and constraint, taken up arms, or joined any insurrection or rebellion against the United States; that you have not adhered to any insurrection or rebellion, giving it aid or comfort; that you have not, directly or indirectly, given any assistance in money, or any other thing, to

any person or persons whom you knew, or had good ground to believe, had joined, or was about to join, said insurrection or rebellion, or had resisted, or was about to resist, with force of arms, the execution of the laws of the United States; and that you have not counselled any person or persons to join any rebellion against, or to resist with force of arms, the execution of the laws of the United States.[55]

Any person who swore falsely was considered to have "committed the crime of perjury, and shall be subject to all pains and penalties declared against the crime."

Also in 1862, the "ironclad test oath of loyalty" was enacted. This act required "every person elected or appointed to any office of honor or profit under the government of the United States . . . , excepting the President of the United States," to subscribe to the test oath, which read in part: "I, A. B., do solemnly swear (or affirm) that I have never voluntarily borne arms against the United States since I have been a citizen thereof; that I have voluntarily given no aid, countenance, counsel or encouragement to persons engaged in armed hostilities, thereto; that I have neither sought nor accepted nor attempted to exercise the functions of any office whatever, under any authority or pretended authority in hostility to the United States. . . ."[56]

Hyman has observed that "[b]y early 1862 the roster of loyalty tests was already impressive. Civil servants, shipmasters, military officers, postal contractors, pensioners, applicants for passports, telegraphers— all swore to their loyalty to the Union. But the story has only begun, for the years to follow witnessed a still wider spread of loyalty tests."[57]

In 1865, the Ironclad test oath was applied to attorneys in the federal courts.[58] Also in 1865, an amended and revised Missouri constitution was adopted containing a Section three, which declared in part:

[N]o person who has ever been in armed hostility to the United States, or to the lawful authorities thereof, or to the government of this State; or has ever given aid, comfort, countenance, or support to persons engaged in any such hostility; or has ever, in any manner, adhered to the enemies, foreign or domestic, of the United States, either by contributing to them, or by unlawfully sending within their lines, money, goods, letter, or information . . . ; or has ever, by act or word, manifested his adherence to the cause of such enemies, or his desire for their triumph over the arms of the United States, or his sympathy with those engaged in exciting or carrying on rebellion against the United States . . . ; or has ever been engaged in guerilla warfare against loyal inhabitants of the United States, or in that description of marauding commonly known as "bushwhacking"; or has ever knowingly and willingly harbored, aided, or countenanced any person so engaged . . . ; nor shall any such person be capable of holding in this State any office of honor, trust, or profit, under its authority; or of being an officer, councilman, director, trustee, or other manager of any corporation, public or private, now existing or hereafter established by its authority; or of acting as a professor or teacher in any educational institution; or in any common or other school; or of holding any real estate or other property in trust for the use of any church, religious society, or congregation. . . . [59]

Section six of the Missouri constitution included an oath of loyalty, which read in part: "I, A. B., do solemnly swear that I am well acquainted with the terms of the third section of the second article of the Constitution of the State of Missouri . . . and have carefully considered the same; that I have never, directly or indirectly, done any of the acts in said section specified; that I have always been truly and loyally on the side of the United States against all enemies thereof, foreign and domestic; that I will bear true faith and allegiance to the United States, and will support the Constitution and laws thereof as the supreme law of the land. . . ."[60]

Finally, Section nine stipulated who was required to take the above oath: "No person shall assume the duties of any state, county, city, town, or other office, to which he may be appointed, otherwise than by vote of the people; nor shall any person, after the expiration of sixty days after this Constitution takes effect, be permitted to practise as an attorney or counsellor at law; nor, after that time, shall any person be competent as a bishop, priest, deacon, minister, elder, or other clergyman of any religious persuasion, sect, or denomination, to teach, or preach, or solemnize marriages, unless such person shall have first taken, subscribed, and filed said oath."[61]

As Thomas Marclay has observed, "The clergy of all denominations were placed in a difficult, if not to say humiliating, position. The constitution required them, in effect, to take out a license to preach. To comply with its provisions, it was contended, would be to concede the power of the state to regulate religion; to refuse to comply, while continuing the functions of the office, would be to disobey the law. . . ."[62] When the deadline for subscribing to the oath ended on September 2, 1865, "it was announced that in St. Louis scarcely one-fourth of the clergy had taken the oath and that no priest or bishop of the Catholic Church or minister of the Methodist Church, south, or of the Christian Church had subscribed to it."[63]

On September 3, John Cummings, a Catholic priest, preached without having subscribed to the required oath; he was indicted, convicted, fined five hundred dollars, and jailed for several days when he refused to pay the fine. Cummings appealed, and the Missouri Supreme Court affirmed the judgment of the lower court. Whereupon Cummings appealed to the United States Supreme Court, which decided for him in January 1867. At the outset of the Court's opinion, Justice Stephen Field noted that while some of the acts against which the oath was directed constituted serious offenses, "some of the acts have never been classed as offenses in the laws of any State, and some of the acts, under many circumstances, would not even be blameworthy. It requires the affiant to deny not only that he has ever 'been in armed hostility to the United States . . . ,' but, among other things, that he has ever, 'by act or word,' manifested his adherence to the cause of the enemies of the United States, foreign or domestic, or his *desire* for their triumph over the arms of the United States, or his *sympathy* with those engaged in rebellion, or has ever *harbored* or *aided* any person engaged in guerrilla warfare against the loyal inhabitants of the United States. . . ."[64]

Justice Field attacked the Missouri oath further by declaring that it was, "for its severity, without any precedent that we can discover":

> In the first place, it is retrospective; it embraces all the past from this day; and, if taken years hence, it will also cover all the intervening period. In its retrospective feature we believe it is peculiar to this country. In England and France there have been test oaths, but they were always limited to an affirmation of present belief, or present disposition towards the government, and were never exacted with reference to particular instances of past misconduct. In the second place, the oath is directed not merely against overt and visible acts of hostility to the government, but is intended to reach words, desires, and sympathies, also. And, in the third place, it allows no distinction between acts springing from malignant enmity and acts which may have been prompted by charity, or affection, or relationship.[65]

The state of Missouri had argued that the oath requirement did not constitute a punishment, but instead was a qualification. Justice Field responded: "The disabilities created by the constitution of Missouri must be regarded as penalties—they constitute punishment." Missouri had contended that "to punish one is to deprive him of life, liberty, or property, and that to take from him anything less than these is no punishment at all." Field retorted:

> The learned counsel [representing Missouri] does not use these terms— life, liberty, and property—as comprehending every right known to the law. He does not include under liberty freedom from outrage on the feelings as well as restraints on the person. He does not include under property those estates which one may acquire in professions, though they are often the source of the highest emoluments and honors. . . . Disqualification from the pursuits of a lawful avocation . . . may also, and often has been, imposed as punishment.[66]

Speaking to the ex post facto nature of the Missouri oath provision, the High Court asserted: "Now, some of the acts to which the expurgatory oath is directed were not offences at the time they were committed. It was no offence against any law to enter or leave the State of Missouri for the purpose of avoiding enrolment or draft in the military service of the United States, however much the evasion of such service might be the subject of moral censure. Clauses which prescribe a penalty for an act of this nature are within the terms of the definition of *ex post facto* law—'they impose a punishment for an act not punishable at the time it was committed.' "[67]

"And this is not all," continued the Court. "The clauses in question subvert the presumptions of innocence, and alter the rules of evidence, which heretofore, under the universally recognized principle of the common law, have been supposed to be fundamental and unchangeable. They assume that the parties are guilty; they call upon the parties to establish their innocence; and they declare that such innocence can be shown only in one way—by an inquisition, in the form of an expurgatory oath, into the consciences of the parties."[68]

The Court concludes its opinion with a two-page excerpt from the writings of Alexander Hamilton "in which, with his characteristic fulness and ability, he examines the [expurgatory] oath, and demonstrates that it is not only a mode of inflicting punishment, but a mode in violation of all the constitutional guarantees, secured by the Revolution, of the rights and liberties of the people." Hamilton had written that the oath requirement was "a subversion of one great principle of social security, to wit: that every man shall be presumed innocent until he is proved guilty. This was to invert the order of things; and, instead of obliging the State to prove the guilt, in order to inflict the penalty, it was to oblige the citizen to establish his own innocence to avoid the penalty."[69]

On the same day the United States Supreme Court held invalid the oath involved in *Cummings*—January 14, 1867—it also struck down as unconstitutional a loyalty oath requirement imposed by Congress on attorneys.[70] On January 24, 1865, Congress had passed legislation that stated in part: "No person after the date of this act, shall be admitted to the bar of the Supreme Court of the United States, or at any time after the fourth of March next, shall be admitted to the bar of any Circuit or District Court of the United States, or of the Court of Claims, as an attorney . . . unless he shall have first taken and subscribed the oath prescribed in 'An act to prescribe an oath of office and for other purposes,' approved July 2d, 1862."[71] The oath of office referred to was the 1862 Ironclad test of loyalty.

Augustus Garland, an attorney from Arkansas, was a one-time representative in the House and Senate of the Congress of the Confederate States and "was a member of the senate at the time of the surrender of the Confederate forces to the armies of the United States." In 1865, Garland received from President Andrew Johnson "a full pardon for all offences committed by his participation, direct or implied, in the Rebellion."[72] Before the Civil War, Garland had been admitted "as an attorney and counsellor" of the Supreme Court, and now in 1865 he asked "permission to continue to practise as an attorney and counsellor of the court without taking the oath required by the act of January 24th, 1865 . . . which he is unable to take by reason of the offices he held under the Confederate government."[73]

In deciding for Garland, the United States Supreme Court listed at the outset of its opinion what was prescribed by the required oath that Garland refused to take:

1st. That the deponent has never voluntarily borne arms against the United States since he has been a citizen thereof;

2d. That he has not voluntarily given aid, countenance, counsel, or encouragement to persons engaged in armed hostility thereto;

3d. That he has never sought, accepted, or attempted to exercise the functions of any office whatsoever, under any authority, or pretended authority, in hostility to the United States;

4th. That he has not yielded a voluntary support to any pretended government, authority, power, or constitution, within the United States, hostile or inimical thereto. . . . [74]

All these clauses, said the Court, "relate to past acts. Some of these acts constituted, when they were committed, offences against the criminal laws of the country; others may, or may not, have been offences according to the circumstances under which they were committed, and the motives of the parties." The Court then dealt with the clauses one by one:

> The first clause covers one form of the crime of treason, and the deponent must declare that he has not been guilty of this crime, not only during the war of the Rebellion, but during any period of his life since he has been a citizen. The second clause goes beyond the limits of treason and embraces not only the giving of aid and encouragement of a treasonable nature to a public enemy, but also the giving of assistance of any kind to persons engaged in armed hostility to the United States. The third clause applies to the seeking, acceptance, or exercise not only of offices created for the purpose of more effectually carrying on hostilities, but also of any of those offices which are required in every community, whether in peace or war, for the administration of justice and the preservation of order. The fourth clause not only includes those who gave a cordial and active support to the hostile government, but also those who yielded a reluctant obedience to the existing order, established without their co-operation.[75]

The Court argued that the object of the January 24, 1865, statute was to exclude those "parties who have offended in any of the particulars embraced by these clauses" from "the profession of the law, or at least from its practice in the courts of the United States. As the oath prescribed cannot be taken by these parties, the act, as against them, operates as a legislative decree of perpetual exclusion. And exclusion from any of the professions or any of the ordinary avocations of life for past conduct can be regarded in no other light than as punishment for such conduct."[76]

As in *Cummings*, the *Garland* majority argued that the statute constituted *ex post facto* law: "In the exclusion which the statute adjudges it imposes a punishment for some of the acts specified which were not punishable at the time they were committed; and for other of the acts it adds a new punishment to that before prescribed, and it is thus brought within the further inhibition of the Constitution against the passage of an *ex post facto* law."[77]

Various scholars have concluded that all this coerced oathtaking was ineffectual, counterproductive, demeaning, and divisive. William Russ, writing in the *Mississippi Law Journal* on "The Lawyer's Test Oath

During Reconstruction," begins by saying, "The moral of the story is that, whether it is possible to better the general standing of lawyers as a whole or not, the means about to be discussed is a horrible example of one way which will *not* work."[78] Russ concludes that required oathtaking resulted in an "intolerable" situation: "Professional disqualifications not only produced economic maladjustment, but also infringed upon the right of a guild or profession to earn its daily bread. The situation was made almost intolerable in those states which disabled ministers, teachers, lawyers, and others; it was intolerable not only for those disfranchised, but for the community as a whole. The professions are an integral part of civilized society, and society without the ministration of free, unfettered professions is unthinkable. A test oath is an excellent example of one way in which the law, or any other profession, cannot be improved."[79]

Harold Hyman also concludes in his *Era of the Oath* that the compulsory oath test was a failure: "In 1873, Garrett Davis of Kentucky suggested that Congress offer ' . . . a reward for the discovery of an invention which would provide a proper way for determining loyalty.' His words were an epitaph for the loyalty oaths and loyalty tests of the Civil War and Reconstruction, on epitaph which declared their futility and spotlighted their failure. For the oaths and tests did not mark loyalty."[80] Hyman ends his book by asserting: "And so they failed, these loyalty tests of the Civil War and Reconstruction, for they did not measure loyalty. They failed for the nation, were condemned by the courts, and eventually were discarded. They failed also in the states, where the courts invalidated them or constitutional and legal reform repealed them."[81]

As indicated earlier, Lewis Asper, writing in 1969, during an era when millions of Americans were required to sign loyalty oaths during the "cold war," concluded in his *American Journal of Legal History* article "The Long and Unhappy History of Loyalty Testing in Maryland" that when all this oathtaking during the middle and late nineteenth century in America was all over, "the whole process left the nation feeling a little embarrassed and a little ashamed. Perhaps such a feeling is emerging once again."[82]

During the 1864 U.S. Senate debate on the lawyer's oath, Senator Reverdy Johnson of Tennessee expressed concern about the increasing uses of loyalty oaths, but in the end he voted for passage of the bill creating the lawyer's oath; referring to earlier discussions of the bill, he stated: "We are under the impression, as well as I remember, that if it was necessary to prescribe such an oath to members of the bar, it was equally necessary, and perhaps more necessary . . . , that it should be prescribed to every man in the United States; not only to any man who pursues any other profession, but any man who pursues any calling. The doctor should not be permitted to practice unless he took an oath of this description; the merchant should not be allowed to carry on his particular business; and so in reference to all the relations in which men may be placed in society. But as the honorable member seems to think that it may in some measure serve to render the condition of the country more safe or less perilous than it would be without this oath being taken by the members of the bar, I for one am willing to let him silence his own fears on that subject and let the law be passed. I say, 'Yea.' "[83]

Senator Johnson's seemingly farfetched envisioning of a compulsory oath for "any man who pursues any calling" did materialize a century later when, during the mid-twentieth-century "cold war," federal, state, and local governments instituted loyalty tests, subscribed to by thirteen million five hundred thousand Americans. Writing in 1957, Ralph S. Brown, Jr. put the thirteen million five hundred thousand into perspective: "Taking the total labor force at around 65,000,000, this means that at least one person out of five, as a condition of his current employment, has taken a test oath, or completed a loyalty statement, or achieved official security clearance, or survived some undefined private scrutiny."[84] While the use of oaths was widespread during the seventeenth, eighteenth, and nineteenth centuries, in sheer number of citizens required to participate, it was the twentieth century that deserved the dubious honor of being called the century of coerced oaths and pledges.

One hundred years after the Supreme Court decided in *Cummings* and *Garland* that the oaths required of the clergy and attorneys involved in those cases were unconstitutional, the American courts were confronted with deciding the constitutionality of a variety of federal, state, and local loyalty oaths imposed on, among others, teachers, students, labor leaders, attorneys, scientists, librarians, dead authors (with their oaths being signed by live publishers), municipal employees, and war veterans.

Where seventeenth-century Englishmen were coerced into signing oaths declaring that they did not believe in transubstantiation; and where seventeenth-century colonists were required to acknowledge the divine authority of the Old and New Testaments and the truth of the Christian religion; and where nineteenth-century Civil War and Reconstruction-era loyalty oaths were imposed on legislators, clergy, teachers, and attorneys, twentieth-century governmental authorities required millions of Americans to sign first a positive oath swearing allegiance to the United States of America, and next a disclaimer affidavit swearing they did not believe in, were not members of, and did not support organizations that believe in or teach the overthrow of the government by force.

3

"I Do Solemnly Swear . . ." in Mid-Twentieth-Century America

The search for heretics dominated the political scene in mid-twentieth-century America. The "un-Americans" were subpoenaed to appear before a variety of un-American activities committees and coerced into revealing their political beliefs and associations. Un-Americans were to be identified through the mandatory loyalty oaths. It was a time when citizens were commanded to reveal whether acquaintances were Communists or "acted like Communists"; it was a time when government officials asked whether one believed that socialism was inevitable in the United States; it was a time when the attorney general of the United States compiled a list of 197 "subversive" organizations, and the House Committee on Un-American Activities compiled its own list of 663 "subversive" organizations that included "Communist-front" groups; it was a time when one's loyalty was determined by the answer to the question, "Do you believe a citizen has a right to advocate forceful overthrow of government?"

Writing in 1958 about the widespread use of loyalty tests in the United States, Ralph S. Brown, Jr., devoted several pages to the practices state bar examiners followed when questioning attorneys seeking admission to the bar:

> An interview with the candidate—part of the routine of admission in more than one-third of the states—is the final channel for loyalty testing. A few character committees ask, almost as a matter of course, "Are you a Communist?" Others raise loyalty issues sporadically, or indirectly by way of such catch questions as, "Do you think that Communists are eligible to practice law?" The right answer is "no," for any other answer may lead to further and more suspicious grilling. Other oral inquiries that have been reported range from an embarrassed, "You aren't a Communist or anything, are you?" to the following exchange: "Did you vote for Henry

Wallace in 1948?" "No, I voted for Harry Truman." "Don't tell me that—we don't have the right to ask you that."[1]

While thousands of Americans were ordered to appear before state and federal un-American activities committees to reveal their political beliefs and associations, millions were required, as a condition of employment, to sign loyalty oaths and disclaimer affidavits. Various scholars have pointed to the huge increase in the use of the oaths and affidavits in the 1950s. This increase was observed in 1959 by Harold Hyman, who wrote: "Since Hiroshima. . . . , state and local governments across America have 'discovered' loyalty test oaths. By 1956 no less than forty-two states, and more than two thousand county and municipal subdivisions and state and local administrative commissions, required loyalty oaths from teachers, voters, lawyers, union officials, residents in public housing, recipients of public welfare, and, in Indiana, wrestlers."[2]

In his 1950 article "State Legislatures and Communism: The Current Scene," William Prendegast, after referring to the criminal syndicalism and criminal anarchy statutes passed by legislators earlier in the century, wrote: "More typical of the recent crop of anti-subversive legislation is the law designed to exclude subversive individuals from public employment found in some form in thirty-two states at the beginning of the present year."[3] Writing in 1958, Ralph Brown, Jr., also recognized the significant increase in the use of test oaths: "[T]he legislative itch to do something against communism has been contagious; so the number of states free of employment tests has rapidly declined."[4]

Brown's estimate of thirteen million, five hundred thousand Americans signing loyalty oaths as a condition of employment[5] is very similar to the numbers provided by Thomas I. Emerson, who wrote in 1970: "There are nearly 3,000,000 Federal employees at any one time, virtually all of whom are subject to loyalty tests. Out of some 9,000,000 State and local government employees probably two-thirds, about 6,000,000, engage in work for which a loyalty oath or other loyalty test is required. In addition, about 5,000,000 non-government employees are under Federal loyalty programs. . . . Thus a total of 14,000,000, out of a working force of 70,000,000, are directly affected."[6] Concluding that the loyalty tests have widespread ramifications, Emerson writes: "The overall impact upon freedom of expression can hardly be exaggerated."[7]

When in 1956 the United States Supreme Court declared unconstitutional a California loyalty oath required of war veterans seeking to qualify for property tax exemptions, Justice Black wrote in his concurring opinion about the extensive use of loyalty oaths:

> Government employees, lawyers, doctors, teachers, pharmacists, veterinarians, subway conductors, industrial workers, and a multitude of others have been denied an opportunity to work at their trade or professions for these reasons. Here a tax is levied unless the taxpayer makes an oath that he does not and will not in the future advocate certain things; in Ohio those without jobs have been denied unemployment insurance unless they are willing to swear that they do not hold specific views; and Congress has even attempted to deny public housing to needy families unless they demonstrate their loyalty. These are merely random samples; I will not take time here to refer to innumerable others, such as oaths for hunters and fishermen, wrestlers and boxers and junk dealers.[8]

In 1947, Congress passed legislation that denied some of the benefits of the National Labor Relations Act to unions whose officials did not file with the National Labor Relations Board a "non-Communist" affidavit stating that they are not members "of the Communist Party or affiliated with such party, and that he does not believe in, and is not a member of or supports any organization that believes in or teaches, the overthrow of the United States Government by force or by any illegal or unconstitutional methods."[9]

In 1948, the city of Los Angeles passed Ordinance No. 94,004, which required the following oath from every person who held an office or position in the service of the city:

> I further swear (or affirm) that I do not advise, advocate or teach, and have not within the period beginning five (5) years prior to the effective date of the ordinance requiring the making of this oath or affirmation, advised, advocated or taught, the overthrow by force, violence or other unlawful means, of the Government of the United States of America or of the State of California and that I am not now and have not, within said period, been or become a member of or affiliated with any group, society, association, organization or party which advises, advocates or teaches, or has, within said period, advised, advocated or taught, the overthrow by force, violence or other unlawful means of the Government of the United States of America, or of the State of California. I further swear (or affirm) that I will not, while I am in the service of the City of Los Angeles, advise, advocate or teach, or be or become a member of or affiliated with any group, association, society, organization or party which advises, advocates or teaches, or has within said period, advised, advocated or taught, the

overthrow by force, violence or other unlawful means, of the Government of the United States or of the State of California. . . . [10]

Seventeen employees refused to sign the affidavit and were discharged, whereupon they brought suit asking for reinstatement and back pay. When their case reached the United States Supreme Court, in a 5 to 4 decision the Court declared the required oath constitutional.[11]

With the passage of the National Defense Education Act in 1958, college students applying for loans through the federally administered National Defense Student Loan Program were required to sign first the loyalty oath swearing allegiance to the United States and then to sign a disclaimer affidavit, which read: "I,_____, do solemnly swear (or affirm) that I do not believe in, and am not a member of and do not support any organization that believes in or teaches, the overthrow of United States Government by force or violence or by any illegal or unconstitutional methods."[12] Students who refused to sign the oath and affidavit were denied the educational loans.

In 1949, the state of Florida instituted a loyalty oath required of every employee of the state or its subdivisions; employees who did not subscribe to the oath were immediately discharged. In addition to swearing that they would support the United States and Florida constitutions, each employee was required to swear that "I am not a member of the Communist Party; that I have not and will not lend my aid, support, advice, counsel or influence to the Communist Party; that I do not believe in the overthrow of the Government of the United States or of the State of Florida by force or violence; that I am not a member of any organization or party which believes in or teaches, directly or indirectly, the overthrow of the Government of the United States or of Florida by force or violence." [13] A public-school teacher challenged the constitutionality of the oath, and in 1961 a unanimous United States Supreme Court concluded that the language of the oath was too vague and hence "repugnant to the guaranty of liberty contained in the Fourteenth Amendment."[14]

The loyalty oaths and affidavits were increasingly challenged in the courts, and in the early 1950s the courts generally decided against those who challenged their constitutionality. Just as the courts during this period upheld the contempt citations of those who appeared before the un-American activities committees and refused, invoking the First Amendment, to divulge their beliefs and associations, so too did the courts generally uphold the various local, state, and federal loyalty oaths.

While those who refused to answer HUAC's questions were cited for contempt and sent off to prison, those who refused to sign the oaths and affidavits were not hired or lost their jobs. More often than not, the courts used the same type of arguments to justify and uphold both the loyalty-oath requirements and the convictions of the HUAC witnesses who refused to answer belief and association questions.

When in 1950 a California district court of appeals upheld the constitutionality of the 1948 Los Angeles ordinance requiring anyone in the service of the city to sign a loyalty oath, the court stated that "the principles here involved have been before the courts in the following cases," with *Lawson v. United States* being the first case cited.[15] In June 1949, the United States Court of Appeals had upheld screenwriter John Howard Lawson's contempt-of-Congress conviction for refusal to answer HUAC inquiries into his political beliefs and associations.[16] The California court said that in *Lawson* "the United States Court of Appeals for the District of Columbia held that questions by a Congressional Committee to script writers for motion pictures whether they were or were not communists were pertinent and proper; therefore contumacious witnesses were not protected by the Bill of Rights from answering."[17]

When one year later, on June 4, 1951, the United States Supreme Court also decided against the Los Angeles employees, the High Court argued that the past conduct of a city employee "may well relate to present fitness; past loyalty may have a reasonable relationship to present and future trust. Both are commonly inquired into in determining fitness for both high and low positions in private industry and are not less relevant in public employment. The affidavit requirement is valid."[18] Further, the Court argued that the ordinance did not constitute an ex post facto law: "The ordinance would be *ex post facto* if it imposed punishment for past conduct lawful at the time it was engaged in. Passing for the moment the question whether separation of petitioners from their employment must be considered as punishment, the ordinance clearly is not *ex post facto*."[19]

The "moment" passed, and the High Court declared in the next paragraph: "We are unable to conclude that punishment is imposed by a general regulation which merely provides standards of qualification and eligibility for employment."[20]

Justice Douglas disagreed and declared in his dissenting opinion that punishment was indeed involved when one was discharged for refusing to sign the oath:

> Deprivation of a man's means of livelihood by reason of past conduct, not subject to this penalty when committed, is punishment whether he is a professional man, a day laborer who works for private industry, or a government employee. . . . Petitioners were disqualified from office not for what they are today, not because of any program they currently espouse . . . , not because of standards related to fitness for the office . . . , but for what they once advocated. They are deprived of their livelihood by legislative act, not judicial processes.[21]

Douglas also argued that this case was governed by *Cummings v. Missouri* and *Ex parte Garland*, and he concluded: "We put the case in the aspect most invidious to petitioners. Whether they actually advocated the violent overthrow of Government does not appear. But here, as in the *Cummings* case, the vice is in the presumption of guilt which can only be removed by the expurgatory oath. That punishment, albeit conditional, violates here as it did in the *Cummings* case the constitutional prohibition against bills of attainder."[22]

The Supreme Court's *Garner* decision was handed down on June 4, 1951. On October 18, 1951, the Supreme Court of Oklahoma concluded that Oklahoma's lengthy loyalty oath was constitutional, and in so doing it relied on *Garner* to support its conclusion that the oath was neither a bill of attainder nor an ex post facto law. The Oklahoma oath required the oath-taker to swear, in part, "I am not affiliated directly or indirectly with the Communist Party, the Third Communist International, with any foreign political agency, party, organization or Government, or with any agency, party, organization, association or group whatever which has been officially determined by the United States Attorney General or other authorized agency of the United States to be a communist front or subversive organization. . . ."[23]

In deciding that the oath was constitutional, the Oklahoma Supreme Court asserted:

> A bill of attainder is a legislative act which inflicts punishment without judicial trial. It is contended that the act is a bill of attainder because it punishes one for refusal to take an oath that he has not been a member of listed organizations by vacating his position and denying him compensation. We think the Supreme Court of the United States has answered the

question in *Garner v. Board of Public Works of City of Los Angeles.* . . .
An *ex post facto* law is one which provided a punishment for an act which
was innocent when committed. . . . The [Oklahoma] act is neither a bill of
attainder nor an *ex post facto* law.[24]

However, one year later, on December 15, 1952, the United States
Supreme Court in *Wieman v. Updegraff* unanimously reversed
Oklahoma's supreme court decision, distinguishing this case from *Garner* [and *Adler* and *Gerende*, decided earlier in 1952]: "It is in the context of these decisions that we determine the validity of the oath before
us."[25] One of the questions addressed in those cases had been "whether
the Due Process Clause permits a state, in attempting to bar disloyal
individuals from its employ, to exclude persons solely on the basis of
organizational membership, regardless of their knowledge concerning
the organizations to which they belonged. For, under the statute before
us, the fact of membership alone disqualifies."[26]

Membership alone, said the Court, was not enough to disqualify, for
"membership may be innocent": "A state servant may have joined a
proscribed organization unaware of its activities and purposes. In recent
years, many completely loyal persons have severed organizational ties
after learning for the first time of the character of groups to which they
had belonged. . . . At the time of affiliation, a group itself may be innocent, only later coming under the influence of those who would turn it
toward illegitimate ends."[27]

As to the distinction between this case and *Garner, Adler* and *Gerende*, the Court further stated:

> [U]nder the Oklahoma Act, the fact of association determines disloyalty
> and disqualification; it matters not whether association existed innocently
> or knowingly. To thus inhibit individual freedom of movement is to stifle
> the flow of democratic expression and controversy at one of its chief
> sources. We hold that the distinction observed between the case at bar and
> *Garner, Adler,* and *Gerende* is decisive. Indiscriminate classification of
> innocent with knowing activity must fall as an assertion of arbitrary
> power. The oath offends due process.[28]

Writing a concurring opinion, Justice Black referred to the dangers of
the widespread use of loyalty oaths: "[T]he present period of fear seems
more ominously dangerous to speech and press than was that of the
Alien and Sedition Laws. Suppressive laws and practices are the fashion.
The Oklahoma oath statute is but one manifestation of a national net-

work of laws aimed at coercing and controlling the minds of men. Test oaths are notorious tools of tyranny."[29]

Since the appellants in *Wieman* were members of the faculty and staff of Oklahoma Agricultural and Mechanical College, Justice Frankfurter devoted most of his concurring opinion to the effects of the loyalty oath requirement on teachers: "[T]o require such an oath, on pain of a teacher's loss of his position in case of refusal to take the oath, penalizes a teacher for exercising a right of association peculiarly characteristic of our people. . . . [I]n view of the nature of the teacher's relation to the effective exercise of the rights which are safeguarded by the Bill of Rights and by the Fourteenth Amendment, inhibition of freedom of thought, and of action upon thought, in the case of teachers brings the safeguards of those amendments vividly into operation."[30]

While the city of Los Angeles was requiring oaths from its employees, Maryland was requiring oaths from its political candidates,[31] and Oklahoma was attempting to impose an oath on all state officers and employees, the state of New York was requiring that public-school teachers and employees reveal whether they were members of any of the "subversive organizations" listed by New York's Board of Regents. On March 3, 1952, the United States Supreme Court upheld the constitutionality of New York's "Feinberg Law." In so deciding, the Court, relying on *Garner*, declared: "We adhere to that case."[32]

In deciding against the teachers who had challenged the constitutionality of the Feinberg Law, the High Court argued in *Adler v. Board of Education*:

> It is clear that such persons have the right under our law to (assemble,) speak, think and believe as they will. . . . It is equally clear that they have no right to work for the State in the school system on their own terms. . . . They may work for the school system upon the reasonable terms laid down by the proper authorities of New York. If they do not choose to work on such terms, they are at liberty to retain their beliefs and associations and go elsewhere. Has the State thus deprived them of any right to free speech or assembly? We think not.[33]

In arguing that the state "must preserve the integrity of the schools," the Court stated: "One's associates, past and present, as well as one's conduct, may properly be considered in determining fitness and loyalty. From time immemorial, one's reputation has been determined in part by the company one keeps. In the employment of officials and teachers of the school system, the state may very properly inquire into the company they keep. . . ."[34]

In his dissenting opinion, Justice Black again expressed his concern about the increase in the use of loyalty oaths: "This is another of those rapidly multiplying legislative enactments which make it dangerous—this time for school teachers—to think or say anything except what a transient majority happen to approve at the moment. Basically these laws rest on the belief that government should supervise and limit the flow of ideas into the minds of men."[35]

Justice Douglas, also dissenting, saw the Feinberg Law as proceeding "on a principle repugnant to our society—guilt by association" and as a threat to academic freedom. Of the first concern, he wrote:

> A teacher is disqualified because of her membership in an organization found to be "subversive." The finding as to the "subversive" character of the organization is made in a proceeding to which the teacher is not a party and in which it is not clear that she may even be heard. . . . The irrebuttable charge that the organization is "subversive" therefore hangs as an ominous cloud over her own hearing. The mere fact of membership in the organization raises a prima facie case of her own guilt. She may, it is said, show her innocence. But innocence in this case turns on knowledge; and when the witch hunt is on, one who must rely on ignorance leans on a feeble reed.[36]

As for the effects of the New York requirement on academic freedom, Douglas observed: "What happens under this law is typical of what happens in a police state. Teachers are under constant surveillance; their pasts are combed for signs of disloyalty; their utterances are watched for clues to dangerous thoughts. A pall is cast over the classrooms. There can be no real academic freedom in that environment."[37]

Fifteen years later, on January 23, 1967, the United States Supreme Court overruled *Adler*, declaring in *Keyishian v. Board of Regents* that "constitutional doctrine which has emerged since that decision [*Adler*] has rejected its major premise. That premise was that public employment, including academic employment, may be conditioned upon the surrender of constitutional rights which could not be abridged by direct government action."[38] Justice Brennan, delivering the opinion of the Court, borrowed one of the metaphors Justice Douglas had used in his Adler dissent "Our nation is deeply committed to safeguarding academic freedom, which is of transcendent value to all of us and not merely to the teachers concerned. That freedom is therefore a special concern of the First Amendment, which does not tolerate laws that cast a pall of orthodoxy over the classroom."[39]

In the same year as the United States Supreme Court concluded that New York's requirement that teachers reveal their "subversive" associational ties was constitutional in *Adler*, New York's legislature was in the process of enacting the Security Risk Law, in which it was determined that the New York City Transit Authority was a "security agency." The Security Risk Law provided for the dismissal of any employee who, among other things, held "membership in any organization or group found by the state civil service commission to be subversive." In September 1954, New York subway conductor Lerner "was summoned to the office of the Commissioner of Investigation of the City of New York in the course of an investigation being conducted under the Security Risk Law. Appellant, who had been sworn, was asked whether he was *then* a member of the Communist Party, but he refused to answer and claimed his privilege against self-incrimination under the Fifth Amendment to the Federal Constitution." Lerner was suspended and told that there existed "reasonable grounds" for belief that his "continued employment would endanger national and state security." This finding, he was told, was based on his refusal "to answer questions as to whether or not he was a member of the Communist Party and [invocation of] the Fifth Amendment to the Constitution of the United States."[40]

When Lerner's case reached the United States Supreme Court, his discharge was upheld in a 5–4 decision; Justices Warren, Brennan, Black, and Douglas dissented and applied their dissenting opinions to *Beilan v. Board of Education* which was decided the same day as *Lerner*.

Herman Beilan, who had been a teacher for about twenty-two years in the Philadelphia public-school system, was discharged on the ground of "incompetency," evidenced by his refusal to respond to his superintendent's "request to confirm or refute information as to [his] loyalty and his activities in certain allegedly subversive organizations." Beilan was asked whether he had been the press director of the professional section of the Communist Political Association in 1944, and he declined to answer the question. Further, he "announced he would also decline to answer any other questions 'similar to it,' 'questions of this type,' or 'questions about political and religious beliefs . . . ' "[41]

The Pennsylvania Supreme Court upheld Beilan's dismissal, whereupon he appealed to the United States Supreme Court, which decided, 5–4, against him, the majority asserting, "The only question before us is whether the Federal Constitution prohibits petitioner's discharge for statutory 'incompetence' based on his refusal to answer the Superintendent's questions."[42] The Court answered this question by declaring: "Petitioner blocked from the beginning any inquiry into his Communist activities, however relevant to his present loyalty. The Board based its dismissal upon petitioner's refusal to answer any inquiry about his relevant activities—not upon those activities themselves. It took care to charge petitioner with incompetence, and not with disloyalty. It found him insubordinate and lacking in frankness and candor—it made no finding as to his to his loyalty."[43] The Court concluded that Beilan's discharge "did not violate the Federal Constitution."[44]

Justice Douglas began his dissenting opinion, which applied also to *Lerner*, by arguing:

> The holding of the Court that the teacher in the *Beilan* case and the subway conductor in the *Lerner* case could be discharged from their respective jobs because they stood silent when asked about their Communist affiliations cannot, with due deference, be squared with our constitutional principles. Among the liberties of the citizens that are guaranteed by the Fourteenth Amendment are those contained in the First Amendment. . . . These include the right to believe what one chooses, the right to differ from his neighbor, the right to pick and choose the political philosophy that he likes best, the right to associate with whomever he chooses, the right to join the groups he prefers, [and] the privilege of selecting his own path to salvation.[45]

Emphasizing that *Beilan* and *Lerner* were cases involving persons being punished for their beliefs, Douglas concluded: "In sum, we have here only a bare refusal to testify; and the Court holds that sufficient to show that these employees are unfit to hold their public posts. That makes qualification for public office turn solely on a matter of belief—a notion very much at war with the Bill of Rights."[46]

Justice Brennan also wrote a dissenting opinion, in which he stated that "more is at stake here than the loss of positions of public employment for unreliability or incompetence. Rather, it is the simultaneous public labeling of the employees as disloyal that gives rise to our concern": "In each case a man's honor and reputation are indelibly stained. 'There can be no dispute about the consequences visited upon a person excluded from public employment on disloyalty grounds. In the view of the community, the stain is a deep one; indeed, it has become a badge of infamy.' *Wieman v. Updegraf.* . . . The petitioners thus not only lose their present jobs, but their standing in the community is so undermined as doubtless to cost them most opportunities for future jobs."[47]

At the same time as the United States Supreme Court decided (on June 30, 1958) against subway employee Lerner and schoolteacher Beilan, the High Court decided that two California loyalty oaths, one required of war veterans seeking tax exemptions and another of churches seeking property-tax exemptions, were unconstitutional.[48]

"I do not advocate the overthrow of the Government of the United States or of the State of California by force or violence or other unlawful means, nor advocate the support of a foreign government against the United States in event of hostilities." Such was the wording of the oath required of war veterans claiming property-tax exemptions: "Under California law applicants for such exemption must annually complete a standard form of application and file it with the local assessor."[49] Several honorably discharged veterans of World War II, claiming the veteran's exemption, refused to subscribe to the oath and were denied the exemption. When the case reached the United States Supreme Court, Justice Brennan, delivering the opinion of the Court, argued that the oath requirement interfered with freedom of speech: "It cannot be gainsaid that a discriminatory denial of a tax exemption for engaging in speech is a limitation on free speech. . . . To deny an exemption to claimants who engage in certain forms of speech is in effect to penalize them for such speech. Its deterrent effect is the same as if the State were to fine them for this speech."[50]

To support its position, the state of California relied on earlier Supreme Court loyalty-oath decisions: *Garner v. Bd. of Public Works, Gerende v. Bd. of Supervisors,* and *American Communications Assn. v. Douds.* However, Justice Brennan argued that these cases were not applicable in this case. He concluded: "Believing that the principles of those cases have no application here, we hold that when the constitutional right to speak is sought to be deterred by a State's general taxing program[,] due process demands that the speech be unencumbered until the State comes forward with sufficient proof to justify its inhibition. The State clearly has no such compelling interest at stake as to justify a shortcut procedure which must inevitably result in suppressing protected speech."[51]

In a concurring opinion, Justice Black began: "California, in effect, has imposed a tax on belief and expression. In my view, a levy of this nature is wholly out of place in this country; so far as I know such a thing has never even been attempted before. I believe that it constitutes a palpable violation of the First Amendment, which of course is applicable in all its particulars to the States."[52] Critical of a decade-long acceptance of loyalty oaths, Black wrote: "The result is a stultifying conformity which in the end may well turn out to be more destructive to our free society than foreign agents could ever hope to be. The course which we have been following the past decade is not the course of a strong, free, secure people, but that of the frightened, the insecure, the intolerant."[53]

Justice Douglas also wrote a concurring opinion. His relied in part on Alexander Hamilton's warnings against compulsory oaths and on the High Court's 1867 *Cummings* decision striking down as unconstitutional a Missouri oath required of clergy among others. Hamilton, said Douglas, called the loyalty test "a subversion of one great principle of social security: to wit, that every man shall be presumed innocent until he is proved guilty."[54] Douglas warned of intrusions on the right to believe what one chooses and the right of conscience: "When we allow government to probe his [citizen's] beliefs and withhold from him some of the privileges of citizenship because of what he thinks, we do indeed 'invert the order of things,' to use Hamilton's phrase. . . . What a man thinks is of no concern to government. 'The First Amendment gives freedom of mind the same security as freedom of conscience.' "[55]

California law also required churches seeking property-tax exemptions for "real property and buildings used solely and exclusively for religious worship" to subscribe to the same loyalty oath required of the veterans. The First Unitarian Church of Los Angeles, in refusing to subscribe, argued that the oath was forbidden by the Federal Constitution. On the same day as the High Court decided for the veterans, it also decided for the Unitarian Church, with Justice Brennan delivering the opinion of the Court: "For the reasons expressed in *Speiser v. Randall*, we hold that the enforcement through procedures which place the burdens of proof and persuasion on the taxpayer is a violation of due process."[56]

As in *Speiser*, Justice Douglas wrote a concurring opinion in which he stated that what he had said in *Speiser* applied in this case. Douglas also argued that "there is a related ground on which the decision in these *Unitarian* cases should rest." He then cited a relevant principle of that church: "The principles, moral and religious, of the First Unitarian Church of Los Angeles compel it, its members, officers and minister, as a matter of deepest conscience, belief and conviction, to deny power in the state to compel acceptance by it or any other church of this or any other oath of coerced affirmation as to church doctrine, advocacy or beliefs."[57]

Concluding that the test oaths were an anathema in our society, Douglas wrote: "We stated in *Girouard v. United States* . . . : 'The test oath is abhorrent to our tradition.' . . . The reason for that abhorrence is the supremacy of conscience in our constitutional scheme. As we state in *Board of Education v. Barnette* . . . , 'If there is any fixed star in our constitutional constellation, it is that no official, high or petty, can prescribe what shall be orthodox in politics, nationalism, religion, or other matters of opinion or force citizens to confess by word or act their faith therein.' "[58]

At the same time as the United States Supreme Court was deciding that Pennsylvania's Beilan and New York's Lerner could be required to reveal their political associations and beliefs and that California's Speiser and Unitarian Church could not be required to sign the California loyalty oath, the General Assembly of Arkansas was passing legislation that required every public-school teacher in Arkansas to file annually an affidavit listing every organization to which he or she belonged or had contributed to in the preceding five years. As summarized by the United States District Court, the state's Act 10

> provides in substance that no person shall be employed or elected to employment as a superintendent, principal or teacher in any public school in Arkansas, or as an instructor, professor or teacher in any public institution of higher learning in that State until such person shall have submitted to the appropriate hiring authority an affidavit listing all organizations to which he at the time belongs and to which he has belonged during the past five years, and also listing all organizations to which he at the time is paying regular dues or is making regular contributions, or to which within the past five years he has paid such dues or made such contributions.[59]

B. T. Shelton, a teacher employed in the Little Rock public-school system for twenty-five years, refused to file the affidavit, and his contract was not renewed. He and others challenged the constitutionality of the oath. Shelton was a member of the National Association for the Advancement of Colored People (NAACP), but evidence presented at his trial "showed that he was not a member of the Communist Party or of any organization advocating the overthrow of the Government by force."[60]

The United States district court upheld the act as constitutional, concluding that the information required by the state was relevant in determining the fitness and competency of teachers; in deciding for Arkansas, the district court relied heavily on *Garner, Adler, Beilan,* and *Lerner:* "A public employer has a right to know the organizations to which its employees, including school teachers, belong or have belonged or to which they are making or have made financial contributions. This right has been recognized in *Garner . . . , Adler . . . , Beilan . . . , and Lerner.*"[61] Shelton argued that "Act 10 deprives teachers of Arkansas of their rights to personal, associational, and academic liberty, protected by the Due Process Clause of the Fourteenth Amendment from invasion by state action."[62]

When the case reached the United States Supreme Court, it decided on December 12, 1960, in a 5–4 decision, for Shelton. The High Court recognized that "there can be no question of the relevance of [a] State's inquiry into the fitness and competence of its teachers"; however, the Court went on: "It is not disputed that to compel a teacher to disclose his every associational tie is to impair that teacher's right of free association, a right closely allied to freedom of speech and a right which, like free speech, lies at the foundation of a free society."[63]

Justice Stewart, delivering the opinion of the Court, was especially concerned about "the unlimited and indiscriminate sweep of the statute":

> The scope of the inquiry required by Act 10 is completely unlimited. The statute requires a teacher to reveal the church to which he belongs, or to which he has given financial support. It requires him to disclose his political party, and every political organization to which he may have contributed over a five-year period. It requires him to list, without number, every conceivable kind of associational ties—social, professional, political, avocational, or religious. Many such relationships could have no possible bearing upon the teacher's occupational competence or fitness.[64]

The Court's opinion concluded with the assertion that "[t]he statute's comprehensive interference with associational freedom goes far beyond what might be justified in the exercise of the State's legitimate inquiry into the fitness and competency of its teachers."[65]

During the 1960s, the United States Supreme Court was confronted with several more cases dealing with loyalty oaths required of teachers, in these cases in Florida, Washington, Arizona, Maryland, and New

York. In each case, the High Court decided for the teachers who had challenged the constitutionality of the oath.

While *Shelton v. Tucker* was a 5–4 decision, nine months later the High Court unanimously declared unconstitutional a Florida oath that required the oathtaker to swear not only that he or she would support the Constitution, but also "that I have not and will not lend my aid, support, advice, counsel or influence to the Communist Party; that I do not believe in the overthrow of the Government of the United States or of the State of Florida by force or violence; that I am not a member of any organization or party which believes in or teaches, directly or indirectly, the overthrow of the Government of the United States or of Florida by force or violence."[66]

The Florida Supreme Court had concluded that the oath requirement was constitutional, declaring in its opinion that the Florida statute did not suffer from vagueness: "Certainly the instant statute is perfectly clear in its requirements. There could be no doubt in the minds of anyone who can read English as to the requirements of the statute and the effect of a failure to comply."[67]

What was "perfectly clear" to the Florida Supreme Court was not so clear to the United States Supreme Court, which attacked the "extraordinary ambiguity of the statutory language": "The provision of the oath here in question . . . says nothing of advocacy of violent overthrow of state or federal government. . . . The provision is completely lacking in these or other terms susceptible of objective measurement. Those who take this oath must swear, rather, that they have not in the unending past ever knowingly lent their 'aid,' or 'support,' or 'advice,' or 'counsel' or 'influence' to the Communist Party. What do these phrases mean?"[68]

Justice Stewart, writing for the unanimous Court, then asked a series of questions to point out the "extraordinary ambiguity of the statutory language":

> Could one who had ever cast his vote for such a candidate [Communist] safely subscribe to this legislative oath? Could a lawyer who had ever represented the Communist Party or its members swear with either confidence or honesty that he had never knowingly lent his "counsel" to the Party? Could a journalist who had ever defended the constitutional rights of the Communist Party conscientiously take an oath that he had never lent the Party his "support"? Indeed, could anyone honestly subscribe to this oath who had ever supported any cause with contemporaneous knowledge that the Communist Party also supported it?[69]

The Court concluded with an affirmation of the constitutional rights of public employees: "It is enough for the present case to reaffirm 'that constitutional protection does extend to the public servant whose exclusion pursuant to a statute is patently arbitrary or discriminatory.' *Wieman v. Updegraff. . . .* 'The fact . . . that a person is not compelled to hold public office cannot possibly be an excuse for barring him from office by state-imposed criteria forbidden by the Constitution.' *Torcaso v. Watkins. . . .*"[70]

The *Torcaso* citation with which Justice Stewart concluded *Cramp* came from the Court's opinion in *Torcaso v. Watkins,* decided six months before *Cramp.* Roy Torcaso had refused to take a Maryland oath required of persons seeking a commission to become a notary public; the oath was not a non-Communist oath, but an oath requiring an assertion that he believed in the existence of God. As a condition for becoming a notary public, Torcaso was required to state: "I, Roy R. Torcaso, do declare I believe in the existence of God."[71] Torcaso was willing to take that part of the oath in which he promised to "support the Constitution of the United States." As a result of his refusal to assert his belief in the existence of God, he was denied the commission, whereupon he brought suit.

When the case reached the Maryland Court of Appeals, it decided against Torcaso, arguing that "the petitioner is not compelled to believe or disbelieve, under threat of punishment or other compulsion. True, unless he makes the declaration of belief he cannot hold public office in Maryland, but he is not compelled to hold office."[72] The Maryland court also argued: "[I]t seems clear that under our Constitution disbelief in a Supreme Being, and the denial of any moral accountability for conduct, not only renders a person incompetent to hold public office, but to give testimony, or serve as a juror. The historical record makes it clear that religious toleration, in which this State has taken pride, was never thought to encompass the ungodly."[73]

The Maryland court asserted that it found it "difficult to believe that the Supreme Court will hold that a declaration of belief in the existence of God . . . is discriminatory and invalid."[74]

But on June 19, 1961, the United States Supreme Court did hold, unanimously, that the Maryland oath demanding a declaration of belief in the existence of God was invalid. In deciding for Torcaso, the High Court stated: "We repeat and again reaffirm that neither a State nor the Federal Government can constitutionally force a person 'to profess a belief or disbelief in any religion.' Neither can constitutionally pass laws or impose requirements which aid all religions as against non-believers, and neither can aid those religions based on a belief in the existence of God as against those religions founded on different beliefs."[75]

Justice Black, writing for the unanimous Court, responded directly to Maryland's argument that Torcaso was "not compelled to believe or disbelieve, under threat of punishment or other compulsion" and that he was not "compelled to hold office": "The fact . . . that a person is not compelled to hold public office cannot possibly be an excuse for barring him from office by state-imposed criteria forbidden by the Constitution. . . . This Maryland religious test for public office unconstitutionally invades the appellant's freedom of belief and religion and therefore cannot be enforced against him."[76]

The 1961 United States Supreme Court had come a long way from *Adler* in 1952, in which it had asserted that those who did not choose to sign the New York oath had, of course, the right to assemble, speak, think, and believe as they will, but that "[i]t is equally clear that they have no right to work for the State in the school system on their own terms. They may work for the school system upon the reasonable terms laid down by the proper authorities of New York. If they do not choose to work on such terms, they are at liberty to retain their beliefs and associations and go elsewhere. Has the State thus deprived them of any right to free speech or assembly? We think not."[77]

In 1955, the state of Washington had begun requiring state employees to sign a loyalty oath, including teachers already required to sign an oath of allegiance. This latter oath had been instituted in 1931 and required teachers to subscribe to the following: "I solemnly swear (or affirm) that I will support the constitution and laws of the United States of America and of the State of Washington, and will by precept and example promote respect for the flag and the institutions of the United States of America and the State of Washington, reverence for law and order and undivided allegiance to the government of the United States."[78]

As of 1955, teachers were required to sign a second oath, which read in part:

> I certify that I have read the provisions of RCW 9.81.010 (2), (3), and (5); RCW 9.81.060 . . . which are printed on the reverse hereof; that I am not a subversive person as therein defined; and
>
> I do solemnly swear (or affirm) that I am not a member of the Communist Party or knowingly of any other subversive organization.

I understand that this statement and oath are made subject to the penalties of perjury.[79]

The Washington Revised Code, 9.81.010 (5) defined a "subversive person" as follows:

"Subversive person" means any person who commits, attempts to commit, or aids in the commission, or advocates, abets, advises or teaches by any means any person to commit, attempt to commit, or aid in the commission of any act intended to overthrow, destroy or alter, or to assist in the overthrow, destruction or alteration of, the constitutional form of the government of the United States, or of the state of Washington, or any political subdivision of either of them by revolution, force, or violence; or who with knowledge that the organization is an organization as described in subsections (2) and (3) hereof, becomes or remains a member of a subversive organization or a foreign subversive organization.[80]

The constitutionality of the two Washington oaths was challenged by approximately sixty-four members of the University of Washington staff, faculty, and student body. On February 9, 1963, the United States District Court decided that the 1955 loyalty oath was constitutional, arguing that "[a]cademic freedom of inquiry and the fearless pursuit of truth and knowledge, wherever they may lead, is not possible for an individual who is fettered by dedicated membership in an association whose purpose is violent overthrow or destruction of our constitutional form of government, the very guardian of our rights and freedoms. . . . Education, not indoctrination, is the function of a university teacher."[81]

Those who challenged the constitutionality of the oaths argued that "the structure and language of the oath is vague, leaving plaintiffs uncertain of the sweep of the statute and the kind of conduct or association which will disqualify an individual from public employment." The district court responded: "It is our view that a reasonable construction of the statutory language does not leave the meaning uncertain or vague—in any event not to the extent that the statute must or should be held unconstitutional in an action such as this. The words used are to be understood in accordance with the ordinary meaning of the words in current usage."[82] The meaning of "abet," "assist" and "by any means," asserted the district court, "as used in the statute, is free of ambiguity."[83]

But the statute was not "free of ambiguity," said the United States Supreme Court on June 1, 1964, when it reversed the district court decision. Justice White, delivering the opinion of the Court, devoted a significant portion of its opinion to the issue of vagueness: "Appellants contend in this Court that the oath requirements and the statutory provisions on which they are based are invalid on their face because their language is unduly vague, uncertain and broad. We agree with this contention and therefore, without reaching the numerous other contentions pressed upon us, confine our considerations to that particular question."[84]

Justice White turned to *Cramp*, in which the Court had "invalidated an oath requiring teachers and other employees of the State to swear that they had never lent their 'aid, support, advice, counsel or influence to the Communist Party' because the oath was lacking in 'terms susceptible of objective measurement' and failed to inform as to what the State commanded or forbade."[85] The Washington oath, said the Court, suffered from "similar infirmities": "Persons required to swear they understand this oath may quite reasonably conclude that any person who aids the Communist Party or teaches or advises known members of the Party is a subversive person because such teaching or advice may now or at some future date aid the activities of the Party."[86]

The Court asked some of the same questions as it had asked in *Cramp*: "Does the statute reach endorsement or support for Communist candidates for office? Does it reach a lawyer who represents the Communist Party . . . ?" The Washington statute, concluded the Court, "like the one at issue in *Cramp*, is unconstitutionally vague."[87] Further, asked the Court, "Is it subversive activity . . . to attend and participate in international conventions of mathmeticians and exchange views with scholars from Communist countries?"[88]

At the same time as it struck down the 1955 oath, the High Court also declared the 1931 oath unconstitutional because of vagueness.

> The oath exacts a promise that the affiant will, by precept and example, promote respect for the flag and the institutions of the United States and the State of Washington. The range of activities which are or might be deemed inconsistent with the required promise is very wide indeed. The teacher who refused to salute the flag or advocated refusal because of religious beliefs might well be accused of breaching his promise. . . . Even criticism of the design or color scheme of the state flag or unfavorable comparison of it with that of a sister State or foreign country could be deemed disrespectful and therefore violative of the oath. And what are 'institutions' for the purposes of this oath? . . . The oath may prevent a professor from criticizing his state judicial system or the Supreme Court

or the institution of judicial review. Or it might be deemed to proscribe advocating the abolition, for example, of the Civil Rights Commission, the House Committee on un-American Activities, or foreign aid.[89]

Justice White ended the *Baggett* opinion with the same citation from *Torcaso* that concluded the Court's *Cramp* opinion: "The fact . . . that a person is not compelled to hold public office cannot possibly be an excuse for barring him from office by state-imposed criteria forbidden by the Constitution."[90]

One year before the United States Supreme Court decided *Baggett*, the Arizona Supreme Court decided, on May 1, 1963, against school-teacher Barbara Elfbrandt, who had refused to sign Arizona's loyalty oath, which read:

> I, (type or print name), do solemnly swear (or affirm) that I will support the Constitution of the United States and the Constitution and laws of the State of Arizona; that I will bear true faith and allegiance to the same, and defend them against all enemies, foreign and domestic, and that I will faithfully and impartially discharge the duties of the office of (name of office) according to the best of my ability, so help me God (or so I do affirm).[91]

Elfbrandt, "a teacher and a Quaker, decided she could not in good conscience take the oath, not knowing what it meant and not having any chance to get a hearing at which its precise scope and meaning could be determined."[92]

While at first glance the oath appeared to be a standard "positive oath," with no inquiry into "un-American" political associations and beliefs, the Arizona legislature "put a gloss on the oath by subjecting to prosecution for perjury and for discharge from public office anyone who took the oath and who 'knowingly and wilfully becomes or remains a member of the communist party of the United States or its successors or any of its subordinate organizations' or 'any other organization' having for 'one of its purposes' the overthrow of the government of Arizona . . . where the employee had knowledge of the unlawful purpose."[93]

The United States Supreme Court vacated the judgment of the Arizona court and "remanded the cause for reconsideration in light of *Baggett v. Bullitt*." The Arizona Supreme Court reconsidered, and on December 30, 1964, again decided against Elfbrandt, declaring: "It is our conclusion that the portions of the Arizona act here considered do not forbid or require conduct in terms so vague that men and women of common intelligence must necessarily guess at the meaning and differ as to their application."[94]

Arizona Supreme Court Justice Bernstein dissented, arguing that freedom of association was inhibited by the Arizona oath authorizing act that contained a provision that prohibited membership in "any other organization having for *one* of its purposes the overthrow by force or violence of the government of the state of Arizona or any of its political subdivisions." To illustrate his concern, Justice Bernstein provided an example:

> Let us consider a scientist, a teacher in one of our universities. He could not know whether membership is prohibited in an international scientific organization which includes members from neutralist nations and Communist bloc nations—the latter admittedly dedicated to the overthrow of our government and which control the organization—even though access to the scientific information of the organization is available only to its members. . . . Though all might agree that the principal purpose of such an organization is scientific, the statute makes his membership a crime if any subordinate purpose is the overthrow of the state government. The vice of vagueness here is that the scientist cannot know whether membership in the organization will result in prosecution . . . or in honors from his university for the encyclopedic knowledge acquired in his field in part through his membership.[95]

The case went back to the United States Supreme Court, and on April 18, 1966, the High Court decided, 5–4, for Elfbrandt. Justice Douglas, delivering the opinion of the Court, was especially concerned that the Arizona statute brought with it "guilt by association": "Nothing in the oath, the statutory gloss, or the construction of the oath and statutes given by the Arizona Supreme Court, purports to exclude association by one who does not subscribe to the organization's unlawful ends. Here as in *Baggett v. Bullitt* . . . , the 'hazard of being prosecuted for knowing but guiltless behavior' is a reality."[96] Justice Douglas concluded the Court's opinion by asserting: "A law which applies to membership without the 'specific intent' to further the illegal aims of the organization infringes unnecessarily on protected freedoms. It rests on the doctrine of 'guilt by association' which has no place here. . . . Such a law cannot stand."[97]

The following year, on January 23, 1967, New York's complex of loyalty laws, described by Justice Brennan as a "regulatory maze," were struck down by the United States Supreme Court in a 5–4 decision. Over

a decade earlier, the New York State Board of Regents had been directed
by the state to compile a list of "subversive" organizations and to provide rules and regulations related to membership in such organizations
and employment in New York's schools. In 1956, the New York college
professor was required to sign the Feinberg Certificate "declaring that he
had read the Regents Rules and understood that the Rules and the statutes constituted terms of employment, and declaring further that he was
not a member of the Communist Party, and that if he had ever been a
member he had communicated that fact to the President of the State
University. This was the certificate that appellants [professors] Hoch-
field, Maud, Keyishian, and Garver refused to sign."[98]

While the Feinberg Certificate was rescinded in June 1965, the professors were informed "of disqualification which flowed from membership
in a listed 'subversive' organization." They were further informed:
"Should any question arise in the course of such inquiry such candidate
may request . . . a personal interview. Refusal of a candidate to answer
any question relevant to such inquiry by such officer shall be sufficient
ground to refuse to make or recommend appointment."[99] When the case
reached the United States Supreme Court, Justice Brennan, delivering the
opinion of the Court, declared: "The change in procedure in no wise
moots appellants' constitutional questions raised in the context of their
refusal to sign the now abandoned Feinberg Certificate. The substance
of the statutory and regulatory complex remains and from the outset
appellants' basic claim has been that they are aggrieved by its application."[100]

The Court majority argued that the wording in the challenged laws
was vague and led to uncertainty as to what was prohibited:

> We do not have the benefit of a judicial gloss by the New York courts
> enlightening us as to the scope of this complicated plan. In light of the
> intricate administrative machinery for its enforcement, this is not surpris-
> ing. The very intricacy of the plan and the uncertainty as to the scope of
> its proscriptions make it a highly efficient *in terrorem* mechanism. It would
> be a bold teacher who would not stay as far as possible from utterances
> or acts which might jeopardize his living by enmeshing him in this intricate
> machinery. The uncertainty as to the utterances and acts proscribed in-
> creases that caution in "those who believe the written law means what it
> says."[101]

Having relied on the ominous machinery metaphor, Brennan then added
a metaphoric maze to emphasize the difficulty of getting through all the

rules and regulations related to the loyalty-oath process in New York: "The regulatory maze created by New York is wholly lacking in 'terms susceptible of objective measurement.' . . . It has the quality of 'extraordinary ambiguity' found to be fatal to the oaths considered in *Cramp* and *Baggett*. . . . Vagueness of wording is aggravated by prolixity and profusion of statutes, regulations, and administrative machinery, and by manifold cross-references to interrelated enactments and rules."[102]

Fifteen years earlier, in 1952, the High Court had upheld in *Adler* the part of the Feinberg Law that made Communist Party membership prima facie evidence of disqualification. In 1967, Brennan wrote in *Keyishian*: "[C]onstitutional doctrine which has emerged since that decision has rejected its major premise. That premise was that public employment, including academic employment, may be conditioned upon the surrender of constitutional rights which could not be abridged by direct government actions."[103] Quoting from *Sherbert v. Verner*, a 1963 Supreme Court decision related to the firing of a Seventh Day Adventist who would not work on Saturday and was denied unemployment benefits, Justice Brennan wrote: "It is too late in the day to doubt that the liberties of religion and expression may be infringed by the denial of or placing of conditions upon a benefit or privilege."[104]

As to the validity of New York's barring employment to members of the listed "subversive" organizations, Justice Brennan wrote: "Here again constitutional doctrine has developed since *Adler*. Mere knowing membership without a specific intent to further the unlawful aims of an organization is not a constitutionally adequate basis for exclusion from such positions as those held by appellants."[105] The New York laws suffered from vagueness, declared Brennan, but also from overbreadth.[106]

The sharp division of the Court became evident in the first sentence of the dissenting opinion written by Justice Clark (joined by Justices Harlan, Stewart, and White): "The blunderbuss fashion in which the majority couches 'its artillery of words,' together with the morass of cases it cites as authority and the obscurity of their application to the question at hand, makes it difficult to grasp the true thrust of its decision."[107]

The strongly worded dissenting opinion continued on in metaphorical language: "It is clear that the Feinberg Law, in which this Court found 'no constitutional infirmity' in 1952, has been given its death blow today. . . . [R]egardless of its correctness, neither New York nor the several

States that have followed the teaching of *Adler* . . . , for some 15 years, can ever put the pieces together again. No court has ever reached out so far to destroy so much with so little."[108]

Referring to such Court decisions as *Garner, Adler, Beilan*, and *Lerner*, Justice Clark argued: "In view of this long list of decisions covering over 15 years of this Court's history, in which no opinion of the Court even questioned the validity of the *Adler* line of cases, it is strange to me that the Court now finds that the 'constitutional doctrine which has emerged since . . . has rejected [*Adler's*] major premise.' With due respect, as I read them, our cases have done no such thing."[109]

What was at stake here, asserted Clark, was the "self-preservation" of the State: "I regret to say—and I do so with deference—that the majority has by its broadside swept away one of our most precious rights, namely, the right of self-preservation. Our public educational system is the genius of our democracy. The minds of our youth are developed there and the character of that development will determine the future of our land. Indeed, our very existence depends upon it."[110]

Professor Howard Whitehill was another academic who received constitutional protection in 1967, when the United States Supreme Court decided, 6–3, to strike down Maryland's loyalty oath, which he had refused to sign when offered a teaching position at the University of Maryland. The oath Whitehill refused to sign read: "I,———, do hereby . . . certify that I am not engaged in one way or another in the attempt to overthrow the Government of the United States, or the State of Maryland, or any political subdivision of either of them, by force or violence. I further certify that I understand the aforegoing statement is made subject to the penalties of perjury. . . ."[111]

Justice Douglas, delivering the opinion of the Court, indicated at the outset that

> the question is whether the oath is to be read in isolation or in connection with the Ober Act . . . which by §§ 1 and 13 defines a "subversive" as " . . . any person who commits, attempts to commit, or aids in the commission, or advocates, abets, advises or teaches by any means any person to commit, attempt to commit, or aid in the commission of any act intended to overthrow, destroy or alter, or to assist in the overthrow, destruction or *alteration* of, the constitutional form of the government of the United States, or of the State of Maryland, or any public subdivision of either of them, *by revolution, force or violence*; or who is a *member of a*

subversive organization or a foreign subversive organization, as more fully defined in this article."[112]

It was the majority's conclusion that the Maryland oath must be considered "with reference to §§ 1 and 13, not in isolation."[113]

Douglas argued that some of the language appearing in the oath and in the Ober Act was much too vague and too broad. He asked: "Would a member of a group that was out to overthrow the Government by force or violence be engaged in that attempt 'in one way or another' within the meaning of the oath, even though he was ignorant of the real aims of the group and wholly innocent of any illicit purpose? We do not know; nor could a prospective employee know, save as he risked a prosecution for perjury."[114]

Douglas argued that the "continuing surveillance which this type of law places on teachers is hostile to academic freedom. . . . The restraints on conscientious teachers are obvious."[115] The subjects of vagueness, overbreadth, and academic freedom came together at the conclusion of the Court's opinion: "The lines between permissible and impermissible conduct are quite indistinct. Precision and clarity are not present. Rather we find an overbreadth that makes possible oppressive or capricious application as regimes change. That very threat . . . , may deter the flowering of academic freedom as much as successive suits for perjury."[116]

In the middle of the nineteenth century, attorneys were subjected to the Ironclad loyalty oath, imposed by Congress on attorneys. One hundred years later, oathtaking was again imposed, in state after state, when attorneys sought admission to the bar. On February 23, 1971, the United States Supreme Court handed down three decisions related to oaths and questionnaires requiring attorneys applying for admission to the bar in Arizona, Ohio, and New York to reveal political beliefs and associational ties.

In *Baird v. State Bar of Arizona*, the High Court decided for Sara Baird, a graduate of the Stanford Law School who willingly answered a question that required her to reveal all organizations with which she had been associated since she was sixteen years old, but refused to "state whether she had ever been a member of the Communist Party or any organization 'that advocates overthrow of the United States Government by force or violence.' "[117] On the basis of this refusal, the Arizona Bar Committee declined to process her application and would not recommend her admission to the bar.

In announcing the judgment of the Court, Justice Black (joined by Justices Douglas, Brennan, and Marshall) referred to the two decades of loyalty-oath cases that had come before the Supreme Court and led to conflicts and divisions "concerning the power of States to refuse to permit applicants to practice law in cases where bar examiners have been suspicious about applicants' loyalties and their view on Communism and revolution [a reference to attorneys refusing to answer associational questions when appearing before bar examiners[118]]. This has been an increasingly divisive and bitter issue for some years, especially since Senator Joseph McCarthy from Wisconsin stirred up anti-Communist feelings and fears by his 'investigations' in the early 1950's."[119]

Continuing his opinion, Black observed that the courts had been dealing for years with cases "involving inquisitions about beliefs and associations and refusals to let people practice law and hold public or even private jobs soley because public authorities have been suspicious of their ideas. Usually these denials of employment have not been based on any overt acts of misconduct or lawlessness, and the litigation has continued to raise serious questions of alleged violations of the First Amendment and other guarantees of the Bill of Rights."[120] Among the cases Black cites are *Adler, Beilan, Elfbrandt, Keyishian, Shelton, Speiser,* and *Wilkinson.* "The foregoing cases and others," he continued, "contain thousands of pages of confusing formulas, refined reasonings, and puzzling holdings that touch on the same suspicions and fears about citizenship and loyalty."[121]

In giving Baird First Amendment protection, Black argued:

[T]his young lady was asked by the State to make a guess as to whether any organization to which she ever belonged "advocates overthrow of the United States Government by force or violence." There may well be provisions of the Federal Constitution other than the First Amendment that would protect an applicant to a state bar from being subjected to a question potentially so hazardous to her liberty. But whether or not there are other provisions that protect her, we think the First Amendment does so here.[122]

In addition to arguing that Arizona's inquiries discouraged "citizens from exercising rights protected by the Constitution," Black argued that "when a State seeks to inquire about an individual's beliefs and associations a heavy burden lies upon it to show that the inquiry is necessary to protect a legitimate state interest." In this case, said Black, Baird "has already supplied the Committee with extensive personal and professional information to assist its determination."[123]

Noting that Baird had listed in answering one of the questionnaire inquiries such organizations as "Church Choir; Girl Scouts, Girls Athletic Association; Young Republicans; Young Democrats; Stanford Law Association; Law School Civil Rights Research Council," Black asserts that the State Bar of Arizona "does not state which of these organizations may threaten the security of the Republic."[124]

With his heavy reliance on the First Amendment in deciding for Baird, Black alluded to previous uses of the First Amendment by persons who refused to reveal their political beliefs and associations: "Some of what has been written is reconcilable with what we have said here and some of it is not. Without detailed reference to all prior cases, it is sufficient to say we hold that views and beliefs are immune from bar association inquisitions designed to lay a foundation for barring an applicant from the practice of law. Clearly Arizona has engaged in such questioning here."[125]

The alignment of the High Court was the same (5–4) in *In re Stolar*, a case decided the same day as *Baird*. Justice Black again announced the judgment of the Court, in this case involving Martin Stolar, a New York University Law School graduate who, when he applied to the Ohio Bar for admission to practice law in that state, refused to answer the following questions on the Ohio application form:

7. List the names and addresses of all clubs, societies or organizations of which you are or have been a member since registering as a law student.

12. State whether you have been, or presently are . . . (g) a member of any organization which advocates the overthrow of the government of the United States by force. . . .

13. List the names and addresses of all clubs, societies or organizations of which you are or have been a member.[126]

Stolar's application to take the Ohio bar examination was denied on the basis of his refusal to answer the above questions.

Stolar, who had previously been licensed to practice law in New York, had answered the New York question, "Do you believe in the principle underlying the form of government of the United States?" with "Yes." He had also answered the New York inquiry, "State whether you have been or are a member of any party or organization engaged in propagating or pledged to effect changes in the form of government provided for by the United States Constitution, or in advancing the interests of a foreign country. If so, state the facts fully." His answer had been no.[127]

Justice Black observed that Stolar had "supplied the Ohio committee with extensive personal and professional information as well as numerous character references to enable it to make the necessary investigation and determination. Moreover, even though irrelevant to his fitness to practice law, Stolar's answers to questions on the New York application provided Ohio with substantially the information it was seeking by Questions 7, 12(g), and 13."[128] Clearly and directly, Black asserted that Ohio

> may not require an applicant for admission to the Bar to state whether he has been or is a "member of any organization which advocates the overthrow of the government of the United States by force." As we noted above, the First Amendment prohibits Ohio from penalizing a man solely because he is a member of a particular organization. . . . Since this is true, we can see no legitimate state interest which is served by a question which sweeps so broadly into areas of belief and association protected against government invasion."[129]

Justice Stewart wrote a short concurring opinion: "Ohio's Questions 7 and 13 are plainly unconstitutional under *Shelton v. Tucker*. . . . In addition, Question 12(g) suffers from the same constitutional deficiency as does Arizona's Question 27 in *Baird v. State Bar of Arizona*. . . . For these reasons I agree that the judgment before us must be reversed."[130]

In the third oath case decided on February 23, 1971, *Law Students Research Council v. Wadmond*, Justice Stewart, who had joined Justices Black, Brennan, Douglas, and Marshall in deciding for Baird and Stolar, now joined Justices Burger, Blackmun, Harlan, and White to comprise the majority upholding the New York oath required of applicants for admission to the Bar of New York. Among the inquiries objected to by the applicants in this case were:

> 26. (a) Have you ever organized or helped to organize or become a member of any organization or group of persons which, during the period of your membership or association, you knew was advocating or teaching that the government of the United States or any state or any political subdivision thereof should be overthrown or overturned by force, violence or any unlaw-

ful means?————If your answer is in the affirmative, state the facts below.

   (b) If your answer to (a) is in the affirmative, did you, during the period of such membership or association, have the specific intent to further the aims of such organization or group of persons to overthrow or overturn the government of the United States or any state or any political subdivision thereof by force, violence or any unlawful means?

27. (a) Is there any reason why you cannot take and subscribe to an oath or affirmation that you will support the constitution of the United States and of the State of New York? If there is, please explain.

   (b) Can you conscientiously, and do you, affirm that you are, without any mental reservation, loyal to and ready to support the Constitution of the United States?[131]

Justice Stewart, writing for the majority, argued that "Question 26 is precisely tailored to conform to the relevant decisions of this Court. . . . We have held that knowing membership in an organization advocating the overthrow of the Government by force or violence, on the part of one sharing the specific intent to further the organization's illegal goals, may be made criminally punishable." "Surely," said Stewart, "a State is constitutionally entitled to make such an inquiry of an applicant for admission to a profession dedicated to the peaceful and reasoned settlement of disputes between men, and between a man and his government."[132]

As for Question 27, Stewart concluded that "the question is simply supportive of the appellee's task of ascertaining the good faith with which an applicant can take the constitutional oath."[133]

Justice Black, joined by Justice Douglas, declared in his dissenting opinion: "In my view, the First Amendment absolutely prohibits a State from penalizing a man because of his beliefs. . . . Hence, a State cannot require that an applicant's belief in our form of government be established before he can become a lawyer."[134] Further, Black stated that he failed "to see how the majority's approval of these questions [26 and 27] can be reconciled with *Baird* . . . and *In re Stolar*. . . ."[135]

Justice Marshall, joined by Justice Brennan, stated in his dissenting opinion that there were three difficulties with Question (26)(a):

First, Question 26(a) is undeniably overbroad in that it covers the affiliations of those who do not adhere to teachings concerning unlawful political change, or are simply indifferent this aspect of an association's activities. . . . Second, no attempt has been made to limit Question 26(a) to associational advocacy of concrete, specific, and imminent illegal acts, or to associational activity that creates a serious likelihood of harm through imminent illegal conduct. . . . Third, would-be Bar applicants are left to wonder whether particular political acts amount to 'becom[ing] a member' of a 'group of persons'—law students and others, when embarking on associational activities, must guess whether the association's teaching fall within the nebulous formula of Question 26(a), or more to the point, whether their own assessment of an association's teaching would coincide with that of screening officials. . . . The indefinite scope of Question 26(a) expectedly operates to induce prospective applicants to resolve doubts by failing to exercise their First Amendment rights.[136]

For a quarter of a century, governmental demands that millions of American citizens sign loyalty oaths to declare their loyalty, sign disclaimer affidavits to declare they were not disloyal, and reveal political beliefs and associations as a condition of employment led to hundreds of court cases determining the constitutionality of the oaths and affidavits. Beginning in the mid-1960s, court after court, federal and state, found the disclaimer affidavits unconstitutional, while at the same time declaring the "positive" oaths constitutional. One by one, state disclaimer affidavits were found unacceptable by the courts. In addition to the Supreme Court cases already cited, these cases included the following:

June 19, 1965: Idaho's oath, said a United States district court, "failed to meet the due process requirements of the Fourteenth Amendment."[137]

October 1, 1965: Georgia's statute requiring all teachers in the public schools to sign a loyalty oath, said a United States district court, was unconstitutional; citing especially *Cramp* and *Baggett*, the court stated: "The oath must allow public servants to know definitely what is and what is not disloyal. They may not be required to guess on penalty of loss of position or liberty; hence the oath must be couched in language setting a clear standard, and it must be directed to activity, either as an individual or through organizational membership, wherein the overthrow of the federal or state government by force or violence is advocated."[138]

October 4, 1966: Oregon's teacher loyalty oath was held to be unconstitutional by the Supreme Court of Oregon: "Our decision is controlled by *Baggett v. Bullitt. . . ."*[139]

April 24, 1967: Colorado's loyalty oath required of college professors was struck down by a United States district court: "The Court concludes as a matter of law that the statute requiring the plaintiff to take the oath in question, when construed in the light of *Baggett v. Bullitt . . .* , is violative of due process because the oath is unduly vague, uncertain and broad. . . ."[140]

March 24, 1967: The New Hampshire Supreme Court declares that state's loyalty oath required of public servants unconstitutional: "We can see no way to distinguish the oath before us from the oath declared invalid in *Baggett v. Bullitt. . . ."*[141]

August 30, 1967: The Texas nonsubversive loyalty oath is declared unconstitutional by a United States district court: "We find that Section 1 of Article 6252-7 [asking about membership in the Communist Party and Communist front organizations, etc.] suffers from the same 'impermissible overbreadth' which afflicted the statutory provisions struck down in *Elfbrandt* and *Keyishian*."[142]

September 11, 1967: The Kansas loyalty oath required of state employees is declared unconstitutional by a United States district court: "We conclude that K.S.A. 21-305 [the oaths of public officers and employees and the provision for dismissal for failure to sign] to the extent that it proscribes mere membership in an organization advocating the overthrow by violence of the government of the United States or of the state, without any showing of specific intent to further the aims of such organization, suffers from the 'overbreadth' denounced in *Keyishian*, and is therefore unconstitutional."[143]

December 4, 1968: A District of Columbia loyalty oath required of members of Federal City College of D.C. is declared unconstitutional by the United States district court in D.C.: "The statute as applied requires a college instructor to take an oath that he is not and will not knowingly become a member of an organization that advocates the overthrow of our constitutional form of government. Such a requirement has more than once been declared unconstitutional by the Supreme Court."[144]

June 13, 1969: An Illinois loyalty affidavit required of state employees is declared unconstitutional by a United States district court: "Clearly, it is too late in the day to resurrect the premise that public employment, or compensation therefor, may be conditioned upon the surrender of constitutional rights that could not be abridged by direct governmental action. . . . In sum, the constitutional issues raised in these actions have been fully and finally determined by the Supreme Court in *Keyishian, Elfbrandt* and *Whitehill.* . . . We are, therefore, left with no alternative but to conclude that the Illinois oath . . . must fall as being a derogation of the First and Fourteenth Amendment rights of the plaintiffs [schoolteachers]."[145]

October 30, 1969: A Florida loyalty oath is declared unconstitutional by a United States district court, except the part of the oath that requires the oathtaker to swear: "I will support the Constitution of the United States and of the State of Florida; *** that I do not believe in the overthrow of the Government of the United States or of the State of Florida by force or violence."[146]

June 24, 1970: California's loyalty oath for teachers is declared unconstitutional by a United States district court: "The Court, having heard oral argument and considered the briefs herein, finds the oath promulgated by § 13121 to be essentially indistinguishable from the one declared unconstitutional in *Baggett.* The Court thus feels itself foreclosed from considering the arguments advanced by the State."[147]

December 29, 1970: Mississippi's loyalty questionnaire asking if one is a "subversive" person, required of state employees, is declared unconstitutional by a United States district court: "We think that the concluding paragraph of the majority opinion in *Bullitt* succinctly and precisely states the basis for our holding the Mississippi Subversive Activities Act to be unconstitutional because the language therein is unduly vague, uncertain and broad. . . ."[148]

Where the oaths and affidavits imposed by state legislators earlier were held constitutional by the courts on the basis of what the United States Supreme Court had decided in *Garner, Adler, Grende,* and *Beilan,* during the 1960s and 1970s the oaths were being declared unconstitutional in court after court on the basis of *Baggett, Shelton, Elfbrandt, Cramp, Keyishian,* and *Whitehill.*

This switch also occurred in state courts. For instance, in 1952, the California Supreme Court decided in *Pockman v. Leonard* that the California loyalty oath required of state employees was constitutional. In so deciding, the court declared: "Nearly all of the contentions made by petitioner [a San Francisco State College professor] concerning asserted violations of federal constitutional guarantees are answered adversely to him by recent decisions of the United States Supreme Court."[149] Whereupon the California court cited *Adler, Garner,* and *American*

Communications Ass'n, followed by the assertion that "a person's associates, as well as his conduct, are relevant factors in determining fitness and loyalty, and the state, under its police power, may properly limit a person's freedom of choice between membership in such organizations and employment in the school system."[150] Fifteen years later, the same California court concluded that essentially the same California oath was unconstitutional: "On the authority of *Keyishian . . . ,* and *Elfbrandt . . . ,* it must be held that the oath required [in this case] is invalid. *Pockman v. Leonard . . . ,* holding to the contrary, is overruled."[151]

While in the 1960s the courts increasingly declared unconstitutional those oaths that required the oath-taker to reveal political associations and beliefs—to declare, "I am not a member of any organization which believes in or teaches the overthrow of the United States Government by force or violence," and to assert, "I will promote respect for the flag and respect for law and order"—the "positive oaths," also challenged, were held to be constitutional. On June 2, 1967, a United States district court upheld an oath required of teachers and professors in New York, several of whom had refused to sign the oath, which read: "I do solemnly swear (or affirm) that I will support the constitution of the United States of America and the constitution of the State of New York, and that I will faithfully discharge, according to the best of my ability, the duties of the position of (title of position and name or designation of school, college, university or institution to be here inserted), to which I am now assigned."[152]

In deciding against the professor who challenged the constitutionality of the oath, the district court argued that the United States Supreme Court, "in striking down so called 'negative loyalty oath' requirements of the states, has never suggested that the First Amendment proscribes any form of oath or affirmation required of teachers. See e.g., *Elfbrandt. . . ."*[153] The district court concluded that "the language of Section 30002 [which included the oath] is simple and clear in its import" and did not "suffer the vice of vagueness."[154]

As for the argument that the contested oath interfered with the teachers' freedom of speech, the court stated: "[W]e interpret the statute to impose no restrictions upon political or philosophical expressions by teachers in the State of New York. A state does not interfere with its teachers by requiring them to support the governmental systems which shelter and nourish the institutions in which they teach, nor does it restrict its teachers by encouraging them to uphold the highest standards of their chosen profession."[155] In 1968, the United States Supreme Court affirmed this decision.[156]

Another "positive oath," this one required of teachers and employees of the University of Colorado, was held constitutional by a United States district court in 1967. The Colorado oath read: "I solemnly swear or affirm that I will support the Constitution of the State of Colorado and of the United States of America and the laws of the State of Colorado and of the United States."[157] The oath, said the district court, was "not vague and indefinite so as to be in violation of the Fourteenth Amendment. . . . The oath in question is plain, straight-forward and unequivocal. A person taking it is not left in doubt as to his undertaking."[158] Further, said the court, the oath does not have any "tendency to curtail freedom of expression as guaranteed by the First Amendment."[159] "So we hold," concluded the court, "that an oath to support the constitution and laws of the state and nation does not and cannot run counter to First Amendment freedoms."[160] Again, the United States Supreme Court affirmed the positive loyalty oath.[161]

In 1969, another Colorado loyalty oath, worded slightly differently than the above Colorado oath and "required of every person employed to teach in state public schools or institutions of higher learning," was held to be constitutional by a United States district court. The oath in this later case read: "I solemnly (swear) (affirm) that I will uphold the constitution of the United States and the constitution of Colorado, and I will faithfully perform the duties of the position upon which I am about to enter."[162] The district court concluded that this oath "is not unduly vague. . . . It is not a sweeping and improper invasion of plaintiffs' rights of free association and expression."[163] Again, the United States Supreme Court affirmed the decision of the lower court.[164]

On January 19, 1971, Sari Knopp Biklen, a Quaker, was discharged from her teaching position as a result of her refusal to sign the oath required by New York, which read: "I do solemnly swear (or affirm) that I will support the constitution of the United States of America and the constitution of the State of New York, and that I will faithfully discharge, according to the best of my ability, the duties of the position of (title of position and name or designation of school, college, university or institution to be here inserted), to which I am now assigned."[165] Biklen had "informed the Director of Personnel of the City School District that her religious and conscientious beliefs prevented her from signing the required oath or affirmation."[166]

In a personal statement, Biklen presented the reasons upon which her refusal was based; she said, in part:

> My decision was one of conscience. I have tried to teach the children in my class that each of us has a conscience, and that we need to learn to listen to it and to act upon it. If I don't act upon my conscience I would be a hypocrite. . . . The contents of the oath are irrelevant to me in my stand. I stand opposed in principle to all loyalty oaths.
>
> 1. I believe that loyalty oaths contradict individual freedoms of expression and belief guaranteed in the Bill of Rights.
> 2. I have a commitment to humanist ideals and values rather than to the state. Free man is not the creature of the state; the state is his creation.
> 3. Loyalty oaths have possible incriminating effects and were used for such purposes during the McCarthy era of the early 1950s.
> 4. Our commitment is best determined by our actions, rather than by our signature. My background as a Quaker has taught me to try to lead a meaningful life rather than to talk or to sign oaths about it.
> 5. Loyalty oaths have nothing to do with good teaching.
> 6. Loyalty oaths presume that people are guilty of being disloyal unless they have signed. . . .
>
> I am challenging this law because I see it as a potentially dangerous one—one which goes against the principles of freedom, liberty and democracy upon which our country was founded. . . . [167]

The United States district court's response was: "[I]t is clearly inappropriate to ruminate about the mixed socio-political, philosophical or personal objections of the plaintiff. She has stated that it is offensive to her religious convictions and that it may also offend her in other ways is not our concern. Neither are we concerned about her Quaker orthodoxy."[168] Relying on *Knight, Hosack*, and *Ohlson*, the district court argued: "With all respect for Sari Knopp Biklen's sincerity and conscientious conviction, we hold that her complaint must be dismissed. The constitutionality of this support oath has been repeatedly sustained by the Supreme Court of the United States against First Amendment attacks by public school teachers."[169]

The court then turned to the question of "whether the state has a compelling interest in requiring plaintiff Biklen to make an affirmation that is antithetic to her personal beliefs." Doing some balancing of interests, the court concluded: "That the state has a compelling interest in assuring the fitness and dedication of its teachers is a self-evident proposition. Accordingly, it may demand that those aspiring to labor in the sensitive area of the classroom be willing to affirm their support of its government systems. This affirmation does not inquire into one's present beliefs, political or religious. It is merely promissory."[170] In 1972, the United States Supreme Court affirmed the decision.[171]

Also in 1972, the Supreme Court decided 4–3 (Powell and Rehnquist took no part in this case) that a Massachusetts loyalty oath required of all state employees was constitutional. Lucretia Peteros Richardson, a research sociologist at the Boston State Hospital, had refused to take the required oath, and her employment was terminated. The oath she refused to take read: "I do solemnly swear (or affirm) that I will uphold and defend the Constitution of the United States of America and the Constitution of the Commonwealth of Massachusetts and that I will oppose the overthrow of the government of the United States of America or of this Commonwealth by force, violence or by any illegal or unconstitutional method."[172]

Unlike Biklen, Richardson won at the district court level, with the court concluding that there was nothing improper with the first part of the oath ending with "Massachusetts," but that there was vague language in the second part: "We find the phrase 'oppose the overthrow' fatally vague and unspecific. The word 'oppose' has a number of common meanings, running from the negative, 'not favor,' or 'refrain from,' to the affirmative, viz., to take active steps to restrain the conduct of others."[173]

The district court also saw ambiguity in "I will oppose the overthrow of the government of the United States of America or of this Commonwealth by force, violence or any illegal method." The Commonwealth of Massachusetts had argued: "[I]n the event that a clear and present danger arose of the actual overthrow of the government, ***the public employee [would] be required to use reasonable means at his disposal to attempt to thwart that effort. What he might do in such circumstances could range from the use of physical force to speaking out against the downfall of the government."[174] The language of the second part of the oath, concluded the District Court, was "hopelessly vague" and, said the court, "it is . . . well settled employment cannot be conditioned upon an unintelligible oath."[175]

The United States Supreme Court reversed this decision, concluding that the Massachusetts oath was "constitutionally permissible." Chief

Justice Burger, delivering the opinion of the Court, asserted: "We view the second clause of the oath as essentially the same as the first."[176] As for the ambiguity of the second part of the oath, Burger wrote:

> Plainly "force, violence or . . . any illegal or unconstitutional method" modifies "overthrow" and does not commit the oath taker to meet force with force. Just as the connotatively active word "support" has been interpreted to mean, simply a commitment to abide by our constitutional system, the second clause of this oath is merely oriented to the negative implication of this notion; it is a commitment not to use illegal and constitutionally unprotected force to change the constitutional system. . . . That the second clause may be redundant is no ground to strike it down; we are not charged with correcting grammar but with enforcing a constitution.[177]

Noting that there had been no prosecutions under the statute since its 1948 enactment, Burger saw the oath as "no more than an amenity" and responded to the contention that the oath could lead to threatened prosecutions or harassment by stating that those who held such fears "would do well to bear in mind that many of the hazards of human existence that can be imagined are circumscribed by the classic observation of Mr. Justice Holmes, when confronted with the prophecy of dire consequences of certain judicial action, that it would not occur 'while this Court sits.' "[178]

Justice Marshall, joined by Justice Brennan, argued in a dissenting opinion that the second part of the oath was "impermissibly vague and overbroad." He explained:

> The most striking problem with the oath is that it is not clear whether the last prepositional phrase modifies the verb "oppose" or the noun "overthrow." Thus, an affiant cannot be certain whether he is swearing that he will "oppose" governmental overthrow by utilizing every means at his disposal, including those specifically prohibited by the laws or constitutions he has sworn to support, or whether he has merely accepted the responsibility of opposing illegal or unconstitutional overthrows. The first reading would almost surely be unconstitutional since it is well established that a State cannot compel a citizen to waive the rights guaranteed him by the Constitution in order to obtain employment. . . . This reading would also make the second half of the oath inconsistent with the first half. It is far from clear to me which reading the Massachusetts Legislature intended.[179]

Expressing aversion to both types of oaths, negative and positive, Marshall wrote: "The Court's prior decisions represent a judgment that simple affirmative oaths of support are less suspect and less evil than negative oaths requiring a disaffirmance of political ties, group affiliations, or beliefs. . . . Yet, I think that it is plain that affirmative oaths of loyalty, no less than negative ones, have odious connotations and that they present dangers."[180] Referring to *Barnette*, the 1943 Supreme Court decision striking down West Virginia's compulsory flag salute, Marshall stated: "The Constitution severely circumscribes the power of government to force its citizens to perform symbolic gestures of loyalty."[181]

Notwithstanding Justice Marshall's claim, for three decades in the middle of the twentieth century federal, state, and local government officials did force American citizens to "perform symbolic gestures of loyalty," whether through the required loyalty oaths and affidavits, the compulsory flag salute required of schoolchildren, or the coerced testimony before the un-American activities committees.

All of this coerced expression involved more than intrusions on freedom of speech, freedom of association, and academic freedom; what was at stake was the dignity of the individual, the right to be free from state-imposed humiliation and degradation. When in 1952 a high-school teacher in Pennsylvania refused to sign that state's loyalty oath, he explained: "In a day when the impulse to conform, to acquiesce, to go along, is the instrument used in subjecting men to dictatorial rule throughout the world, non-conformity—with a religious motivation—becomes a means of preserving the dignity of man. Although I am neither communist nor subversive, I must say 'No' to the spirit of the Oath."[182]

In his review of the fate of several professors who were able to keep their jobs after they agreed to sign the required disclaimer affidavits, Lionel S. Lewis refers to the "degrading inquisitorial practices and public humiliation": "Not only were these five principals made to affirm their loyalty publicly, but their tenure was revoked. . . . Authorities could continue to check to make sure that they had truly repudiated their political beliefs. Not surprisingly, one discernible reaction to degrading inquisitorial practices and public humiliation seemed to be a diminished interest in political matters. An attorney in one case assured the regents that his clients had 'no desire to engage in any political affray from now on.' "[183]

In his condemnation of test oaths, Professor Ralph S. Brown, Jr., also refers to the coercion and humiliation accompanying this "symbolic gesture of loyalty": "The test oath is a form of intellectual coercion that singles out a particular heresy for ritual condemnation without contributing anything to its detection and correction. It seems to be true that some people do not mind periodically raising their right hand and attesting to a variety of things that they are not, have not been, and will not be. That others regard such exercises as humiliating, the willing oath-takers find hard to understand. But our current experience with loyalty oaths shows once again that those who refuse to subscribe to them are more often than not people of stout conscience whom we should cherish rather than punish."[184]

As one looks back into history, it is evident that test oaths have long constituted an assault on human dignity. Professor Harry Kalven, Jr., has written of oath-taking and past indignities: "The very idea of an oath, regardless of its terms, evokes from many people stubborn and bitter opposition. History furnishes numerous examples of men refusing on principle to take an oath although they could readily and honestly swear to its terms. In brief, the test oath has come down to us with a bad name. It is much as though men today react against a symbol of past indignities buried in a history long forgotten."[185]

In 1950, Supreme Court Justice Jackson recognized the indignity that was being imposed by the government when it required labor officials to sign loyalty oaths; but he concluded that the "public welfare" outweighed "any affront to individual dignity":

> I am aware that the oath is resented by many labor leaders of unquestioned loyalty and above suspicion of Communist connections, indeed by some who have themselves taken bold and difficult steps to rid the labor movement of Communists. I suppose no one likes to be compelled to exonerate himself from connections he has never acquired. I have sometimes wondered why I must file papers showing I did not steal my car before I can get a license for it. But experience shows there are thieves among automobile drivers, and that there are Communists among labor leaders. The public welfare, in identifying both, outweighs any affront to individual dignity.[186]

The difficulty of Jackson's analogy is that one part deals with criminal behavior (auto theft), while the other part addresses beliefs and associations that are not criminal. But even more important to note is his subordination of "individual dignity" to the nebulous "public welfare."

Nowhere in the scores of United States Supreme Court decisions related to loyalty oaths and affidavits does there appear the argument that the freedom not to speak, the right to remain silent, protected the non-signers. Nowhere is it argued that to coerce the citizen to sign an oath is an affront to human dignity. While Justice Brennan spoke eloquently on protecting human dignity, he voted to strike down loyalty oaths and disclaimer affidavits not because they were an affront to human dignity, but because they were intrusions on freedom of association, freedom of speech, and academic freedom; further, he and other Justices argued that the oaths and affidavits suffered from vagueness and overbreadth.

When Justice Brennan was asked to identify his favorite judicial opinion, he refused, but he was willing to say that "high on the list of the Court's accomplishments during my tenure were a panoply of opinions protecting and promoting individual rights and human dignity."[187] Our Constitution, Brennan has written, is "a charter of human rights and human dignity."[188] Further, he has stated: "In my time, it was the 'living' Constitution, infused with a vision of human dignity, that prohibited local police from ransacking a home without a warrant (in 1961) and forbade state prosecutors to compel an accused to convict himself with his own words (in 1964)."[189]

While human dignity prohibits police from "ransacking a home without a warrant," that same human dignity does not prohibit government officials and legislators from ransacking the citizen's mind and conscience.

4

From "I Pledge Allegiance . . ." to "Are You a Member of . . . ?"

While mid-twentieth century United States was caught up in the frenzy of imposing loyalty oaths on millions of American adults, the first half of the century was caught up in imposing the compulsory flag salute on America's schoolchildren. By 1920, several states had passed legislation that provided that a flag-salute ritual was to begin some school days.[1] In 1919, the state of Washington added the following requirement to its school code: "Every board of directors of the several districts of this state shall procure a United States flag . . . , and shall cause appropriate flag exercises to be held in every school at least once in each week at which exercises the pupils shall recite the following salute to the flag: 'I pledge allegiance to my flag and to the republic for which it stands, one nation indivisible, with liberty and justice for all.' "[2] As David Manwaring has indicated, "Failure of a school officer or teacher to carry out this provision was declared adequate for dismissal, and a punishable misdemeanor as well. Roughly similar laws were enacted by Delaware in 1925, New Jersey in 1932, and Massachusetts in 1935."[3]

A compulsory flag-salute case came out of Pennsylvania in 1935, beginning its way to the United States Supreme Court. On November 6, 1935, twelve-year-old Lillian Gobitis and her ten-year-old brother, Walter Gobitis, refused to participate in their seventh-and fifth-grade flag-salute rituals because, as Jehovah's Witnesses, they had been brought up to believe that the flag salute was forbidden by Scripture, especially by Exodus 20:3-5: "Thou shalt have no other gods before me. Thou shalt not make unto thee any graven image, or any likeness of any thing that is in heaven above, or that is in the earth beneath, or that is in the water under the earth. Thou shalt not bow down thyself to them, nor serve them. . . ." Because they refused to utter the pledge and to salute, Lillian and William Gobitis were expelled from school, for their refusal to participate in the flag salute ritual was defined by the school-board regulation as "insubordination": "That the Superintendent of the Minersville Public Schools be required to demand that all teachers and pupils of said schools be required to salute the flag of our country as part of the daily exercises. That refusal to salute the flag shall be regarded as an act of insubordination and shall be dealt with accordingly."[4]

Having been expelled, the Gobitis children were forced to seek their education elsewhere; Pennsylvania law provided that "every parent of any child of school age who fails to comply with the provisions of the act regarding compulsory attendance is guilty of a misdemeanor."[5] The Gobitis parents placed the children in private schools, but this resulted in a financial burden on the family, and hence Mr. Gobitis brought suit to enjoin the public-school authorities from continuing to require participation in the flag-salute ritual as a condition of his children's attendance at the Minersville public school; a bill of complaint was filed on May 3, 1937.

On December 1, 1937, a United States district court in Pennsylvania decided against the school district and ordered the case to trial. In so doing, the court said: "The liberty protected by the due process clause of the Fourteenth Amendment undoubtedly includes the liberty to entertain any religious belief, to practice any religious principle, and to do any act or refrain from doing any act, on conscientious grounds, which does not endanger the public safety, violate the laws of morality or property or infringe on personal rights."[6]

During the trial in February 1938, district court judge Maris asked the attorney representing the school district a series of questions, including the following questions about the sincerity of the Gobitis children:

Q. Do you feel that these views [that the flag salute is not a religious exercise] to the contrary here held by these two pupils are not sincerely held?
A. I feel that they were indoctrinated.
Q. Do you feel their parents' views were not sincerely held?
A. I believe they are probably sincerely held, but misled; they are perverted views.[7]

On June 18, 1938, Judge Maris handled down his decision in favor of Gobitis, reiterating some of what he had said in his earlier decision: "We . . . held that the minor plaintiffs have a right to attend the public schools and that to require them, as a condition of the exercise of that right, to participate in a ceremony which runs counter to religious convictions sincerely held by them, would violate the Pennsylvania Constitution and infringe the liberty guaranteed them by the Fourteenth Amendment. . . ."[8]

Identifying coerced speech with totalitarianism, Judge Maris declared: "Our country's safety surely does not depend upon the totalitarian idea of forcing all citizens into one common mold of thinking and acting or requiring them to render lip service of loyalty in a manner which conflicts with their sincere religious convictions. Such a doctrine seems to me utterly alien to the genius and spirit of our nation and destructive of that personal liberty of which our flag itself is the symbol."[9]

After Judge Maris handed down his final decision on June 18, 1938, the Minersville school board voted on June 28 to appeal to the United States Court of Appeals. The Gobitis children were refused readmission to the school while the appeal was pending. Charles E. Roudabush, the superintendent of schools, strongly condemned the district court decision and came out with a public statement in which he declared: "Boys and girls who do not acknowledge allegiance to their country of birth are aliens, and do not belong in the public schools which are tax supported. . . . [Teachers have] as much right to teach and require the elements of patriotism as a parent has to indoctrinate the children with false religion. . . ."[10]

When the United States Court of Appeals handed down its decision on November 10, 1939, it was very clear from the first few paragraphs of Judge Clark's opinion that the court was deciding against the school district. His first sentence read: "Eighteen big states have seen fit to exert their power over a small number of little children. . . ." A footnote indicated the number of "little children" affected: "According to the latest casualty lists circa. 120." After providing the text of the regulation the children had violated by refusing to salute the flag, Judge Clark stated: "The appellees, a little girl of 13 and a little boy of 12, refused to salute the flag of 'their country' on the appropriate occasion. They stood in respectful silence while the other children submitted to the 'requirement' and they were 'dealt with accordingly' by being expelled."[11]

Judge Clark identified the religious group the students belonged to as "Russellites, or more colloquially, Earnest Bible students." Referring to the persecution of Jehovah's Witnesses in Nazi Germany, Judge Clark cited Adolf Hitler's words: "I consider them quacks. I dissolve the Earnest Bible Students in Germany; their property I dedicate to the people's welfare; I will have all their literature confiscated.' Pronouncement of A. Hitler, April 4, 1935."[12]

Clark's identification of the appellees as "a little girl of 13 and a little boy of 12," and his mention of the small "number of little children" in "eighteen big states" in a note referring to the "latest casualty lists," along with his identification of Adolf Hitler as one of those who persecuted Jehovah's Witnesses, made the court's decision immediately evident. Judge Clark, after recognizing the liberty of conscience, added: "As indicated by their decisions, our courts consider that the peace and good order of the community must prevail over conscience, (a) wherever its mental or physical health is affected, (b) wherever a violation of its sense of reverence makes a breach of the peace reasonably foreseeable, and (c) wherever the 'defense of the realm is imperiled.' "[13] The examples he provides include statutes requiring the physical examination of schoolchildren and the vaccination, and others regulating the exhumation of dead bodies, the suppression of mail fraud, and polygamy. The flag salute, declared Judge Clark, "unlike the other exercises of the police power, negative and positive, which we have mentioned, is of at least doubtful efficacy and, as applied to [the] appellees, plainly lacking in necessity."[14]

In concluding, Judge Clark reminded us that William Penn "came to the new country because his refusal to subordinate religious scruples to educational coercion led to his expulsion from Oxford University. . . ."[15] Further, Clark quoted from a letter George Washington had written to the Religious Society Called Quakers in 1789: "I assure you very explicitly, that in my opinion the conscientious scruples of all men should be treated with great delicacy and tenderness; and it is my wish and desire, that the laws may always be as extensively accommodated to them, as a due regard to the protection and essential interests of the nation may justify and permit." Drawing on Washington's language, Judge Clark ended the court's opinion thusly: "The appellant School Board has failed to 'treat the conscientious scruples' of all children with that 'great delicacy and tenderness.' We agree with the father of our country that they should and we concur with the learned District Court in saying that they must."[16]

In January 1940, the school district decided to appeal to the United State Supreme Court, and on March 4, the High Court granted a writ of certiorari. Three months later, on June 3, 1940, the Supreme Court decided 8-1 in favor of the Minersville school board. While violence had previously been directed against Jehovah's Witnesses across the nation, the Court's decision contributed to a substantial increase in these attacks. David Manwaring reports in *Render Unto Caesar: The Flag-Salute Controversy* that "the outburst that followed June 3 was impressive. Incidents in June and after were worse and much more numerous."[17] Jehovah's Witnesses were beaten when they refused to salute the flag; a mob burned one of the Witnesses' Kingdom Halls; Witnesses' cars were overturned and burned; a Witness was tarred and feathered; a Witness was abducted and castrated; Witnesses attending a convention were attacked with guns, pipes, and screwdrivers; and at times, Witnesses received little or no police protection.[18]

The United States Supreme Court decided in *Minersville School Dist. v. Gobitis*, on June 3, 1940, that the state had the constitutional power to coerce public-school students, in this case members of the Jehovah's Witness faith, to declare publicly what they did not believe, to participate in a ritual that they found to be a degrading invasion of conscientious scruples. Justice Frankfurter, writing for the majority, justified the imposition of such coercion by arguing that religious freedom was not absolute: "Conscientious scruples have not, in the course of the long struggle for religious toleration, relieved the individual from obedience to a general law not aimed at the promotion or restriction of religious beliefs. The mere possession of religious convictions which contradict the relevant concerns of a political society does not relieve the citizen from the discharge of political responsibilities."[19] Emphasizing the need for promoting and establishing national unity, Frankfurter wrote: "We are dealing with an interest inferior to none in the hierarchy of legal values. National unity is the basis of national security."[20]

Frankfurter's emphasis on establishing national unity through the compulsory flag salute continued to the end of his opinion. As he saw it, the compulsory salute was related to preserving "ultimate values of civilization": "The preciousness of the family relation, the authority and independence which give dignity to parenthood, indeed the enjoyment of all freedom, presupposes the kind of ordered society which is summarized by our flag. A society which is dedicated to the preservation of these ultimate values of civilization may in self-protection utilize the educational process for inculcating those almost unconscious feelings which bind men together in a comprehending loyalty, whatever may be their lesser differences and difficulties."[21]

The lone dissenting justice, Harlan Stone, minimized the necessity to use the compulsory flag salute to achieve national unity. There were, he argued, other ways of achieving this goal:

> [E]ven if we believe that such compulsions will contribute to national unity, there are other ways to teach loyalty and patriotism which are the sources of national unity, than by compelling the pupil to affirm that which he does not believe and by commanding a form of affirmance which violates his religious convictions. Without recourse to such compulsion the state is free to compel attendance at school and require teaching by instruction and study of all in our history and in the structure and organization of our government, including the guaranties of civil liberty which tend to inspire patriotism and love of country. I cannot say that government here is deprived of any interest or function which it is entitled to maintain at the expense of the protection of civil liberties by requiring it to resort to the alternatives which do not coerce an affirmation of belief.[22]

Justice Stone was especially concerned about the coercion imposed on the students by the state; the words "coerce," "compulsion," and "compel" appear over twenty times in his six-page dissenting opinion, as in "the state seeks to coerce these children," "by compelling the pupil to affirm," and "compulsory affirmation of the desired belief"; his last sentence reads: "With such scrutiny I cannot say that the inconveniences which may attend some sensible adjustment of school discipline in order that the religious convictions of these children may be spared, presents a problem so momentous or pressing as to outweigh the freedom from compulsory violation of religious faith which has been thought worthy of constitutional protection."[23]

In contrast, Justice Frankfurter's majority opinion never refers to the students' flag salute as "compulsory" or as a "coercion." In Frankfurter's language, "the local Board of Education required both teachers and pupils to participate in this ceremony," and Gobitis "sought to enjoin the authorities from continuing to exact participation in the flag-salute ceremony as a condition of his children's attendance at the Minersville school."[24]

Where Frankfurter saw the "binding tie of cohesive sentiment" as the "ultimate foundation of a free society,"[25] and "the preciousness of the family relation, the authority and independence which give dignity to parenthood" as the "ultimate values of civilization,"[26] Stone emphasized the "freedom of the human mind and spirit." In his dissenting opinion Stone asserts: "The guaranties of civil liberty are but guaranties of freedom of the human mind and spirit and of reasonable freedom and opportunity to express them. . . . The very essence of the liberty which they guaranty is the freedom of the individual from compulsion as to what he shall think and what he shall say. . . ."[27] Later in his opinion, Stone writes of preserving the "freedom of the mind and spirit": "The Constitution expresses more than the conviction of the people that democratic processes must be preserved at all costs. It is also an expression of faith and a command that freedom of mind and spirit must be preserved, which government must obey, if it is to adhere to that justice and moderation without which no free government can exist."[28]

Frankfurter's emphasis on the compulsory flag salute as necessary to establish national unity and patriotism led legal scholar Robert Cushman to write in 1941: "All of the eloquence by which the majority extol the ceremony of flag saluting as an expression of patriotism turns sour when used to describe the brutal compulsion which requires a sensitive and conscientious child to stultify himself in public." In contrast, writes Cushman, "Mr. Justice Stone's opinion deserves a place in the classic literature of civil liberty."[29]

One effect of the Court's *Gobitis* decision was an increase in the number of communities and states requiring students to participate in the flag-salute ritual. New flag-salute regulations were instituted and more stringent penalties were established, as reported by David Manwaring:

> The flag salute requirement spread in a variety of ways. Many communities passed new salute regulations in direct response to the *Gobitis* ruling. . . . Some communities showed their first interest quite late, passing regulations as late as 1941 or 1942. Mississippi passed a new flag-salute law in 1942. In mid-1941, the Oklahoma State Superintendent of Schools interpreted that state's 1921 flag-exercise statute to require the orthodox flag-salute ceremony in all public and private schools, and held that pupils refusing to give the regular salute and pledge might be expelled. A number of Massachusetts communities already requiring the salute announced that they were considering 'firmer action' in light of *Gobitis*. The Washington Attorney General overruled his earlier official opinion advising school authorities to refrain from expelling conscientiously motivated non-saluters. Attorneys general in eight other states also issued official opinions upholding the constitutionality of old or new flag-salute regulations.[30]

According to Witness sources, writes Manwaring, "expulsions took place in all forty-eight states and totaled more than 2,000 by 1943."[31]

On June 8, 1942, United States Supreme Court Justices Black, Douglas, and Murphy took the unusual step of writing a dissenting opinion not directly related to *Jones v. City of Opelika*, a case dealing with a city licensing ordinance requiring the payment of a license fee, which affected the door-to-door sale of books and pamphlets by the Jehovah's Witnesses. In *Opelika* the High Court decided, 5–4, that the licensing ordinance was constitutional; Justice Murphy wrote a dissenting opinion, joined by Chief Justice Stone and Justices Black and Douglas, arguing that the Witnesses' freedoms of speech, press, and religion had been violated. What was unusual was that in addition to adhering to this dissenting opinion directly related to *Opelika*, Black, Douglas, and Murphy took the opportunity to "attach" another opinion, in which they declared in a short paragraph that they now believed that *Gobitis* had been "wrongly decided."[32]

One month after the dissenting justices said in *Opelika* that *Gobitis* had been "wrongly decided," the Kansas Supreme Court decided for Jehovah's Witness parents found guilty of violating the Kansas truancy law when their children refused to salute the flag and were expelled. A "truant officer filed a complaint against the parents under the compulsory education law. A trial was had in the juvenile court, where they were found guilty. They appealed to the district court, where a trial was had, and they were again found guilty."[33] The Kansas Supreme Court, in deciding for the Witnesses, referred to the "separate opinion" of the three justices in *Opelika*:

> Counsel for the state cite and rely upon *Minersville School District v. Gobitis*. . . . Obviously, this is the case referred to in the letter of the county superintendent which Miss Turrill gave Mrs. Smith to read. We note, without comment as to its effect, that in the later case of *Jones v. City of Opelika* . . . three of the justices who had concurred in the opinion of the court in the Gobitis case, in a separate opinion stated: "Since we joined in the opinion of the Gobitis case, we think this is an appropriate occasion to state that we now believe that it was also wrongly decided."[34]

Within three months, the Witnesses were in court again, challenging the constitutionality of a West Virginia regulation ordering that the flag salute become "a regular part of the program of activities in the public schools . . . and that all teachers as defined by law in West Virginia and pupils in such schools shall be required to participate in the salute, honoring the Nation represented by the Flag; provided, however, that refusal to salute the Flag be regarded as an act of insubordination, and shall be dealt with accordingly."[35] Walter Barnette and other Jehovah's Witnesses brought suit "in behalf of themselves and their children and all other persons in the State of West Virginia in like situation . . . to secure an injunction restraining the State Board of Education from enforcing against them a regulation of the Board requiring children in the public schools to salute the American flag."[36]

On October 6, 1942, a United States district court in West Virginia, deciding for Barnette, granted the injunction. While it recognized that the United States Supreme Court had upheld the flag salute requirement in 1940 in *Gobitis*, the district court indicated that it could not ignore what the dissenting justices had said in their 1942 separate opinion in *Opelika*; writing for a unanimous court, district court judge Parker declared:

> Ordinarily we would feel constrained to follow an unreversed decision of the Supreme Court of the United States, whether we agreed with it or not. . . . The developments with respect to the Gobitis case, however, are such that we do not feel it is incumbant upon us to accept it as binding authority. Of the seven justices now members of the Supreme Court who participated in that decision, four have given public expression to the view that it is unsound, the present Chief Justice in his dissenting opinion rendered therein and three other justices in a special dissenting opinion in *Jones v. City of Opelika*. . . . [37]

The clear and present danger test played a significant role in the district court's decision, a test relied upon by Justice Jackson when the case reached the United States Supreme Court. The district court did recognize that there were limitations on "what a man may do or refrain from doing in the name of religious liberty": "He must render to Caesar the things that are Caesar's as well as to God the things that are God's. He may not refuse to bear arms or pay taxes because of religious scruples, nor may he engage in polygamy or any other practice directly harmful to the safety, morals, health or general welfare of the community."[38] Having said this, however, the court, applying the clear and present danger test, stated: "To justify the overriding of religious scruples . . . there must be a clear justification therefore in the necessities of national or community life. Like the right of free speech, it is not to be overborne by the police power, unless its exercise presents a clear and present danger to the community."[39]

The clear and present danger test was invoked again by the district court when it declared: "[I]f speech tending to overthrow of the government but not constituting a clear and present danger may not be forbidden because of the guaranty of free speech, it is difficult to see how it can be held that conscientious scruples against giving a flag salute must give way to an educational policy having only indirect relation, at most, to the public safety. Surely, it cannot be that the nation is endangered more by the refusal of school children, for religious reasons, to salute the flag than by the advocacy on the part of grown men of doctrines which tend towards the overthrow of the government."[40]

Towards the end of its opinion, the district court still again turned to the clear and present danger test to support its decision: "As fine a ceremony as the flag salute is, it can have at most only an indirect influence on the national safety; and no clear and present danger will result to anyone if the children of this sect are allowed to refrain from saluting because of their conscientious scruples, however groundless we may personally think these scruples to be."[41]

Then, in a strongly worded concluding paragraph, Judge Parker asserted: "The salute to the flag is an expression of homage of the soul. To force it upon one who has conscientious scruples against giving it, is petty tyranny unworthy of the spirit of this Republic and forbidden, we think, by the fundamental law. This court will not countenance such tyranny but will use the power at its command to see that rights guaranteed by the fundamental law are respected."[42]

Within three weeks, the school board decided to appeal to the United States Supreme Court, and the High Court heard oral argument in *Barnette* on March 11, 1943. A few weeks later, another state supreme court had decided for parents of the Jehovah's Witness faith whose children had refused to salute the flag in the state of Washington. The Washington Supreme Court, noting, as had the district court in *Barnette* and the Kansas Supreme Court in *State v. Smith*, that three United States Supreme Court justices had declared that *Gobitis* had been "wrongly decided," decided for the Jehovah's Witness parents whose three children had refused to salute the flag and as a result had been taken from the parents and declared wards of the court by a superior court judge, who placed the children with their elder sister.[43]

Referring to "the recent case *Jones v. Opelika*," the Washington Supreme Court stated: "Mr. Chief Justice Stone again dissenting, as did

Mr. Justice Murphy, Mr. Justice Black, and Mr. Justice Douglas, the three last named justices deeming it an appropriate occasion to state that in their opinion the *Gobitis* case, in which they concurred, had been wrongly decided."[44] Quoting extensively from Chief Justice Stone's *Gobitis* dissenting opinion, the Washington court declared that "it is difficult to refrain from quoting at length from Chief Justice Stone's dissent in the *Gobitis* case, as the basic principles which we deem controlling in the case at bar are therein so clearly and forcefully stated."[45]

The Washington court then went back to Roman history for an example of the punishment of Christians who refused to "offer incense before the statue of the emperor": "The early Christians, while recognizing the sovereignty of the emperor, refused to perform this ceremony, deeming it idolatrous. ... A refusal to perform the rite was equivalent to an affirmation that the one refusing was a Christian, and subject to the severe penalties of the Roman law. A phrase, or the making of a gesture, which to most people may seem either right or possibly unimportant, may to others appear to be of great significance."[46] The court concluded: "The section of the code above quoted, which requires school children to repeat the form of words constituting the salute to the flag, as set forth in the law, may not be enforced as against the children of the petitioners in these proceedings."[47]

By the time the United States Supreme Court heard the oral arguments in *Barnette*, then, various lower courts had already begun to undermine *Gobitis*. On June 14, 1943, the United States Supreme Court decided, 6–3, against the West Virginia State Board of Education and for the Barnette children.[48] Lillian Gobitis, by then twenty years old, has written: "In the *Barnette* case, we felt more optimistic this time, like there's a light at the end of the tunnel. We *never* thought it would come to court again. ... So the atmosphere changed, and the Court was won over on Flag Day—June 14, 1943. We really never thought that day would come."[49]

The Court's *Barnette* decision received mixed reactions, and Justice Jackson's majority opinion was praised by some for its eloquence and criticized by others for its questionable arguments.[50] Thomas I. Emerson saw Jackson's *Barnette* arguments protecting the Jehovah's Witnesses as going beyond religion and the flag salute; Emerson wrote in 1970:

> In the end the Jackson opinion extends the unqualified protection of the First Amendment. It would forbid any compulsion to affirmation of belief,

under any circumstances. This can be the only meaning of Justice Jackson's famous concluding paragraph: "If there is any fixed star in our constitutional constellation, it is that no official, high or petty, can prescribe what shall be orthodox in politics, nationalism, religion, or other matter of opinion or force citizens to confess by word or act their faith therein. If there are any circumstances which permit an exception, they do not now occur to us."[51]

Besides this "fixed star in our constitutional constellation" metaphor, there appear in Jackson's opinion other concepts and principles that would lead one to conclude that the First Amendment forbids "any compulsion to affirmation of belief, under any circumstances." After a discussion of the West Virginia statute, the expulsion of the Barnette children, the punishment imposed on them, and the Biblical passages upon which the students based their objections to the compelled flag salute, Justice Jackson argues that "the freedom asserted by these appellees does not bring them into collision with rights asserted by any other individual. It is such conflicts which most frequently require intervention of the State to determine where the rights of one end and those of another begin. But the refusal of these persons to participate in the ceremony does not interfere with or deny rights of others to do so. Nor is there any question in this case that their behavior is peaceable and orderly."[52]

It is the coercion imposed by the state that Jackson argues against, not the instilling of patriotism and love of country: "Here . . . we are dealing with a compulsion of students to declare a belief. They are not merely made acquainted with the flag salute so that they may be informed as to what it is or even what it means. The issue here is whether this slow and easily neglected route to aroused loyalties constitutionally may be short cut by substituting a compulsory salute and slogan."[53]

Recognizing that the kind of coerced speech imposed here by the state was known to the "framers of the Bill of Rights," Jackson states: "Here it is the State that employs a flag as a symbol of adherence to government as presently organized. It requires the individual to communicate by word and sign his acceptance of the political ideas it thus bespeaks. Objection to this form of communication when coerced is an old one, well known to the framers of the Bill of Rights."[54] At this point, Jackson inserts a footnote: "Early Christians were frequently persecuted for their refusal to participate in ceremonies before the statue of the emperor or other symbol of imperial authority."[55]

The clear and present danger test is brought to bear when Jackson argues that the children's refusal to salute the flag did not create any such danger:

> It is now a commonplace that censorship or suppression of expression of opinion is tolerated by our Constitution only when the expression presents a clear and present danger of action of a kind the State is empowered to prevent and punish. It would seem that involuntary affirmation could be commanded only on even more immediate and urgent grounds than silence. But here the power of compulsion is invoked without any allegation that remaining passive during a flag salute ritual creates a clear and present danger that would justify an effort even to muffle expression. To sustain the compulsory flag salute we are required to say that a Bill of Rights which guards the individual's right to speak his own mind, left it open to public authorities to compel him to utter what is not in his mind.[56]

Jackson's condemnation of coerced expression is not limited to its relation to religion: "Nor does the issue as we see it turn on one's possession of particular religious views or the sincerity with which they are held. While religion supplies appellees' motives for enduring the discomforts of making the issue in this case, many citizens who do not share these religious views hold such a compulsory rite to infringe constitutional liberty of the individual."[57]

In response to Frankfurter's *Gobitis* argument that the compelled flag salute was justified in light of the nation's interest in maintaining a strong government and establishing unity, Jackson wrote: "Without promise of a limiting Bill of Rights it is doubtful if our Constitution could have mustered enough strength to enable its ratification. To enforce those rights today is not to choose weak government over strong government. It is only to adhere as a means of strength to individual freedom of mind in preference to officially disciplined uniformity for which history indicates a disappointing and disastrous end."[58]

Since it was a legislative act that imposed the compulsory flag salute, Jackson asserted that there are fundamental rights that "may not be submitted to vote; they depend on the outcome of no elections": "The very purpose of a Bill of Rights was to withdraw certain subjects from the vicissitudes of political controversy, to place them beyond the reach of majorities and officials and to establish them as legal principles to be applied by the courts. One's right to life, liberty, and property, to free speech, a free press, freedom of worship and assembly, and other fundamental rights may not be submitted to vote; they depend on the outcome of no elections."[59]

Frankfurter had argued in *Gobitis* that "national unity is the basis of national security," that the authorities have "the right to select appropriate means for its attainment," and hence that "such compulsory measures toward 'national unity' are constitutional." Jackson replied in *Barnette*: "National unity as an end which officials may foster by persuasion and example is not in question. The problem is whether under our Constitution compulsion as here employed is a permissible means for its achievement."[60]

Jackson then presents a brief history of past futile efforts to achieve unity through compulsion:

> Ultimate futility of such attempts to compel coherence is the lesson of every such effort from the Roman drive to stamp out Christianity as a disturber of its pagan unity, the Inquisition as a means to religious and dynastic unity, the Siberian exiles as a means to Russian unity, down to the fast failing efforts of our present totalitarian enemies. Those who begin coercive elimination of dissent soon find themselves exterminating dissenters. Compulsory unification of opinion achieves only the unanimity of the graveyard.[61]

Jackson concludes by asserting that in this nation coerced speech—the compulsory flag salute—is not necessary to instill patriotism and achieve unity: "[W]e apply the limitations of the Constitution with no fear that freedom to be intellectually and spiritually diverse or even contrary will disintegrate the social organization. To believe that patriotism will not flourish if patriotic ceremonies are voluntary and spontaneous instead of a compulsory routine is to make an unflattering estimate of the appeal of our institutions to free minds."[62]

Justice Jackson's majority opinion was, for the most part, immediately praised, and in subsequent decades that praise continued to be expressed by various legal scholars. In 1992, professor Bruce Ackerman referred to "Robert Jackson's great opinion in the second Flag Salute Case, *West Virginia State Board of Education v. Barnette*."[63] Also in 1992, professor Rodney Smolia wrote: "Justice Jackson's opinion for the Court in *Barnette* is among the most eloquent pronouncements ever on First Amendment freedoms."[64]

Professor Henry Abraham's praise of Jackson's opinion increased over the years. In the second edition of his *Freedom and the Court*, published in 1972, Abraham wrote: "The closing paragraphs of the Jackson opinion for the Court contain some of the most significant language ever used by an opinion assignee. Stressing the futility of compelling conformity and coherence in such sacred First Amendment guarantees of the freedom of belief, conscience, and expression, Jackson warned that 'those who begin coercive elimination of dissent soon find themselves exterminating dissenters. Compulsory unification of the opinion achieves only the unanimity of the graveyard.' "[65] Ten years later, in the fourth edition of *Freedom and the Court*, Abraham elevated his praise of Jackson's language, calling it "both seminal and magnificent": "The closing paragraphs of the Jackson opinion for the Court contain language both seminal and magnificent. Stressing the futility of compelling conformity and coherence in such sacred First Amendment guarantees as the freedoms of belief, conscience, and expression, the great stylist warned. . . ."[66]

Eloquent as Jackson's ideas and language may have been, his *Barnette* opinion did not entirely fulfill its promise. Jackson had eloquently declared that "no official, high or petty, can prescribe what shall be orthodox in politics, nationalism, religion, or other matters of opinion or force citizens to confess by word or act their faith therein." However, before the end of the decade in which these words were written, American citizens were being forced to "confess by word or act" in matters related to politics, religion, and nationalism.

Before the end of the decade, citizens were required to assert whether they were members or supporters of any organizations that believed in or taught the overthrow of the government, or they were required to publicly reveal the organizations to which they belonged or coerced into naming names. Those who refused to assert what the government demanded were punished, if not by imprisonment, then by being blacklisted, losing their jobs, or being publicly ostracized. Referring to the loyalty oaths that required citizens to reveal their political views and associational ties, Franklyn Haiman has written: "What is even more puzzling about these loyalty oath opinions of the Supreme Court than the haziness of the border between positive and test oaths is the utter absence of any reference to the right of silence which had been enunciated in the Jehovah's Witnesses' flag ritual case in 1943. When loyalty oaths were struck down in the 1960s it was on the grounds of vagueness, guilt by association, or discriminatory conditions of public employment."[67]

Thomas I. Emerson's reading of Jackson's *Barnette* opinion led him to apply the *Barnette* principles and concepts to the state and federal loyalty-oath cases: "All these oaths, like the pledge of allegiance to the flag, seek to compel a public avowal of belief and are subject to the same objections as those upheld by the Supreme Court in *Barnette*."[68] But the promise of *Barnette* arguments being applied to the loyalty oaths and government inquiries compelling citizens to reveal their political beliefs and associations did not materialize. While the clear and present danger test was used in *Barnette* to give protection to the Barnette children, that same test was never used to protect those who refused to sign the test oaths or those who refused to answer HUAC-type inquiries into political beliefs and associations. While the *Barnette* Court declared that "no official, high or petty, can prescribe what shall be orthodox in politics, nationalism, religion, or other matters of opinion or force citizens to confess by word or act their faith therein," that concept was not applied to provide constitutional protection to those who refused to sign the test oaths or answer HUAC-type inquiries.

With the 1940s came a significant increase in state demands that citizens reveal their political and religious associations and beliefs. As Carl Beck has indicated, "In 1947 and 1948 the Committee on Un-American Activities began to exercise more fully the powers given to it by the Congress. In 1947 the committee conducted nine different hearings, took testimony from ninety-seven individuals, and cited thirteen for contempt."[69] Between 1945 and 1957, the committee "held at least 230 public hearings, at which over 3,000 persons testified, of whom over 100 were cited for contempt."[70]

Writing in 1958, Ralph S. Brown demonstrated just how widespread the loyalty-oath requirement had become: "While constitutional oaths have been common for public school teachers since before World War I, the advent of full-blown loyalty oaths has been fairly recent. Today twenty-four states and two U.S. territories impose test oaths on all public employees, including teachers."[71] Brown calculated that "at least one person in five" in the labor force had, as a condition of employment, "taken a test oath, or completed a loyalty statement, or achieved official security clearance, or survived some undefined private scrutiny."[72]

In 1947, four years after *Barnette*, the passage of the Taft-Hartley Act required officers of labor unions to sign loyalty affidavits indicating that they were not members of the Communist Party or supporters of any organizations that believed in or taught the overthrow of the government by force or by any illegal or unconstitutional methods. They also had to declare that they did not "believe in" such overthrow. In 1950, the

United States Supreme Court decided in *American Communications Assn. v. Douds* that the oath requirement was constitutional. In so deciding, the Court concluded that this governmental inquiry into organizational ties and political beliefs did not involve a free speech issue, that the clear and present danger test did not apply in this case.[73] Where seven years earlier the Supreme Court had relied on the clear and present test in *Barnette* to protect the freedom not to speak, in 1950 the High Court saw the clear and present danger test as an irrelevant "mechanical test" in deciding whether labor union officials were free not to speak.[74]

Jackson concurred in part and dissented in part in *Douds*: "I conclude that today's task can only be discharged by holding that all parts of this oath which require disclosure of overt acts of affiliation or membership in the Communist Party are within the competence of Congress to enact and that any parts of it that call for a disclosure of belief unconnected with any overt act are beyond its power."[75] While he agreed with the majority of the Court that the oath could be required of labor leaders, Jackson went on to express misgivings about that part of the oath which proscribed beliefs:

> [E]fforts to weed erroneous beliefs from the minds of men have always been supported by the argument which the Court invokes today, that beliefs are springs to action, that evil thoughts tend to become forbidden deeds. Probably so. But if power to forbid acts includes power to forbid contemplating them, then the power of government over beliefs is as unlimited as its power over conduct and the way is open to force disclosure of attitudes on all manner of social, economic, moral and political issues.[76]

Referring to his *Barnette* opinion, Jackson declared: "I adhere to views I have heretofore expressed ... , that our Constitution excludes both general and local governments from the realm of opinions and ideas, beliefs and doubts, heresy and orthodoxy, political, religious or scientific."[77]

Writing a strong dissenting opinion, Justice Black asserted at the outset in his first paragraph: "Individual freedom and governmental thought-probing cannot live together."[78] The test oath being required in this act, said Black, "was passed to exclude certain beliefs from one arena of the national economy," and "it was quite natural to utilize the test oath as a weapon." Drawing on history, he continued: "History attests the efficacy of that instrument [the test oath] for inflicting penalities and disabilities on obnoxious minorities. It was one of the major devices used against the Huguenots in France, and against 'heretics' during the Spanish Inquisition. It helped English rulers identify and outlaw Catholics, Quakers, Baptists, and Congregationalists—groups considered dangerous for political as well as religious reasons. And wherever the test oath was in vogue, spies and informers found rewards far more tempting than truth."[79]

On February 18, 1947, newly elected congressman Richard M. Nixon delivered his first speech on the floor of the House of Representatives, a speech in which he argued that the House adopt the report of the House Committee on Un-American Activities citing songwriter Gerhard Eisler for contempt of Congress because of his refusal to testify before the committee. It became clear from Nixon's speech that he and the committee were interested in exposing and punishing more than Communists: "I think that every member of the House is in substantial agreement with the Attorney General in his recent statements on the necessity of rooting out Communist sympathizers from our American institutions."[80] Nixon was interested in rooting out not only "Communist sympathizers," but also employees who "follow the Communist line": "Certainly no stronger case could be made for the proposition that there is no place in the United States, for governmental employees who follow the Communist line or any other line which advocates the overthrow of the Government by force and violence."[81] The House voted to cite Eisler for contempt, and he was sentenced to one year in jail and fined one thousand dollars. However, once he was out on bail, Eisler left the country.

According to HUAC, one of the "American institutions" that needed its "Communist sympathizers" rooted out was the film industry. In the autumn of 1947, HUAC began its inquiry into the political beliefs and associations of some Hollywood writers and directors, ten of whom refused to answer the inquiries and were subsequently cited for contempt, jailed, and blacklisted. One of these writers was John Howard Lawson, who expressed, in an opening statement he had prepared but was not allowed to present at the hearing, his strong objections to the "indecent smear tactics" used by the committee: "I want to speak of a writer's integrity—the integrity and professional ethics that have been so irresponsibly impugned at these hearings. In its illegal attempt to establish a political dictatorship over the motion picture industry, the Committee has tried to justify its probing into the thought and conscience of individuals on the ground that these individuals insert allegedly 'subversive' lines or scenes in motion pictures." Later in his statement, Lawson again emphasized "integrity" and "conscience": "[M]y integrity as a writer is obviously an integral part of my integrity as a citizen. . . . I am like most Americans in resenting interference with my conscience and belief."[82]

Screenwriter Albert Malz, another of the Hollywood Ten cited for contempt and jailed, was asked about scripts he had written and whether he was now or had been a member of the Communist Party. At one point in the 1947 HUAC investigation, Malz was asked: "Are you a member of the Screen Writers Guild?" Malz responded: "Next you are going to ask me what religious group I belong to." He was then asked: "Do you object to answering whether or not you are a member of the Screen Writers Guild?" Malz answered: "I have not objected to answering that question. On the contrary, I point out that next you are going to ask me whether or not I am a member of a certain religious group and suggest that I be blacklisted from an industry because I am a member of a group you don't like."[83]

Malz's fears that HUAC would soon be asking questions related to religion were not totally unfounded. As early as 1948, it was clear that HUAC was interested in "subversives" in the churches of America. In 1948, the committee issued a pamphlet titled *100 Things You Should Know About Communism and Religion.*[84]

On March 5, 1947, Leon Josephson refused to testify before a subcommittee of HUAC chaired by Nixon and was cited for contempt and jailed. In deciding against Josephson, the United States Court of Appeals argued that Congress has a legitimate interest in investigating "un-American propaganda." Dissenting judge Clark, concerned about the vagueness of "un-American propaganda," wrote: "[T]he recent movie investigation found the necessary un-American qualities for which the Committee was searching in films which placed bankers in an unfavorable light or talked 'against the free enterprise system.' "[85]

The year 1947 brought not only the Taft-Hartley loyalty oath, the contempt citations against the Hollywood Ten, and the jailing of Leon Josephson, but also President Truman's Executive Order 9835, which provided that "[t]here shall be a loyalty investigation of every person entering the civilian employment of any department or agency of the executive branch of the Federal Government." The attorney general compiled a list of 108 "communist organizations," but the executive order punished more than membership; Part V, 2.(f) of the executive order stated:

Activities and associations of an applicant or employee which may be considered in connection with the determination of disloyalty may include one or more of the following:

(f) Membership in, affiliation with or sympathetic association with any foreign or domestic organization, association, movement, group or combination of persons, designated by the Attorney General as totalitarian, fascist, communist, or subversive, or as having adopted a policy of advocating or approving the commission of acts of force or violence to deny other persons their rights under the Constitution of the United States, or as seeking to alter the form of government of the United States by unconstitutional means.[86]

Not to be outdone, HUAC published its own *Guide to Subversive Organizations and Publications,* which was revised in 1961; the *Guide's* introduction indicated that "Communist-front" organizations were listed, along with "outright Communist enterprises":

This Guide is basically a compilation of organizations and publications which have been declared to be Communist-front or outright Communist enterprises in official statements by Federal legislative and executive authorities, and by various State and Territorial investigating committees. In this document, the Committee on Un-American Activities revises and brings up to date a similar compilation published under the same title, "Guide to Subversive Organizations and Publications" on January 2, 1957. The Guide lists a total of 663 organizations or projects and 122 publications cited as Communist or Communist front by Federal Agencies; and 155 organizations and 25 publications cited as Communist or Communist front by State or Territorial investigating committees.[87]

The revised 1961 edition of the *Guide* listed an additional 249 organizations.

The inquiries into citizens' past and present political beliefs and associations went far beyond, "Are you a member of the Communist Party?" In 1950, when the United States Supreme Court decided against Dorothy Bailey, who had gone to court after she had lost her job as a civil-service employee after being determined to be disloyal, United States Court of Appeals judge Edgerton wrote a dissenting opinion that began: "Without trial by jury, without evidence, and without even being allowed to confront her accusers or to know their identity, a citizen of the United States has been found disloyal to the government of the United States."[88] Judge

Edgerton expressed concern about the types of questions that citizens were required to answer:

> In loyalty hearings the following questions have been asked of employees against whom charges have been brought. "Do you read a good many books?" "What books do you read?" "What magazines do you read?" "What newspapers do you buy or subscribe to?" "Do you think that Russian Communism is likely to succeed?" "How do you explain the fact that you have an album of Paul Robeson records in your home?" "Do you ever entertain Negroes in your home?" "Is it not true that you lived next door to and therefore were closely associated with a member of the I.W.W.?" A record filed in this court was taken to task for membership in Consumers Union and for favoring legislation against racial discrimination. The record in the present case contains the follow colloquy between a member of the Regional Board and the present appellant: "Mr. Blair: Did you ever write a letter to the Red Cross about the segregation of blood? Miss Bailey: I do not recall. Mr. Blair: What was your personal position about that? Miss Bailey: Well, the medical———. Mr. Blair: I am asking yours."[89]

Such inquiries by the state, Judge Edgerton concluded, were intrusions upon freedom of thought: "Appellant's dismissal abridges not only freedom of speech but freedom of thought. Whatever disloyalty means in the present connection, it is not speech but a state of mind. The appellant was dismissed for thinking prohibited thoughts. A constitution that forbids speech control does not permit thought control."[90]

In 1956, the New Hampshire Supreme Court decided against Professor Paul Sweezy, who had been cited for contempt when he refused to answer questions related to his political beliefs and the political associations of his wife and others, questions put to him by the attorney general of New Hampshire, who had been authorized as a one-man legislative investigating committee looking into subversive activities in New Hampshire. Among the questions Sweezy refused to answer were: "Was she, Nancy Sweezy, your wife, active in the formation of the Progressive Citizens of America?" "Was Nancy Sweezy then working with individuals who were then members of the Communist Party?" "Didn't you tell the class at the University of New Hampshire on Monday, March 22, 1954, that Socialism was inevitable in this country?" "Did you advocate Marxism at that time?" "Did you in this last lecture on March 22 or in any of the former lectures espouse the theory of dialectical materialism?"[91]

In 1957, the United States Supreme Court reversed the judgment of the New Hampshire Supreme Court, and Chief Justice Earl Warren, announcing the judgment of the High Court, declared: "[T]o summon a witness and compel him, against his will, to disclose the nature of his past expressions and associations is a measure of governmental interference in these matters. These are rights which are safeguarded by the Bill of Rights and the Fourteenth Amendment. We believe that there unquestionably was an invasion of petitioner's liberties in the areas of academic freedom and political expression—areas in which government should be extremely reticent to tread."[92]

On June 19, 1958, Joseph Papp (Joseph Papirofsky), producer of the New York Shakespeare Festival and employed as a stage manager by CBS, was before HUAC and refused to answer some questions related to Communist Party membership. He was asked by Representative Morgan Moulder: "Do you have the opportunity to inject into your plays or into the acting or the entertainment supervision which you have any propaganda in any way which would influence others to be sympathetic with the Communist philosophy or the beliefs of Communism?" Moulder then asked: "Have you undergone any change in your beliefs, in your philosophies or social beliefs, and the form of government we should have, during the past two years? Have you changed your opinion in that connection?"

> *Papirofsky:* Changed my opinion from what?
> *Moulder:* In your philosophy of government or form of government we should have.
> *Papirofsky:* My opinions change constantly, and they have changed from time to time on many, many subjects.
> *Moulder:* You understand, of course, the Communist philosophy is antispiritual, antireligious, and is very much in conflict with our system in the American form of government and the American way of life. Do you agree with that?
> *Papirofsky:* I am not antispiritual or antireligious in any way.[93]

In a case involving the suspension of an employee of the United States Department of Interior whose loyalty had come into question, the interrogator inquired into his views on racial equality and the constitutional rights of "Negroes and Jews." The suspended employee had "an M.A. in Fine and Industrial Arts and a Ph.D. in Education. . . . His duties required him to teach basic subjects and crafts. These duties required a fluency in the unusual native tongue [of the "trust territory"]. He had five to six Americans and approximately sixty natives on his staff. He had no access to secret Governmental documents."[94] In 1954, the employee was suspended, the reasons for the suspension being "[t]hat during the years 1941 to 1945, inclusive, but not limited thereto, you were either a member of, affiliated with, or in sympathetic association with the Communist Party, and members of the Communist Party, including but not limited to the following particulars as to such affiliation and sympathetic association...."[95] Inquiries were made about the employee's voting record:

Q.: How many times did you vote for him (Norman Thomas), if you care to say?
A. Never.
Q. How about Henry Wallace?
A. Once (in 1948).
Q. Did you become active in the Progressive Party?
A. ... I did, but not as any official or not as any member of the Party.

In addition to being asked about his voting record, the employee was asked about his views on the United Nations:

Q. The file indicates that you were quite hepped up over the One World ideas?
A. ... I am still interested in the idea of world cooperation among all people in order that we may have peace, but I am ... cynical now about its possibilities.
Q. At one time or two, you were a strong advocate of the United Nations. Are you still?
A. I am still.[96]

After his dismissal in 1954, the employee "did manual labor at $1.00 to $2.00 per hour" and in 1955 was working as "a designer of swimming pools at $100.00 a week."[97]

On August 18, 1955, folksinger Pete Seeger appeared before HUAC and refused to answer a series of questions related to his political associations and acquaintances and to events at which he had performed. He refused to answer the questions "Have you been a member of the Communist Party since 1947?" and "Are you acquainted with V. J. Jerome?" Seeger responded: "I have already told you, sir, that I believe my associations, whatever they are, are my own private affairs." The chairman of

HUAC, Representative Walter, then asked Seeger: "I direct you to answer the question. Did you sing this particular song ["Wasn't That A Time"] on the Fourth of July at Wingdale Lodge in New York?" Seeger responded: "I have already given you my answer to that question, and all questions such as that. I feel that is improper to ask about my associations and opinions. I have said that I would be voluntarily glad to tell you any song, or what I have done in my life." Chairman Walter shot back: "I think it is my duty to inform you we don't accept this answer and the others."[98] Seeger was cited for contempt and given a prison sentence, which was overturned in 1962 by the United States Court of Appeals.[99]

When theologian Willard Uphaus appeared before HUAC on May 23, 1955, he refused to answer questions related to his political beliefs and associations and was subsequently imprisoned for a year. Uphaus, who had advocated the admission of Communist China into the United Nations, was asked: "And your point of view at that time, and now, Doctor, is that Red China, Communist-controlled, atheistic, godless China, should be admitted into the council of the nations of the world in the United Nations?" Uphaus answered: "I just admit that the present government of China be admitted. I don't put all the adjectives in."[100] The following colloquy then took place:

> Arens [HUAC chief counsel]: And you are familiar with the words from the Song of David? "Blessed is the man that walketh not in the counsel of the ungodly, nor standeth in the way of sinners, nor sitteth in the seat of the scornful?"
>
> Uphaus: That was his point of view.
>
> Arens: Whose point of view?
>
> Uphaus: The person who wrote it.
>
> Arens: You do not concur with David in the book of Psalms?
>
> Uphaus: I have a basic disagreement with a lot that I read in the Bible.
>
> Arens: I assume you feel that David was in error when he said: "Blessed is the man that walketh not in the counsel of the ungodly, nor standeth in the way of sinners, nor sitteth in the seat of the scornful."
>
> Uphaus: Is this a theological seminar today?
>
> Arens: You came with a Bible today. You have been waving it around in front of this committee.

> *Uphaus:* Will you give me time to discuss the theology of that verse you quoted?[101]

Arens then dropped the subject and asked Uphaus questions related to his writings and the peace conferences he had attended.

In a written statement submitted to HUAC, Uphaus criticized the committee's practices and procedures: "If the Un-American Activities Committee, through questioning or other pressure, concerns itself with my conduct in accordance with any religious views, or seeks to make moral judgments about my views, it infringes on my free exercise of religion as guaranteed by the First Amendment, and it goes contrary to the social creed of the Methodist Church. . . . The present practice, in and out of government, of exposing people or trying to repress and frighten them is both undemocratic and un-Christian. It violates the sacredness of the individual personality and poisons social and international relations."[102] Objecting to the committee's inquiries into his associations and acquaintances, Uphaus stated that he would "not join in any campaign to make outcasts or pariahs out of persons because of their political opinions," whereupon he cited Biblical passages condemning "tale-bearing or raising false reports": "THOU SHALT NOT RAISE A FALSE REPORT; PUT NOT THINE HAND WITH THE WICKED TO BE AN UNRIGHTEOUS WITNESS," Exodus 23:1; "THOU SHALT NOT GO UP AND DOWN AS A TALE-BEARER AMONG THY PEOPLE," Leviticus 19:16; "BE NOT A WITNESS AGAINST THY NEIGHBOR WITHOUT CAUSE: AND DECEIVE NOT WITH THY LIPS." Proverbs 24:28.[103]

In 1954, the attorney general of New Hampshire, conducting the state's inquiries into un-American activities, demanded that Uphaus turn over to the state the names and addresses of all the paid employees of the World Fellowship Center, "an organization to promote religious unity through contact between representatives of all living faiths." Uphaus was also asked for the names of persons who had attended World Fellowship summer camps in New Hampshire. He refused to comply with the attorney general's command, was subsequently cited for contempt, and was to remain in prison until "purged of his contempt." In 1959, the United States Supreme Court upheld Uphaus's conviction. He spent one year in prison and was released on December 11, 1960, at the age of seventy.[104]

While some who refused to utter what the state demanded did so because such coerced speech would have a chilling effect on speech and association and lead to conformity and regimented thinking, still others refused to speak because what was involved were matters of conscience, dignity, privacy, and personal integrity. Uphaus saw coerced speech as a violation of the "sacredness of the individual personality," and he contended that the attorney general's "action is a direct invasion of Christian conscience, an authority higher than that of the State, because my conscience tells me that to give the names and addresses of people who, to my knowledge, have never done anything to injure their country and who came to World Fellowship solely for vacation, recreation and friendly discourse, would turn me into a contemptible informer."[105]

If, as a Christian, Uphaus could not become an informer, it was also impossible for Zero Mostel, as a Jew, to become an informer when HUAC demanded that he name names. "Mostel, the son of a rabbi, explained that he couldn't inform, because as a Jew, if I inform, I can't be buried in sacred ground."[106]

When Lillian Hellman appeared before HUAC on May 21, 1952, she refused to answer questions about her association with the Communist Party and questions about her acquaintances. She was asked: "Were you at any time a member at large of the Communist Party?" She replied: "I refuse to answer . . . on the same grounds [self-incrimination]." The following colloquy took place:

> *Mr. Tavenner [HUAC staff member]:* Were you acquainted with V. J. Jerome?
> *Miss Hellman:* I refuse to answer on the same grounds.
> *Mr. Tavenner:* John Howard Lawson?
> *Miss Hellman:* I refuse to answer on the same grounds.
> *Mr. Tavenner:* Are you now a member of the Communist Party?
> *Miss Hellman:* No, sir.
> *Mr. Tavenner:* Were you ever a member of the Communist Party?
> *Miss Hellman:* I refuse to answer, Mr. Tavenner, on the same grounds.[107]

In a letter to Representative John Wood, chairman of HUAC, Hellman explained her unwillingness to become an informer. "To hurt innocent people whom I have known many years ago in order to save myself," she said, is "inhuman and indecent and dishonorable."[108] And then, in her now-famous line, she added: "I cannot and will not cut my conscience to fit this year's fashions, even though I long ago came to the conclusion that I was not a political person and could have no comfortable place in any political group."[109]

It was also a matter of conscience for playwright Arthur Miller, who refused to name names when he appeared before HUAC on June 21, 1956:

> *Mr. Scherer [Congressman]:* There is a question before the witness—namely, to give the names of those individuals who were present at this Communist Party meeting. There is a direction on the part of the Chairman to answer that question. Now, so that the record may be clear, I think we should say to the witness, Witness, would you listen?
>
> *Mr. Miller:* Yes.
>
> *Mr. Scherer:* We do not accept the reasons you gave for refusing to answer the question, and it is the opinion of the Committee that, if you do not answer the question, you are placing yourself in contempt.
>
> (*the witness confers with his counsel*)
>
> *Mr. Scherer:* That is an admonition that this Committee must give you in compliance with the decisions of the Supreme Court. Now, Mr. Chairman, I ask that you again direct the witness to answer the question.
>
> *The Chairman:* He has been directed to answer the question, and he gave us an answer we just do not accept.
>
> *Mr. Arens [HUAC staff]:* Was Arnaud d'Usseau chairman at this meeting of Communist Party writers which took place in 1947 at which you were in attendance?
>
> *Mr. Miller:* All I can say, sir, is that my conscience will not permit me to use the name of another person.[110]

When asked to provide the names of people attending "meetings with the Communist Party writers" sixteen years earlier, in "1939 or 1940," Miller refused and explained: "Mr. Chairman, I understand the philosophy behind this question and I want you to understand mine. When I say this, I want you to understand that I am not protecting the Communists or the Communist Party. I am trying to, and I will, protect my sense of myself. I could not use the name of another person and bring trouble on him. These were writers, poets, as far as I could see, and the life of a writer, despite what it sometimes seems, is pretty tough. I wouldn't make it any tougher for anybody. I ask you not to ask that question."[111] Representative Jackson's response was: "May I say that moral scruples, however laudable, do not constitute legal reason for refusing to answer the question. I certainly endorse the request for direction."[112]

Actor Larry Parks begged HUAC not to force him to name names. During the morning HUAC session on March 21, 1951, he pleaded with the committee not to force him to "really crawl through the mud to be an informer."[113] Francis Chaney, married to Ring Lardner, Jr., said in an interview: "When Larry finally broke down, it was heartbreaking. The way in which he did it was sad and so awful because the poor son of a bitch never did work again. Nothing good ever happened to him. He had this thing on his back for the rest of his life."[114]

In his letter advocating noncooperation with the un-American activities committees, Albert Einstein argued that the refusal to testify before the committees should not be based on the Fifth Amendment, "but on the assertion that it is shameful for a blameless citizen to submit to such an inquisition and that this kind of inquisition violates the Constitution."[115] However, hundreds of witnesses appearing before the HUAC type committees did invoke the Fifth Amendment. In "The Fifth Amendment Plea Before Congressional Committees Investigating Subversion," Daniel Pollitt indicates that "during the years 1953 and 1954 some 365 witnesses relied upon the fifth amendment in refusing to answer questions relating to Communist Party membership, association with 'Communist Front' organizations and/or illegal, seditious or subversive activities."[116] Hundreds who invoked the Fifth Amendment when inquiries were made into their political beliefs and associations found themselves under a cloud of suspicion, were blacklisted, and/or lost their jobs.

During this period, the United States Supreme Court asserted again and again that no conclusion can be drawn about the guilt or innocence of the individual who relies on the Fifth Amendment when asked by government to reveal political beliefs and associations. In 1955, in deciding for Thomas J. Quinn, who had refused to say, when appearing before HUAC in 1949, whether he had ever been a member of the Communist Party, the High Court declared:

> [T]he Self Incrimination Clause "must be accorded liberal construction in favor of the right it was intended to secure." Such liberal construction is particularly warranted in a prosecution of a witness for refusal to answer, since the respect normally accorded the privilege is then buttressed by the presumption of innocence accorded a defendant in a criminal trial. To

apply the privilege narrowly or begrudgingly—to treat it as a historical relic, at most merely to be tolerated—is to ignore its development and purpose.[117]

One year later, in *Ullmann v. United States*, the United States Supreme Court reiterated the importance and meaning of the Fifth Amendment while also deciding against William Ullmann, who had refused to answer grand jury questions related to his knowledge of espionage and conspiracy to commit espionage:

> It is relevant to define explicitly the spirit in which the Fifth Amendment's privilege against self-incrimination should be approached. This command of the Fifth Amendment ("nor shall any person . . . be compelled in any criminal case to be a witness against himself. . . .") registers an important advance in the development of our liberties—"one of the great landmarks in man's struggle to make himself civilized." Time has not shown that protection from the evils against which this safeguard was directed is needless and unwarranted. This constitutional protection must not be interpreted in a hostile or niggardly spirit. Too many, even those who should be better advised, view this privilege as a shelter for wrongdoers. They too readily assume that those who invoke it are either guilty of crime or commit perjury in claiming the privilege. Such a view does scant honor to the patriots who sponsored the Bill of Rights as a condition to acceptance of the Constitution by the ratifying states.[118]

One month after the High Court decided against Ullmann, it decided for Professor Harry Slochower, who, while willing to answer questions about his associations and beliefs since 1941, refused to answer Senate Internal Security Subcommittee questions concerning his organizational memberships during 1940 and 1941. As a result of his refusal to answer the committee's questions, Slochower was discharged from his position as associate professor at Brooklyn College. In *Slochower v. Board of Education*, the United States Supreme Court emphasized that the silence of a person who invokes the Fifth Amendment must not be viewed as imputing guilt: "At the outset we must condemn the practice of imputing a sinister meaning to the exercise of a person's constitutional right under the Fifth Amendment. . . . The privilege against self-incrimination would be reduced to a hollow mockery if its exercise could be taken as equivalent either to a confession of guilt or a conclusive presumption of perjury."[119]

The Supreme Court's continued assurance that invoking the Fifth Amendment did not imply guilt, however, was not accepted by many

Americans; the popular presumption was that the person who relied on the Fifth Amendment must have "something to hide" and was afraid of incriminating himself or herself. In 1957, President Dwight Eisenhower stated that the person relying on the Fifth Amendment must have "something he doesn't want to tell": "I personally don't want to comment on the right of a citizen to take the Fifth Amendment because I have no doubt that in some instances it is absolutely a basic safeguard of American liberty or it would not have been written as the Fifth Amendment to the Constitution; although I must say I probably share the common reaction [that] if a man has to go to the Fifth Amendment, there must be something he doesn't want to tell."[120]

In March 1953, Senator Joseph McCarthy's Senate Permanent Subcommittee on Investigations of the Subcommittee on Government Operations was investigating whether books written by Communists or Communist sympathizers were being purchased and shelved in U.S. State Department libraries around the world. Witnesses appearing before the McCarthy committee were questioned about their political associations and beliefs. Those who relied on the Fifth Amendment when refusing to answer the committee's questions were reminded again and again by McCarthy and other committee members that to do so could only mean that they were Communists.

On March 27, 1953, university professor Bernhard J. Stern, seven of whose books were "in use in the State Department information program, being located at some 63 information centers around the world," was questioned by Senators McCarthy and Symington:

Senator Symington: Do you think that a man who refuses to say whether or not he has been a member of an organization which has as its primary motive or one of its primary motives the destruction of our way of government is still a person who can be a good teacher of American youth?

Mr. Stern: My answer is, Senator, that since no inference can be drawn from a refusal to answer under the Fifth Amendment, that your question is irrelevant. . . .

The Chairman: Well, I think it is a relevant question and you will be ordered to answer it unless you think your answer might tend to incriminate you.

Mr. Stern: [W]hen a person refuses to answer a question under the Fifth Amendment, he is merely exercising his privileges, and . . .

therefore no inferences can be drawn. And therefore it is irrelevant from the point of whether a person should teach or not teach.

Senator Symington: Then why do you say you are not a Communist?

Mr. Stern: Because I am not.

Senator Symington: Then why do you not say you were not? If it is irrelevant in one case, why is it not relevant in both cases?

The Chairman: May I interrupt at this time? I would like to state that the witness has made the statement that no inference can be drawn from his refusal to answer a question on the ground of self-incrimination cannot be used against you in a criminal proceeding. However, when you tell us that you will not answer a certain question because you honestly believe that if you told us the truth that it would tend to incriminate you, inferences are drawn not only by this committee but by the public, I believe, as a whole. When you say no inference can be drawn, you are correct if you refer to a criminal trial, but not to an investigation.

Mr. Stern: Inferences can be drawn, but they may not be justifiable inferences.[121]

In 1953, Professor Stern's *Medical Services by Government* and *Medicine in Industry* were removed from United States Information Service libraries around the world.

Two days after Stern appeared before McCarthy's committee, anthropology professor Gene Weltfish, whose book *Races of Mankind* (co-authored with Ruth Benedict) was found in "50 Information Center overseas libraries," was questioned by Roy Cohn (committee chief counsel) and Senators McCarthy, Mundt, McClellan, and Symington:

Mr. Cohn: And were you a member of the Communist Party at the time you wrote this book?

Miss Weltfish: I invoke the Fifth Amendment, because I do not want to enter into an area of political manipulation at this time.

Mr. Cohn: Mr. Chairman, I would suggest that that is not a proper claim of privilege under the Fifth Amendment. The question is: When Professor Weltfish wrote this book which was in use until March 15, anyway, in the State Department information centers, was she a member of the Communist Party?

The Chairman: What is your answer to that, Doctor?

Miss Weltfish: On the basis that it might tend to incriminate me, because of the present atmosphere, I invoke the Fifth Amendment.

The Chairman: Let me ask you this: First, I think you should know that while your refusal to answer whether you were a Communist or not could not be used against you in a criminal court, when you come before this committee, which is an investigating body, and you say: "I won't tell you whether I am a Communist, because if I told the truth it would tend to incriminate me," the inference that any reasonable man draws is that you must be a member of the Communist Party, because if you were not a member you could say "No"; that would not incriminate you. Let me ask you this question. First did you answer the question as to whether you attended Communist Party meetings with other professors, or have you refused to answer that?[122]

When in 1953 the U.S. Information Service libraries were directed to remove "undesirable" books, "only one of the directives specifically listed authors. It included sixteen names, without mention of any of their specific works. The nearest to a common denominator was plainly the fact that most of those listed had refused at one time or another to tell Federal investigators, often the McCarthy subcommittee, if they were or had been Communists."[123]

Professor Gene Wiltfish was among the sixteen on the list, which also included Herbert Aptheker, Earl Browder, Howard Fast, Philip S. Foner, and Dashiell Hammett. Hammett's *The Maltese Falcon* and *The Thin Man*, along with works by Langston Hughes, Alan Barth, Theodore White, Owen Lattimore, Lillian Hellman, and others, were removed from U.S. Information Service libraries abroad. Books, like their authors, were condemned as "un-American" and blacklisted.

Numerous college and university professors who invoked the Fifth Amendment soon found themselves without jobs. In the introduction to his *Cold War on Campus,* Lionel S. Lewis begins with the story of a chemist on the faculty of Rensselaer Polytechnic Institute. Invoking the First and Fifth Amendments, this man refused to answer some HUAC questions about his political, associational ties and activities. The university dismissed the professor, with the board of trustees concluding that he was "unfit" and had "forfeited his right to continue as an assistant professor upon the faculty." What is significant, writes Lewis, "is that the case was by no means an isolated incident. Beginning about a half dozen years earlier, and continuing for another three years after 1953 (that is, during a decade from 1947 to 1956), it was commonplace to hear about campus investigations of alleged political radicals and of firings, near firings, or forced resignations."[124]

In 1948, when several University of Washington professors refused to tell that state's un-American activities committee, the Canwell Committee, whether they were Communists and refused to name names, they became subjects of a university "trial," and as a result three were fired and three were put on two-year probation.[125] Two professors at Rutgers University were dismissed in 1952 as a result of their invoking the Fifth Amendment when they refused to answer questions related to political affiliations put to them by the Senate Internal Security Subcommittee. The university's board of trustees unanimously agreed that "professors could not use their constitutional privilege to invoke the Fifth Amendment and remain on the faculty"; the board contended that the refusal to answer the investigating committee's questions "impaired" confidence in the professors' "fitness to teach."[126]

In 1953, physicist Byron Darling at Ohio State University, when asked questions by HUAC about his and others' political beliefs and associations, refused to answer, basing his refusal on the Fifth Amendment. Within days, he was suspended by Ohio State University President Howard Bevis, after which the board of trustees fired the physicist because his " 'public refusal to answer pertinent questions' was itself sufficient grounds for his dismissal."[127]

Professor of Philosophy Barrows Dunham was dismissed by Temple University in 1952 after he relied on the Fifth Amendment when queried by HUAC. While Dunham was constitutionally justified in invoking the Fifth Amendment, his case, as Ellen Schrecker has observed, revealed, "as did those of Darling and other Fifth Amendment witnesses fired in the spring of 1953, that to use the privilege during a congressional investigation was to court academic unemployment."[128] Reed College Professor of Philosophy Stanley Moore invoked the Fifth Amendment when he appeared "before HUAC in June 1954 and was fired by the school's board of trustees in August."[129]

Actors, screenwriters, and directors who invoked the Fifth Amendment were also subjected to firings and blacklisting. Actor Jeff Corey "took the Fifth" and as a result was blacklisted for over a decade: "I remember hearing the 1947 hearings, the Hollywood Ten. I knew those guys and I trembled, I had the shakes. I knew it was going to be bad. And coincident with that, I had the best period of my career. I did *Abe Lincoln in Illinois.* . . . I did *Home of the Brave* and did one film after another. But I knew that it would catch up with us. And it did in 1951. I was blacklisted twelve years. I think I was the first one to go back to work."[130]

Actor Zero Mostel was blacklisted after he "took the Fifth" in 1955. When he appeared before HUAC on October 14, 1955, Mostel was asked: "Were you a member of the Communist Party or of a Communist faction of the Party in 1938 in the state of California?" Mostel responded: "That question I have to answer several ways. Obviously I was never in California until 1942. But on all questions about my political affiliations I wish to rely upon my constitutional privileges under the Fifth Amendment." The following colloquy then took place:

Mr. *Jackson [Representative]:* I ask that direction be given inasmuch as the witness has volunteered the information that he was not in Los Angeles or in the state of California at that time.

Mr. *Doyle [Representative]:* You understand, Witness, we are not satisfied with the answer you have given as a sufficient answer, and therefore I direct you to expressly answer the question.

Mr. *Mostel:* I decline to answer that question on my constitutional privilege.

Mr. *Tavenner [HUAC investigator]:* During the period of your membership in 1948 [in Actors Equity Association in New York City] were you aware of an effort made by a group of individuals within the Actors Equity to solicit the assistance of Actors Equity in behalf of the eleven Communists on trial under the Smith Act in the City of New York?

Mr. *Mostel:* I decline to answer that question on the previously stated constitutional grounds.

Mr. *Tavenner:* Have you at any time been aware of the existence of an organized group of members of the Communist Party in the City of New York who were members—or, at least, most of whom were members—of Actors Equity?

Mr. *Mostel:* I have to decline to answer that question as well, on my constitutional privileges.[131]

As an actor, Mostel, unlike screenwriters who wrote under assumed names or sold their scripts through "fronts," did not have the option of working anonymously. As he declared: "I am a man of thousand faces, all of them blacklisted."[132]

Screenwriter Paul Jarrico relied on the Fifth Amendment when he refused to answer HUAC questions, and as a result he was blacklisted and denied credit by Howard Hughes and RKO for coauthoring the script for *The Las Vegas Story*; as reported by Larry Ceplair and Steven Englund, "On November 26, 1952, Superior Court judge Orlando Rhodes ruled that Jarrico's refusal to answer HUAC's questions constituted a violation of the moral clause [in his RKO contract]. He stated that taking the Fifth Amendment to avoid testifying had come to be associated in the public mind with Communist Party membership or sympathy, either of which rendered the invoker an 'object of public disgrace, obloquy, ill-will and ridicule.'"[133]

As Leonard G. Ratner has aptly observed, "Penalizing a person for asserting the self-incrimination privilege in effect defeats the privilege. Therefore the constitutional provision creating the privilege must protect an individual not only from punishment for invoking the privilege. Since deprival of livelihood is a form of punishment, it would seem that neither the federal government . . . nor any state having a self-incrimination clause in its own constitution could validly discharge a public employee for exercising the privilege."[134] Yet that was precisely what was occurring in mid-twentieth-century America: employees were being deprived of livelihood, a form of punishment, upon invoking the Fifth Amendment when appearing before the state and federal un-American activities committees. In reference to the dismissals of professors who "took the Fifth," Lionel S. Lewis has accurately pointed out, "Academic authorities did what civic authorities could not. . . . They substituted economic punishment for the criminal punishment that the Fifth Amendment is designed to prevent."[135]

Those who "took the Fifth" when appearing before the HUAC-type committees did so for various reasons, the least of which was the fear of self-incrimination. Daniel Pollitt identified some of the reasons witnesses relied on the Fifth Amendment:

1. Belief that the question infringes on the Witness' freedom of speech, association or conscience.

2. Fear that answering a particular question would "waive" the right to refuse to answer questions concerning the identity of others.
3. Fear of perjury indictment if questions were answered in negative.
4. Desire to protect the integrity of the Fifth Amendment or to support the position of others who had relied on it.
5. Belief that reliance on the Fifth Amendment is the only safe way to refuse to cooperate with the committee.
8. Fear that an answer would cause public humiliation, economic hardship, or social ostracism.[136]

Pollitt concluded his study by asserting that "it may be said that the facts developed here indicate that the term 'Fifth Amendment Communist' has little basis in fact. . . ."[137]

Hence in mid-twentieth-century America, because there was no "freedom not to speak" available, witnesses appearing before the various un-American activities committees relied on what was available, the Fifth Amendment, even though their reasons for "taking the Fifth" had little or nothing to do with "self-incrimination." The witnesses who relied on the First Amendment went to jail; those who relied on the Fifth Amendment lost their jobs.

Had a freedom not to speak been available, there would have been much less presumption of guilt of those compelled to say, "I refuse to answer by invoking the Fifth Amendment against self-incrimination." There is a significant difference between refusing to answer HUAC inquiries on the grounds of self-incrimination and refusing to answer by invoking a freedom not to speak. One may choose to invoke the freedom not to speak not because of concern about self-incrimination, but because one does not want to be coerced into becoming an informer, because one believes that just as a citizen has a freedom to speak, so does he or she have the freedom not to speak. The freedom not to speak, having nothing to do with self-incrimination, thus can be invoked without immediately casting doubt on the presumption of innocence. The very word "incriminate" carries with it both the denotation and the connotation of wrongdoing. "Freedom not to speak" does not.

"Incriminate" is derived from the Latin: *in* + *crimen*. It is defined in *Ballentine's Law Dictionary* as "To charge with a crime. . . . To make it appear that one is guilty of a crime."[138] In *Black's Law Dictionary*, it means "To charge with a crime; to expose to an accusation or charge of crime. . . ."[139] Nothing in the words "freedom not to speak" connotes anything resembling a crime. However, maintaining silence based on the invocation of the Fifth Amendment even though one's silence involves no hiding of a crime or wrongdoing has led to inferences of guilt. The stigmatizing of the individual who invokes the Fifth Amendment is far greater than any stigmatizing that might come from invoking the freedom not to speak.

The problem is further compounded when the agents and authority of the state are used to convey the idea that invoking the Fifth Amendment implies guilt. The United States Supreme Court spoke to this point in *Griffin v. California* (1965) when it decided that it was improper for a trial court to instruct a jury that while a defendant has a constitutional right not to testify, the jury "may take that failure into consideration as tending to indicate the truth of such evidence [against him] and as indicating that among the inferences that may be reasonably drawn therefrom those unfavorable to the defendant are the more probable."[140] In its elaboration of the impropriety of such an instruction to the jury, the High Court declared: "What the jury may infer, given no help from the court, is one thing. What it may infer when the court solemnizes the silence of the accused into evidence against him is quite another." The Court held that the Fifth Amendment "forbids either comment by the prosecution on the accused's silence or instructions by the court that such silence is evidence of guilt."[141]

Yet in mid-twentieth-century America, agents of the state—a president, senators, representatives, college officials, albeit not judges—asserted that "if a man has to go to the Fifth Amendment, there must be something he doesn't want to tell" and that if a person will not tell whether he or she is a Communist, "the inference that any reasonable man draws is that you must be a member of the Communist Party." To paraphrase *Griffin*, solemnizing the silence of the person who refused to answer HUAC inquiries into guilt was what occurred when the state "judges" publicly asserted, at hearings and "trials," that inferences of guilt could be drawn from silence. What the American public may have inferred, given no help from these state authorities, was one thing. What it may have inferred when these representatives of the state solemnized the person's silence into evidence against him was quite another. The stigma attached to refusing to "incriminate" oneself was given the imprimatur of the state.

Professors, actors, screenwriters, clergy, and others who refused to answer HUAC's inquiries were stigmatized and blacklisted, and they found themselves unemployed. Their silence was evidence of their guilt. The authors who refused to answer Senator Joe McCarthy's committee inquiries were stigmatized, and their books were removed from U.S. State Department libraries around the world.

Through the centuries, not only have heretics been punished for refusing to reveal their beliefs and associations to church and state authorities, but it has been further demanded that their heretical voices be muted by the prohibition or destruction of their works. Sixteenth-century physician and theologian Michael Servetus, who was condemned as a heretic for his denial of the Trinity and rejection of paedobaptism, had "the singular distinction of having been burned by the Catholics in effigy and by the Protestants in actuality."[142] The court that condemned Servetus to death stated in its verdict, "[N]ow in writing [we] give final sentence and condemn you, Michael Servetus, to be bound and taken to Champel and there attached to a stake and burned with your book [*Christianismi Restitutio*] to ashes. And so you shall finish your days and give an example to others who would commit the like."[143] When Servetus refused to recant, when he showed no sign "of amendment"[144] of his "errors," on October 27, 1553, he and his writings, inserted between the chains and his body, were set ablaze.

The document pronouncing the excommunication of Giordano Bruno in 1600 declared that "his books should be publicly burned, and their titles placed upon the *Index*."[145] Thirty-five years after Bruno was sent to stake, Galileo Galilei's books were condemned, blacklisted, and placed on the *Index* after he had been interrogated by the Inquisition, forced to recant, and ordered to declare that "should I know any heretic, or person suspected of heresy, I will denounce him to this Holy Office, or to the Inquisitor."[146]

5

Coerced Speech and Un-American Activities Committees

In mid-twentieth-century America, there was no freedom not to speak to protect the "heretics" who refused to reveal to HUAC-type committees their political beliefs and associations. In those cases where the courts gave constitutional protection to the heretics, the protection was based not on any freedom not to speak, but on the courts' contentions that the inquiries were too vague or too broad, were not "pertinent" or that they constituted a violation of freedom of association or academic freedom. As Carl Beck has observed in his study of the prosecutions initiated by HUAC between 1945 and 1957, the courts "sustained all prosecutions for contempt when the defendant had argued that his rights under the First Amendment were being infringed upon by inquiry into his political activities."[1] Beck concludes that "with minor exceptions those who challenged the authority of the committee on constitutional grounds other than self-incrimination prior to 1957 were convicted of contempt."[2]

In one of the earliest of these cases, *United States v. Josephson*, the United States Court of Appeals decided in 1947 against Leon Josephson, who had refused to testify before HUAC and as a result was cited for contempt and subsequently jailed. As the court of appeals saw it, Josephson's silence was punishable because, among other reasons, "the power of Congress to gather facts of the most intense public concern . . . is not diminished by the unchallenged right of individuals to speak their minds within lawful limits. When speech, or propaganda, or whatever it may at the moment be called, clearly presents an immediate danger to national security, the protection of the First Amendment ceases."[3] The court found acceptable HUAC's investigation into "the extent, character, and objects of propaganda activities in this country, which were designated un-American" and "the diffusion within this country of subversive and Un-American propaganda which attacks the principle of the form of government that is guaranteed by the Constitution."[4]

Judge Clark dissented, emphasizing in his opinion the lack of precise definitions of "un-American" and "subversive." After asserting that "all attempts to explain the meaning of the key word 'un-American,' either on the original creation of the Committee or on its later renewals, have been avoided or opposed," Judge Clark declared that "neither the legislative authority nor the actions pursuant to it suggest or permit any limitations on the investigation of the spoken or written word."[5] As he indicates, HUAC was requiring citizens to reveal beliefs and associations that went beyond being "subversive" and "un-American": "Suffice it to say here that its [HUAC's] range of activity has covered all varieties of organizations, including the American Civil Liberties Union, the C.I.O., the National Catholic Welfare Conference, the Farmer-Labor party, the Federal Theatre Project, consumers' organizations, various publications from the magazine 'Time' to the 'Daily Worker,' and varying forms and types of industry, of which the recent investigation of the movie industry is fresh in the public mind."[6]

To illustrate further HUAC's vague use of "un-American," Judge Clark stated: "As a matter of fact, the testimony at the recent movie investigation found the necessary un-American qualities for which the Committee was searching in films which placed bankers in an unfavorable light or talked 'against the free enterprise system.' "[7]

Going beyond the vagueness issue, Judge Clark turned to the question as to whether the authorization establishing HUAC was compatible with the First Amendment. Applying the clear and present danger test, he wrote,

> Congress has a right to protect the safety of the state when that is endangered; and hence when words "are used in such circumstances and are of such a nature as to create a clear and present danger that they will bring about the substantive evils" against which Congress may legislate, they may be prohibited or penalized. . . . Now, when this country is at peace, it is hard to discern such circumstances of "clear and present danger." Indeed, the teaching of experience, after nearly three decades of a wellnigh pathological fear of "Communism," under constant investigation by Congress . . . might suggest that there was more to be feared from the fear itself than from the supposed danger.[8]

The United States Supreme Court denied certiorari, and Josephson was jailed.

At about the same time the Court of Appeals decided against Josephson, the United States Court of Appeals, D.C., was hearing argument in the case of *Barsky v. United States*. As we have seen, the court again decided against a person who had refused to provide HUAC with records, this time of the Joint Anti-Fascist Refugee Committee. The court, in deciding against Barsky, dealt with several of the same arguments as those that appeared in *Josephson*. However, the court presented something new in relation to the freedom to remain silent:

> It is urged by the appellee Government that freedom of speech does not encompass freedom to remain silent. There is justification for the contention that the latter is freedom of privacy, different in character and governed by different considerations from the constitutionally protected freedom of speech. At least, the basic public policies which underlie the two are different. The public policy which supports freedom of speech is that the safety of democratic government lies in open discussion—discussion of grievances, remedies, of "noxious doctrine" as well as of popular preferences. The public interest in privacy, however, is premised upon the individual's right to the pursuit of happiness. But we do not consider that question and do not rest this decision in any respect upon it. We assume, without deciding, for purposes of this case, that compulsion to answer the question asked by the Congressional Committee would impinge upon speech and not merely invade privacy.[9]

The introduction of the right of privacy, while not applied in this case, was unique, for it was not invoked by any courts in deciding the HUAC and loyalty-oath cases during this mid-twentieth-century inquisition.

Judge Edgerton, dissenting in *Barsky*, placed heavy emphasis on the argument that "the House Committee's investigation abridges freedom of speech and inflicts punishment without trial": "The investigation restricts the freedom of speech by uncovering and stigmatizing expressions of unpopular views. The Committee gives wide publicity to its proceedings. This exposes the men and women whose views are advertised to risks of insult, ostracism, and lasting loss of employment. . . . The Committee's practice of advertising and stigmatizing unpopular views is therefore a strong deterrent to any expression, however private, of such views."[10]

While Judge Edgerton emphasizing freedom of speech to support his dissenting opinion, his language comes close to implicating the right of privacy, although he never refers directly to that right: "The investigation also restricts freedom of speech by forcing people to express views. Freedom of speech is freedom in respect to speech and includes freedom not to speak. 'To force an American citizen publicly to profess any statement of belief' is to violate the First Amendment. . . . Witnesses before the House Committee are under pressure to profess approved beliefs. They cannot express others without exposing themselves to disastrous consequences." Citing from an earlier United States Supreme Court decision, Edgerton declares: "Under our traditions beliefs are personal and not a matter of mere association."[11]

More than other judges deciding HUAC and loyalty-oath cases, Edgerton is concerned about "forcing people to express views," about the "freedom not to speak," about forcing Americans "publicly to profess any statement of belief," and he is certain that "under our traditions beliefs are personal." The majority of the court had said that "public policy which supports freedom of speech is that the safety of democratic government lies in open discussion," while "the public interest in privacy . . . is premised upon the individual's right to the pursuit of happiness." Edgerton's language comes very close to addressing privacy, but his emphasis remains on freedom of speech.

Like Judge Clark in *Josephson*, Edgerton invoked the clear and present danger test:

> There is no evidence in the record that propaganda has created danger, clear and present or obscure and remote, that the government of the United States or any government in the United States will be overthrown by force or violence. . . . The premise that the government must have power to protect itself by discovering whether it is in clear and present danger of overthrow by violence is sound. But it does not support the conclusion that Congress may compel men to disclose their personal opinions, to a committee and also to the world, on topics ranging from communism, however remotely and peaceably achieved, to the "American system of checks and balances," the British Empire, and the Franco government of Spain.[12]

In *Barsky* the court of appeals had said that HUAC could legitimately inquire whether a witness was "a believer in Communism": "We are considering a specific question only, which is whether this Congressional Committee may inquire whether an individual is or is not a believer in Communism or a member of the Communist Party."[13] The court held that "Congress has power to make an inquiry of an individual which may elicit the answer that the witness is a believer in Communism or a member of the Communist Party."[14] No longer was it a matter of whether one refused to reveal whether one was "a member of the Communist Party"; the court now required the witness to reveal whether he or she was "a believer in Communism." It had become an act of contempt of Congress not only to refuse to name names and reveal one's associational ties, but also to refuse to reveal one's political beliefs.

One year after the court of appeals decided against Barsky, the same court, relying heavily on *Barsky*, decided on June 3, 1949, against screenwriters John Howard Lawson and Dalton Trumbo, who, along with eight others, refused to answer HUAC questions related to their political beliefs and associations. Trumbo had refused to answer questions as to "whether or not he was a member of the Screen Writers Guild" and "whether or not he was or had ever been a member of the Communist Party."[15] Expressing its reliance on *Barsky*, the court of appeals declared in *Lawson v. United States*: "We hereby reaffirm the holding of the majority opinion of this court in the Barsky case and adopt its reasoning as applicable to appellants in the present cases." To make sure there was no "mistake or misunderstanding," the court went on to assert: "[W]e expressly hold herein that the House Committee on Un-American Activities, or a properly appointed subcommittee thereof, has the power to inquire whether a witness subpoenaed by it is or is not a member of the Communist Party or a believer in Communism and that this power carries with it necessarily the power to effect criminal punishment for failure or refusal to answer that question. . . . [T]his is equally true of the inquiry whether appellants were members of the Screen Writers Guild. . . ."[16]

The United States Supreme Court denied certiorari, and Lawson and Trumbo were imprisoned, along with the other writers and directors who became known as the Hollywood Ten: Albert Malz, Alvah Bessie, Samuel Ornitz, Herbert J. Biberman, Edward Dmytryk, Adrian Scott, Ring Lardner, Jr., and Lester Cole.

As we have seen, other "unfriendly" HUAC witnesses who relied on the First Amendment, not the Fifth, were also cited for contempt of Congress and imprisoned. Earlier we noted that clergyman Willard Uphaus appeared in 1954 before New Hampshire's attorney general, Louis Wyman, who conducted the investigations into un-American activities in New Hampshire. Uphaus was told immediately that he must answer the questions put to him or "take the Fifth." In his autobiography, Uphaus relates his encounter with Wyman:

> Wyman . . . proceeded to inquire in detail about my marital experiences.
> Not even the wide domain he had claimed included this field. Why should
> two innocent women, who knew little or cared less about either politics
> or the work I was now engaged in, be dragged into this man's net of lists
> merely because they had had the misfortune to marry me many years
> before? I could only conclude that the purpose of the questions was to
> disconcert me. I protested. It did me no good. Wyman curtly pointed out
> that "the only basis at the present time upon which the witness may de-
> cline to answer is the ground that his answer, if given, might tend to
> incriminate him." In other words: answer or take the Fifth Amendment.
> Otherwise I would be in contempt.[17]

As noted in chapter 4, Uphaus was then ordered in 1955 to appear before the attorney general again to provide information about World Fellowship, Inc., of which Uphaus was executive director.[18] Uphaus based his refusal on the First and Fourteenth Amendments, the freedoms of religion and conscience, and on "search and seizure" provisions in the New Hampshire Constitution.

On January 5, 1956, Uphaus was brought before the Merrimack County Superior Court in Concord, New Hampshire; he records in his autobiography: "Wyman's purpose was to have the court order me to surrender the guest list, the employees' names and the correspondence files. Then, if I still refused, I would be in contempt of court and subject to a jail sentence."[19] The trial ended with the court clerk reading: "Willard Uphaus is found and adjudged in contempt of this court. Willard Uphaus is ordered committed to the Merrimack County Jail, there to remain until purged of his contempt."[20]

After the case reached the New Hampshire Supreme Court, it concluded on February 28, 1957: "The committal order is terminable upon the witness purging himself of contempt, and is not considered violative of the constitutional provisions relied upon by the defendant."[21] Uphaus appealed. On June 8, 1959, in a 5-4 decision, the United States Supreme Court decided against him, the High Court emphasizing the governmental interest in self-preservation, "the ultimate value of any society":

> [T]he governmental interest in self-preservation is sufficiently compelling
> to subordinate the interest in associational privacy of persons who, at least

to the extent of the guest registration statute, made public at the inception the association they now wish to keep private. In light of such a record we conclude that the State's interest has not been "pressed, in this instance, to a point where it has come into fatal collision with the overriding" constitutionally protected rights of appellant and those he may represent.[22]

Joined by Chief Justice Warren and Justices Black and Douglas, Justice Brennan wrote a dissenting opinion in which he spoke of Uphaus's "interest in privacy as it relates to freedom of speech and assembly": "We deal here with inquiries into the areas of free speech and assemblage where the process of compulsory disclosure itself tends to have a repressive effect. . . . We deal only with the power of the State to *compel* such disclosure. . . . Here we must demand some initial showing by the State sufficient to counterbalance the interest in privacy as it relates to freedom of speech and assembly. On any basis that has practical meaning, New Hampshire has not made such a showing here. I would reverse the judgment of the New Hampshire Supreme Court."[23]

The First Amendment did not save Willard Uphaus. As described in chapter 4, Uphaus was imprisoned for one year and released on December 11, 1960.

On the same day as the United States Supreme Court decided against Willard Uphaus, it also decided against Lloyd Barenblatt, who had been cited for contempt of Congress when he relied on the First Amendment in refusing to answer HUAC questions related to his associational ties. On June 28, 1954, several "friendly" witnesses appeared before HUAC, beginning with Francis X. T. Crowley, who provided the committee with names of students at the University of Michigan who he said belonged to campus political organizations. Crowley was followed by witnesses he had named as being associated with the Communist Party through the Haldane Club. The witnesses relied on the Fifth Amendment when refusing to answer HUAC's questions about their associational ties and beliefs.

But college instructor Lloyd Barenblatt, who had been named by Crowley, did not rely on the Fifth Amendment when called to testify. Barenblatt had prepared a statement, "Objection to jurisdication of the committee on un-american activities and to questions propounded by it," which asserted at the outset: "I, Lloyd Barenblatt, having been subpenaed [sic] before the Committee on Un-American Activities, by subpena [sic] dated the 28th day of May 1954, returnable on the 28th day of June 1954, hereby respectfully object to the power and jurisdiction of this committee to inquire into—(a) My political beliefs; (b) My religious beliefs; (c) Any other personal and private affairs; (d) My associational activities."[24]

Early in the inquiry, when it became clear that Barenblatt was going to decline to answer questions related to his beliefs and associations, Representative Clyde Doyle said to Barenblatt: "I am in no position to give you legal advice, but I know from the record that you are an instructor in a certain very distinguished college, by reputation, at least, and wouldn't it be a magnificent thing if you could take the position that if you ever were a member of the Communist Party, that you say so frankly and clean up and get out of that embarrassing situation and then start from there? Wouldn't that do you and the country a lot of good today." Representative Velde, praising Doyle for providing an "open door" for Barenblatt, declared: "You certainly have given him [Barenblatt] every opportunity, Mr. Doyle, and I think he has had every opportunity before to come clean."[25] However, Barenblatt refused to "come clean."

When HUAC counsel Robert Kunzig asked Barenblatt if he was relying on the Fifth Amendment in declining to answer whether he was a member of the Communist Party, Barenblatt answered: "I do not invoke the Fifth Amendment in declining to answer. I decline to answer on the grounds stated in my objections as presented to the members of this committee, which you have not allowed me to read." Representative Walter then told Barenblatt: "Now, may I inform you that you haven't the right to decline to answer by virtue of any decision of the court. It is because of the Constitution. Now, do you decline to answer because of the constitutional provision?" The interrogation continued:

Mr. Barenblatt: I am declining to answer on constitutional grounds as stated in my objection.

Mr. Velde: But you do not include the Fifth Amendment in your reasons in declining; is that right?

Mr. Barenblatt: You are correct, sir.

Mr. Kunzig: Are you stating in this document which you have just handed us, and which we have had no time to look at at all, that the Fifth Amendment is not included?

Mr. Barenblatt: Not included in my list of objections.

Mr. Kunzig: So you are declining to answer the question as to whether you are now a member of the Communist Party, and you are specifically not giving the Fifth Amendment as a reason for declining?

Mr. Barenblatt: That is correct, sir.

Mr. Kunzig: All right. Now, Mr. Chairman, I respectfully request that the witness be directed to answer the question: Are you now a member of the Communist Party?[26]

Again, Barenblatt refused to answer. As the proceedings progressed, Barenblatt continued to decline to answer HUAC questions, basing his refusals on the document, in which he expressed his objections based on the First, Ninth, and Tenth Amendments, the prohibition against bills of attainder, and the doctrine of separation of powers. The questions he refused to answer included:

Are you now a member of the Communist Party?

Have you ever been a member of the Communist Party?

Now, you have stated that you knew Francis Crowley. Did you know Francis Crowley as a member of the Communist Party?

Were you ever a member of the Haldane Club of the Communist Party while at the University of Michigan?

Were you a member while a student of the University of Michigan Council of Arts, Sciences, and Professions?

Barenblatt's refusal to answer the HUAC questions led to his being cited for contempt of Congress and subsequently tried, found guilty, and sentenced to six months in jail and a two-hundred-fifty-dollar fine. Barenblatt appealed, and the United States Court of Appeals upheld the conviction. When the case reached the United States Supreme Court, it too decided against Barenblatt in a 5–4 decision.[27]

Justice Harlan, delivering the opinion of the Court, argued that HUAC had given Barenblatt ample notice of the pertinency of the committee's questions. Barenblatt had contended that he had not been adequately apprised of the pertinency of the questions to the subject matter of the inquiry being conducted by HUAC. As to Barenblatt's contention that the questions that he refused to answer infringed on his First Amendment rights, Justice Harlan responded by invoking the balancing of interests test; he wrote: "Where First Amendment rights are asserted to bar governmental interrogation[,] resolution of the issue always involves a balancing by the courts of the competing private and public interests at stake in the particular circumstances shown."[28]

After asserting that it is "hardly debatable" that "Congress has wide power to legislate in the field of Communist activity in this country, and to conduct appropriate investigations in aid thereof," Justice Harlan concluded that "the record is barren" of factors which "might sometimes lead to the conclusion that the individual interests at stake were not subordinate to those of the state. . . . We conclude that the balance between the individual and the governmental interests here at stake must be struck in favor of the latter, and that therefore the provisions of the First Amendment have not been offended."[29] As the majority of the Court saw it, "In the last analysis this power [to legislate and conduct investigations] rests on the right of self-preservation, 'the ultimate value of any society.' "[30] As in the case of Willard Uphaus, the First Amendment did not save Barenblatt.

Justice Black wrote a dissenting opinion, joined by Chief Justice Warren and Justice Douglas, rejecting the majority's use of the balancing of interests test:

> [E]ven assuming what I cannot assume, that some balancing is proper in this case, I feel that the Court after stating the test ignores it completely. At most it balances the right of the Government to preserve itself, against Barenblatt's right to refrain from revealing Communist affiliations. Such a balance, however, mistakes the factors to be weighed. In the first place, it completely leaves out the real interest in Barenblatt's silence, the interest of the people as a whole in being able to join organizations, advocate causes and make political "mistakes" without later being subjected to governmental penalties for having dared to think for themselves. It is this right, the right to err politically, which keeps us strong as a nation. . . . It is these interests of society, rather than Barenblatt's own right to silence, which I think the Court should put on the balance against the demands of the Government, if any balancing process is to be tolerated. Instead they are not mentioned, while on the other side the demands of the Government are vastly overstated and called "self-preservation."[31]

Towards the end of his lengthy dissenting opinion, Justice Black stated: "Finally, I think Barenblatt's conviction violates the Constitution because the chief aim, purpose and practice of the House Un-American Activities Committee, as disclosed by its many reports, is to try witnesses and punish them because they are or have been Communists or because they refuse to admit or deny Communist affiliations. The punishment imposed is generally punishment by humiliation and public shame. There is nothing strange or novel about this kind of punishment. It is in fact one of the oldest forms of governmental punishment known to mankind;

branding, the pillory, ostracism and subjection to public hatred [are] but a few examples of it." [32]

Years later, Barenblatt stressed the importance of Black's dissenting opinion: "What was historically important was the minority opinion written by Justice Black. No one reads the majority opinion anymore, but Black's opinion has become history."[33] The effects of the Court's decision are described by Barenblatt: "During the time my case was on appeal, I was working in market research and advertising in New York. I was blacklisted in the academic world and went on Madison Avenue. I did that for about seven years, until I had to report to serve my jail term. I started out in the District of Columbia jail, which was a *horrible* place! Then they sent me to the D.C. workhouse, which is in Occoquan, Virginia. It looked like a small liberal-arts campus on the outside, but inside it was the pits."[34] Barenblatt was finally transferred to the federal prison in Danbury, Connecticut, the same prison to which two of the Hollywood Ten had been sent, Ring Lardner, Jr., and Lester Cole.

"Would I do it over again?" asks Barenblatt. He answers his own question: "Yes, but I'd be better at it! I really think that the American people didn't learn much of anything from the whole McCarthy era. . . . I lost a lot of friends, and it cost me money and jobs. But I stood up at a time when many people kept quiet, or became informers, or left the country. I am *still* an American. I'm glad I took my stand. I don't regret it."[35]

The impact of *Barenblatt* became evident when, six months after the Supreme Court handed down its decision, *Barenblatt* was relied upon by the United States Court of Appeals in deciding against two critics of HUAC who had been cited for contempt of Congress when they refused to answer, on the basis of the First Amendment, HUAC questions about their political associations. On December 10, 1959, the court of appeals decided against Carl Braden and on December 14, 1959, against Frank Wilkinson. Both appealed to the United States Supreme Court, and on February 27, 1961, the High Court decided, 5–4, against both men. Both were imprisoned for twelve months.

Carl Braden appeared before HUAC on July 30, 1958, in response to a subpoena served by HUAC. Early in his testimony, Braden made it clear that he was relying on the First Amendment when he refused to answer HUAC's questions. HUAC Staff Director Richard Arens insisted that Braden answer a question related to a meeting with Harvey O'Connor, who was chairman of the Emergency Civil Liberties Committee, an organization listed by HUAC in its *Guide to Subversive Organizations* as a "front for the Communist Party";[36] Braden refused to comply:

> *Mr. Willis [Representative]:* In other words, you are maintaining your attitude of refusing to answer?
>
> *Mr. Braden:* On the grounds of the First Amendment to the United States Constitution, which protects the right of all citizens to practice beliefs and associations, freedom of the press, freedom of religion, and freedom of assembly. On that ground I stand, sir.
>
> *Mr. Arens:* Now, kindly tell the committee, if you please, sir, are you now, this minute, a member of the Communist Party?
>
> *Mr. Braden:* I stand on my previous position under the First Amendment, that such a question has no pertinency to any legislative purpose and it violates my belief.[37]

Braden was then asked about his involvement in the preparation of an open letter signed by "200 Negro leaders in the South," who expressed alarm at HUAC's appearance in the South to investigate un-American activity in the southern states. The letter, addressed to the House of Representatives, read in part:

> [W]e are alarmed at the prospect of this committee coming South to follow the lead of Senator Eastland, as well as several state investigating committees, in trying to attach the "subversive" label to any liberal white Southerner who dares to raise his voice in support of our democratic ideals.
>
> It was recently pointed out by four Negro leaders who met with President Eisenhower that one of our great needs in the South is to build lines of communication between Negro and white Southerners. Many people in the South are seeking to do this. But if white people who support integration are labeled "subversive" by congressional committees, terror is spread among our white citizens and it becomes increasingly difficult to find white people who are willing to support our efforts for full citizenship. . . .
>
> We therefore urge you to use your influence to see that the House Committee on Un-American Activities stays out of the South—unless it can be persuaded to come in our region to help defend us against those subversives who oppose our Supreme Court, our Federal policy on civil rights for all, and our American ideals of equality and brotherhood.[38]

Mr. Arens then asked Braden: "Now would you kindly answer just 2 questions with reference to this letter? Question number 1 is: What did you, an identified member of the Communist Party, have to do with the letter?" Braden answered: "I will have to stand on my First Amendment rights for private beliefs and association on the grounds that the question has no possible pertinency to any legislation." The questioning of Braden continued:

> *Mr. Arens:* Did you prepare the letter, Mr. Braden?
> *Mr. Willis [Representative]:* Or have anything to do with its preparation?
> *Mr. Braden:* I will have to stand again on the First Amendment, the vagueness of the mandate of the committee, and the pertinency of the investigation and the legislative—.[39]

As noted, Braden was cited for contempt of Congress, found guilty, and sentenced to twelve months in prison. The United States Court of Appeals relied heavily on the *Barenblatt* arguments related to self-preservation, "the ultimate value of any society," and on the *Barenblatt* conclusion that "the balance between the individual and the governmental interests here at stake must be struck in favor of the latter, and that therefore the provisions of the First Amendment have not been offended."[40]

These "principles," said the court of appeals in deciding against Braden, "are applicable and controlling here. The First Amendment does not give to the appellant any right to refuse to answer the questions which are propounded to him by the Committee."[41] The court of appeals again relied on *Barenblatt* to answer Braden's contention that "the Congress had no power to authorize the Committee investigations and that its Rule XI under which the investigation here challenged was conducted was so vague and ambiguous that it could have no constitutional validity." This "contention," said the court of appeals, "has also been put at rest by the Supreme Court in the *Barenblatt* decision."[42]

The day the United States Supreme Court decided against Braden, it also decided against Frank Wilkinson, who had also refused to answer HUAC questions on July 30, 1958. Justice Stewart, delivering the opinion of the Court, stated at the outset of *Braden* that the committee's inquiries were "pertinent of a question under subcommittee inquiry":

> The principal issues raised by the petitioner are substantially identical to those considered in *Wilkinson* and extended discussion is not required in resolving them. Based upon the same record that was brought here in

Wilkinson, we conclude for the reasons stated there that the subjects under subcommittee investigation at the time the petitioner was interrogated were Communist infiltration into basic southern industry and Communist Party propaganda activities in the southern part of the United States. We conclude for the same reasons that the subcommittee's investigation of these subjects was authorized by Congress, that the interrogation was pertinent to a question under subcommittee inquiry, and that the petitioner was fully apprised of its pertinency.[43]

Justice Stewart argued that "*Barenblatt* did not confine congressional committee investigation to overt criminal activity, nor did that case determine that Congress can only investigate the Communist Party itself." The committee, said Stewart, had reason to believe that Braden "was a member of the Communist Party, and that he had been actively engaged in propaganda efforts." Committee inquiries into Communist Party propaganda activities were not, concluded Stewart, "constitutionally beyond the reach of the subcommittee's inquiry. Upon the reasoning and authority of *Barenblatt* . . . , we hold that the judgment is not to be set aside on First Amendment grounds."[44] As in the cases of Uphaus and Barenblatt, the First Amendment did not save Braden.

The same justices who dissented in *Barenblatt* (Warren, Black, Brennan, and Douglas) dissented again in *Braden*. Justice Black devoted part of his dissenting opinion to the majority's argument, which had also appeared in *Barenblatt* and again in *Wilkinson*, that Congress's power to investigate "rests on the right of self-preservation": "I once more deny, as I have found it repeatedly necessary to do in other cases, that this Nation's ability to preserve itself depends upon suppression of the freedoms of religion, speech, press, assembly and petition. But I do believe that the noble-sounding slogan of "self-preservation" rests upon a premise that can itself destroy any democratic nation by a slow process of eating away at the liberties that are indispensable to its healthy growth."[45] Black concluded his dissenting opinion by stating, "I would overrule *Barenblatt*, its forerunners and its progeny, and return to the language of the Bill of Rights."

Just as *Barenblatt* was relied upon by the court of appeals and the United States Supreme Court in upholding Braden's conviction, so too was it relied upon by both courts in upholding the conviction of Frank Wilkinson, who, like Braden, appeared before HUAC and invoked the First Amendment when he refused to answer HUAC questions related to his associational ties. At the outset of his testimony, Wilkinson was asked: "Mr. Wilkinson, are you now a member of the Communist Party?" He answered: "As a matter of conscience and personal responsibility, I refuse to answer any questions of this committee."[46] Wilkinson was then "ordered and directed" to answer the question, "Are you now a member of the Communist Party?" He again refused and told the committee:

> I challenge, in the most fundamental sense, the legality of the House Committee on Un-American Activities. It is my opinion that this committee stands in direct violation by its mandate and by its practices of the First Amendment to the United States Constitution. It is my belief that Congress had no authority to establish this committee in the first instance, nor to instruct it with the mandate which it has.
>
> I have the utmost respect for the broad powers which the Congress of the United States must have to carry on its investigations for legislative purposes. However, the United States Supreme Court has held that, broad as those powers may be, the Congress cannot investigate into an area where it cannot legislate, and this committee tends, by its mandate and by its practices, to investigate into precisely those areas of free speech, religion, peaceful association and assembly, and the press wherein it cannot legislate and therefore cannot investigate.[47]

Wilkinson was cited for contempt of Congress, convicted, and sentenced to twelve months' imprisonment. He appealed, and when his case reached the United States Court of Appeals, the court asserted that his contentions were the same as those made in the *Barenblatt* case and that "there they were resolved against the position asserted by the appellant. It will follow, therefore that unless there be something in the case before us to distinguish it from *Barenblatt*, our decision must be an affirmance."[48] The court found nothing to distinguish this case from *Barenblatt* and concluded: "The activities in which the appellant was believed to be participating presented a more direct threat to the national security than those of which Barenblatt was suspected. The decision in the Barenblatt case is controlling here."[49]

When the case reached the United States Supreme Court, Justice Stewart, writing for the majority, concluded that HUAC's investigation into "Communist infiltration into basic industry in the South, Communist Party propaganda in the South, and foreign Communist party propaganda in the United States" was authorized by Congress. He also concluded that the committee was "pursing a valid legislative purpose" and that the question directed at Wilkinson was "pertinent to the subject matter of the investigation."[50] As to whether HUAC had violated Wilkinson's rights under the First Amendment, Stewart wrote: "We come finally to the claim that the subcommittee's interrogation of the petitioner violated his rights under the First Amendment. The basic issues which this contention raises were thoroughly canvassed by us in *Barenblatt*. Substantially all that was said there is equally applicable here, and it would serve no purpose to enlarge this opinion with a paraphrased repetition of what was in that opinion thoughtfully considered and carefully expressed."[51]

Like the court of appeals, the United States Supreme Court majority found Wilkinson indistinguishable from *Barenblatt*; Justice Stewart brought the Court's opinion to a conclusion thusly: "We conclude that the First Amendment claims pressed here are indistinguishable from those considered in *Barenblatt*, and that upon the reasoning and the authority of that case they cannot prevail. *Affirmed*."[52] As with Uphaus, Barenblatt, and Braden, the First Amendment did not save Wilkinson.

In his dissenting opinion, Justice Black (joined by Warren and Douglas) expressed suspicions about the "protections" of *Barenblatt* that opponents of HUAC would receive; "[I]n my view, the 'protection' afforded by a requirement of some sort of probable cause, even if imposed, is almost totally worthless. In the atmosphere existing in this country today, the charge that someone is a Communist is so common that hardly anyone active in public life escapes it. Every member of this Court has, on one occasion or another, been so designated. . . . If the mere fact that someone has been called a Communist is to be permitted to satisfy a requirement of probable cause, I think it is plain that such a requirement is wholly without value."[53]

As for the majority's contention that "this Court will permit only those abridgments of personal beliefs and associations by Committee inquiry that the Court believes so important in terms of the need of the Committee for information that such need outweighs the First Amendment rights of the witness and the public," Black responded: "The truth of the matter is that the balancing test, at least as applied to date, means that the Committee may engage in *any* inquiry a majority of this Court happens to think could possibly be for a legitimate purpose[,] whether that 'purpose' be the true reason for the inquiry or not. And under the tests of legitimacy that are used in this area, any first-year law-school student worth his salt could construct a rationalization to justify almost any question put to any witness at any time."[54] Black concluded his dissenting opinion with a condemnation of the balancing test used by the Court: "[T]he principles of the First Amendment are stated in precise and mandatory terms and unless they are applied in those terms, the freedoms of religion, speech, press, assembly and petition will have no effective protection. Where these freedoms are left to depend upon a balance to be struck by this Court in each particular case, liberty cannot survive. For under such a rule, there are no constitutional rights that cannot be 'balanced' away."[55]

Several years before the United States Supreme Court decided against Wilkinson, Braden, Barenblatt, and Uphaus, it had decided in favor of two individuals—John Watkins, who had refused to answer HUAC questions, and Paul Sweezy, who had refused to answer questions put to him by New Hampshire's attorney general. But *Watkins v. United States* and *Sweezy v. New Hampshire*, both decided on June 17, 1957, were of no help in keeping Wilkinson, Braden, Barenblatt, and Uphaus from imprisonment. As Thomas I. Emerson has observed: "The indication in *Watkins* and *Sweezy* that the Supreme Court was prepared to develop effective First Amendment safeguards against legislative committees did not materialize. The turning point was *Barenblatt v. United States*[,] decided in 1959."[56]

Others also recognized that the promise of *Watkins* did not materialize. Writing in the *University of Cincinnati Law Review* in 1961, Dean Alfange, Jr., asserted: "[A]lthough the restraints imposed by the *Watkins* decision may have come 'at long last,' they were not to last long. For, on June 8, 1959, just two years after *Watkins*, the Supreme Court handed down another ruling on the subject of congressional investigations, which transmogrified and emasculated that decision. This was *Barenblatt v. United States*, in which the Court, beginning with a fact situation almost identical to *Watkins*, arrived at a conclusion entirely antithetical to it."[57] As Justice Douglas saw it, "[T]he promise contained in the *Watkins* opinion were not kept."[58]

Both Emerson's "safeguards" and Douglas's "promise" are references to the Court's conclusion in *Watkins* that HUAC's questions must serve a legitimate task of Congress, a task that must be clearly articulated, and that the questions directed to the witness and their pertinency must be "made to appear with undisputable clarity." Labor organizer John Watkins had appeared before an HUAC subcommittee and proved willing to answer questions related to monetary contributions he had made, petitions he had signed, and instances of his cooperation with the Communist Party. However, he told the committee that he had "never carried a Communist Party card" and "never accepted discipline and indeed on several occasions opposed their position."[59]

Next, HUAC counsel Robert Kunzig presented a list of names "of people, all of whom were identified as Communist Party members by Mr. Rumsey [a friendly HUAC witness] during his recent testimony in Chicago."[60] When Watkins was asked, "Do you know Harold Fisher to be a member of the Communist Party?," he answered by presenting a statement he had prepared in anticipation of this question:

> I would like to get one thing perfectly clear, Mr. Chairman. I am not going to plead the Fifth Amendment, but I refuse to answer certain questions that I believe are outside the proper scope of your committee's activities. I will answer any questions which this committee puts to me about myself. I will also answer questions about those persons whom I knew to be members of the Communist Party and whom I believe still are. I will not, however, answer any questions with respect to others with whom I associated in the past. I do not believe that any law in this country requires me to testify about persons who may in the past have been Communist Party members or otherwise engaged in Communist Party activity but who to my best knowledge and belief have long since removed themselves from the Communist movement.
>
> I do not believe that such questions are relevant to the work of this committee nor do I believe that this committee has the right to undertake the public exposure of persons because of their past activities. I may be wrong, and the committee may have this power, but until and unless a court of law so holds and directs me to answer, I most firmly refuse to discuss the political activities of my past associates.[61]

Delivering the Court's opinion in *Watkins*, Chief Justice Warren emphasized the need for the committee to make especially clear to the witness the pertinency of the questions: "[W]e remain unenlightened as to the subject to which the questions asked petitioner were pertinent. Certainly, if the point is that obscure after trial and appeal, it was not adequately revealed to petitioner when he had to decide at his peril whether or not to answer. . . . Unless the subject matter has been made to appear with undisputable clarity, it is the duty of the investigative body, upon objection of the witness on grounds of pertinency, to state for the record the subject under inquiry at that time and the manner in which the propounded questions are pertinent thereto."[62]

Subsequently, HUAC continued to ask witnesses the same types of questions it had asked prior to *Watkins*, but whenever a witness refused to answer on the basis of a lack of pertinency, a committee member would ritualistically provide some relationship between the question and the legislative purpose behind the question. For example, one year after *Watkins*, when Braden refused to answer a question put to him at his hearing on July 30, 1958, Staff Director Richard Arens stated: "Mr. Chairman, I respectfully suggest that the witness be ordered and directed to answer; and I should like, for the purpose of making the record absolutely clear, to explain to the witness now the pertinency of the question." Whereupon Arens explained that "it is our understanding that you are now a Communist . . . ," that the committee was considering "tightening the security laws respecting registration of Communists . . . ," and that "there is pending before the Committee on Un-American Activities a series of proposals that are not yet incorporated into legislative form. . . ."[63]

Having satisfied the *Watkins* requirement, Arens continued: "Now, Mr. Chairman, on the basis of that explanation of the pertinency of the question which I have posed to this witness, I respectfully suggest that you now order and direct this witness either to answer the question or to invoke his privileges under the Fifth Amendment against giving testimony which could be used against him in a criminal proceeding." Representative Edwin Willis, chair of the committee, then told Braden: "I think, sir, that a sufficient foundation has been laid to make the question completely pertinent and I direct you to answer the question."[64]

Just as *Watkins* did not save Uphaus, Braden, Wilkinson, and Barenblatt from imprisonment, *Sweezy v. New Hampshire*, decided the same day as *Watkins*, also did nothing to save them, even though Sweezy, too, had refused to answer questions related to his political beliefs and associations. The High Court's decision in favor of Sweezy raised hopes that the Court would now be inclined to provide constitutional protection for those who refused to answer such inquiries. As Chief Justice Warren said in announcing the judgment of the Court in *Sweezy*: "[W]e conclude that the record in this case does not sustain the power of the State to compel the disclosures that the witness refused to make."[65]

On June 3, 1954, Paul Sweezy had appeared before New Hampshire's Attorney General to face an interrogation about his contacts with Communists. While Sweezy affirmed that he was a "classical Marxist" and a "socialist," he refused to answer questions not only related to his political beliefs and the content of his college lectures, but also questions related to his wife's and an acquaintance's associations.[66] While Sweezy had testified that he had never been a member of the Communist Party, he refused to answer the question, "Do you believe in Communism?" Sweezy maintained that "the questions were not pertinent to the matter under inquiry and that they infringed upon an area protected under the First Amendment."[67]

The Superior Court of Merrimack County, New Hampshire, "adjudged him in contempt and ordered him committed to the county jail until purged of the contempt."[68] The New Hampshire Supreme Court upheld the conviction, and Sweezy appealed to the United States Supreme Court.

In deciding for Sweezy on June 17, 1957, Chief Justice Warren in announcing the judgment of the Court argued that the terms "subversive person" and "subversive organizations," as they appeared in the New Hampshire Subversive Activities Act of 1951 were too broad:

> The statute goes well beyond those who are engaged in efforts designed to alter the form of government by force or violence. The statute declares, in effect, that the assistant to an assistant is caught up in the definition. This chain of conduct attains increased significance in light of the lack of a necessary element of guilty knowledge in either stage of assistants. The State Supreme Court has held that the definition encompasses persons engaged in the specified conduct ". . . whether or not done 'knowingly and willfully. . . .' " . . . The potential sweep of this definition extends to conduct which is only remotely related to actual subversion and which is done completely free of any conscious intent to be part of such activity.[69]

Not only were the terms defined too broadly, but the state's inquiries of Sweezy brought it into areas in which government should be "extremely reticent to tread."[70]

The chief justice's opinion moved on to a paragraph subsequently cited again and again in court opinions at various levels of the judiciary;

> The essentiality of freedom in the community of American universities is almost self-evident. No one should underestimate the vital role in a democracy that is played by those who guide and train our youth. To impose any strait jacket upon the intellectual leaders in our colleges and universities would imperil the future of our Nation. No field of education is so thoroughly comprehended by man that new discoveries cannot yet be made. Particularly is that true in the social sciences, where few, if any, principles are accepted as absolutes. Scholarship cannot flourish in an atmosphere of suspicion and distrust. Teachers and students must always

remain free to inquire, to study and to evaluate, to gain new maturity and understanding; otherwise our civilization will stagnate and die.[71]

In his concurring opinion, Justice Frankfurter noted that Sweezy had refused to answer the attorney general's questions "on the ground that, by inquiring into the activities of a lawful political organization, they infringed upon the inviolability of the right to privacy in his political thoughts, actions and associations." Frankfurter emphasized the importance of this right:"For a citizen to be made to forego even a part of so basic a liberty as his political autonomy, the subordinating interest of the State must be compelling. . . . [T]he inviolability of privacy belonging to a citizen's political loyalties has so overwhelming an importance to the well-being of our kind of society that it cannot be constitutionally encroached upon on the basis of so meagre a countervailing interest of the State as may be argumentatively found in the remote, shadowy threat to the security of New Hampshire allegedly presented in the origins and contributing elements of the Progressive Party and in petitioner's relation of these."[72]

While in 1957 the United States Supreme Court gave Professor Sweezy constitutional protection, four years later the High Court did not give constitutional protection to attorneys Raphael Konigsberg and George Anastaplo, who had refused to answer questions related to membership in the Communist Party and as a result were denied admission to the bar, Konigsberg in California and Anastaplo in Illinois.

When Konigsberg had appeared before the California Committee of Bar Examiners, he "introduced . . . evidence as to his good moral character (none of which was rebutted), reiterated unequivocally his disbelief in violent overthrow, and stated that he had never knowingly been a member of any organization which advocated such action. He persisted, however, in his refusals to answer any questions relating to his membership in the Communist Party. The Committee again declined to certify him, this time on the ground that his refusals to answer had obstructed a full investigation into his qualifications."[73] In delivering the opinion of the Court on April 24, 1961, Justice Harlan stated: "We think it clear that the Fourteenth Amendment's protection against arbitrary state action does not forbid a State from denying admission to a bar so long as he refuses to provide unprivileged answers to questions having a substantial relevance to his qualifications."[74]

Konigsberg had argued that "he was privileged not to respond to questions dealing with Communist Party membership because they un-constitutionally impinged upon rights of free speech and association pro-tected by the Fourteenth Amendment."[75] The Court majority's response was: "[G]eneral regulatory statutes, not intended to control the content of speech but incidentally limiting its unfettered exercise[,] have not been regarded as the type of law the First or Fourteenth Amendment forbade Congress or the States to pass, when they have been found justified by subordinating valid governmental interests, a prerequisite to constitu-tionality which has necessarily involved a weighing of the government interest involved."[76]

Justice Black, after presenting an extended attack on "the penurious" balancing test used so often in the loyalty-oath decisions, responded to the majority's argument that the "general regulatory statutes, not in-tended to control the content of speech but incidentally limiting its un-fettered exercise" were not unconstitutional upon a showing of a valid governmental interest:

> [I] cannot agree that the questions asked Konigsberg with regard to his suspected membership in the Communist Party had nothing more than an "incidental" effect upon his freedom of speech and association. Why does the Committee of Bar Examiners ask a bar applicant whether he is or has been a member of the Communist Party? The avowed purpose of such questioning is to permit the Committee to deny applicants admission to the Bar if they "advocate" forcible overthrow of the Government. . . . [I] think the conclusion is inescapable that this case presents the question of the constitutionality of action by the State of California designed to con-trol the content of speech. As such, it is a "direct" and not an "incidental" abridgment of speech.[77]

Black concluded his dissenting opinion with a strong defense of Konigs-berg: "Nothing in this record shows that Konigsberg has ever been guilty of any conduct that threatens our safety. Quite the contrary, the record indicates that we are fortunate to have men like him in this country[,] for it shows that Konigsberg is a man of firm convictions who has stood up and supported this country's freedom in peace and war. . . . He is, therefore, but another victim of the prevailing fashion of destroying men for the views it is suspected they might entertain."[78]

The same day as the High Court decided *Konigsberg*, it also decided—by the same vote of 5-4—against George Anastaplo, a University of Chicago instructor who had passed his Illinois bar examinations but was denied admission to the state's bar because he refused to answer whether he was a member of the Communist Party. He appeared before the Committee of Character and Fitness and "persisted . . . in refusing to answer, among other inquiries, the Committee's questions as to his possible membership in the Communist Party or in other allegedly related organizations."[79] Relying heavily on *Konigsberg*, Justice Harlan, delivering the opinion of the Court, argued that Anastaplo had been "fairly warned that exclusion from admission to practice might follow from his refusal to answer" and that the requirement of due process was "duly met."[80] Anastaplo had refused "on constitutional grounds to answer whether he was affiliated with any church. He answered all questions about organizational relationships so long as he did not know that the organization was 'political' in character. He refused, on grounds of protected free speech and association, to answer whether he was a member of the Communist Party or of any other group named in the Attorney General's list of 'subversive' organizations, including the Ku Klux Klan and the Silver Shirts of America."[81] The Court majority concluded: "We find nothing to suggest that he [Anastaplo] would not be admitted now if he decides to answer, assuming of course that no grounds justifying his exclusion from practice resulted. In short, petitioner holds the key to admission in his own hands. . . . With appropriate regard for the limited range of our authority we cannot say that the State's denial of Anastaplo's application for admission to its bar offends the Federal Constitution."[82]

Justice Black wrote a dissenting opinion (joined by Warren, Douglas, and Brennan) in which he reviewed Anastaplo's background (his education, his air force duty in World War II, his study of law at the University of Chicago) and concluded: "His record throughout his life, both as a student and as a citizen, was unblemished. The personal history form thus did not contain so much as one statement of *fact* about Anastaplo's past life or conduct that could have, in any way, cast doubt upon his fitness for admission to the Bar."[83] In his dissenting opinion Black cited several professors and attorneys who spoke of Anastaplo's "unusually fine character," several of them referring to his "integrity":

> Professor Malcolm P. Sharp of the University of Chicago Law School stated: "No question has ever been raised about his honesty or his integrity, and his general conduct, characterized by friendliness, quiet independence, industry and courage[,] is reflected in his reputation." Professor Roscoe T. Steffen of the University of Chicago Law School said: "I know of no one who doubts his honesty and integrity."

Robert J. Coughlan, Division Director of a research project at the University of Chicago, said: "His honesty and integrity are, in my opinion, beyond question. I would highly recommend him without the slightest reservation for any position involving the highest or most sacred trust. . . ."[84]

Black saw Anastaplo's refusal to answer the committee's questions as an act aimed at helping to preserve this country's freedoms: "The one and only time in which he has come into conflict with the Government is when he refused to answer the questions put to him by the Committee about his beliefs and associations. And I think the record clearly shows that conflict resulted, not from any fear on Anastaplo's part to divulge his own political activities, but from a sincere, and in my judgment correct, conviction that the preservation of this country's freedom depends upon adherence to our Bill of Rights."[85] But the Bill of Rights did not save Anastaplo. While he was not imprisoned, as were Uphaus, Braden, Wilkinson, and Barenblatt, he was denied admission to the bar.

At the conclusion of his dissenting opinion, Black declared: "Too many men are being driven to become government-fearing and time-serving because our Government is being permitted to strike out at those who are fearless enough to think as they please and say what they think." Black footnotes this statement with references to *Barsky, Uphaus, Barenblatt, Wilkinson, Braden,* and *Konigsberg.*

Several years later, Lloyd Barenblatt, who had refused to answer HUAC inquiries about himself and others and was subsequently jailed, described the act of naming names as "an act of contrition": "The treatment of the witnesses by the committee was, without any exaggeration, inquisitional. I was not allowed to make any preliminary statement. I was not allowed to expand or elaborate on any answers. I was not allowed to expand or elaborate on any answers. I was not allowed to confer with my attorney on any matters except legal objections. All they wanted were names! And dates! It was an act of contrition to inform on others."[86] Contrition has been defined as "[s]incere remorse for wrongdoing; repentance."[87] Like the heretics of past centuries, Barenblatt was punished by authorities who sought his repentance.

In 1244, "A Manual for Inquisitors at Carcasonne" provided the following guidance for the treatment of heretics: "We require each and every person who presents himself for confession to abjure all heresy and to take oath that he will tell the full and exact truth about himself and others, living and dead, in the matter of fact or crime of heresy or Waldensianism. . . ."[88] The "Formula for the interrogatory" then provided:

"Thereafter, the person is diligently questioned about whether he saw a heretic or Waldensian, where and when, how often and with whom, and about others who were present; whether he listened to their preaching or exhortation . . . ; whether he knows any other man or woman to have done any of the foregoing. . . ."[89]

In the thirteenth century, "[t]he defiant heretic who persisted in disobedience, or who pertinaciously refused to confess his heresy and asserted his innocence, could not be admitted to penance, and was handed over to the secular arm,"[90] which carried out various degrees of punishment. In the twentieth century, the defiant heretic who refused to "confess his heresy"—to reveal his or her own political beliefs and associations and to name names as an act of contrition when appearing before investigating authorities—was in some cases handed over to the judicial arm, which made the decision to impose punishment; in other instances the heretic was simply blacklisted or denied the right to practice his or her profession. George Anastaplo and Raphael Koningsberg were refused certification to practice law; the Hollywood Ten were imprisoned for up to one year and then blacklisted; Willard Uphaus, Lloyd Barenblatt, Carl Braden, and Frank Wilkinson were sentenced to up to twelve months in jail. They had all refused to "abjure all heresy," and when questioned they refused to say whether they "saw a heretic . . . , where and when, how often and with whom," and to speak about "others who were present."

6

A Freedom Not to Speak

The mid-twentieth-century American "heretics" who relied on the First Amendment faced imprisonment, and those who relied on the Fifth Amendment faced blacklisting and loss of employment. Yet there were others who were not punished when they insisted on remaining silent. At the same time as it was deciding that the state could punish Barenblatt, Wilkinson, Uphaus, et al. for refusing to reveal their political beliefs and associations, the United States Supreme Court decided that the National Association for the Advancement of Colored People (NAACP) could not be required to reveal to the state its membership lists. The arguments presented by the High Court in giving the NAACP constitutional protection apparently did not apply to individuals who refused to reveal their beliefs and associations to the various un-American activities committees.

In *NAACP v. Alabama*, the United States Supreme Court decided unanimously in 1958 that the NAACP could not be required to hand over to the state of Alabama its membership list, and in so deciding the High Court declared: "It is hardly a novel perception that compelled disclosure of affiliation with groups engaged in advocacy may constitute as effective a restraint on freedom of association as the forms of governmental action in the cases above were thought likely to produce upon the particular constitutional rights there involved."[1] While this may not have been a "novel perception," it was neither considered nor applied in the Court's decision against the likes of Braden and Anastaplo.

Another argument presented in *NAACP v. Alabama* that could have been applied in *Barenblatt* et al. was advanced by Justice Harlan when he delivered the opinion of the Court: "Petitioner [NAACP] has made an uncontroverted showing that on past occasions revelation of the identity of its rank-and-file members has exposed these members to economic reprisal, loss of employment, threat of physical coercion, and other manifestations of public hostility."[2] The fates of those who refused to answer the HUAC questions about beliefs and associations, both those who relied on the First Amendment and those who relied on the Fifth Amendment, included just such experiences: economic reprisals, loss of employment, public hostility, and in some cases physical violence. Yet as we have seen, the High Court did not consider these factors when it decided against Barenblatt, whose refusal to answer HUAC questions led to the loss of employment in his life chosen profession; nor did the High Court consider these factors when it decided against the Hollywood Ten, who faced not only imprisonment, but also economic reprisals by being blacklisted.

In 1956, the state of Alabama had demanded that the NAACP turn over the association's financial records and papers, along with the names and addresses of all NAACP members in Alabama. The NAACP refused to comply, contending that the order violated the rights of the association and its members. The Court was especially interested in protecting the freedom of association, declaring that "it is immaterial whether the beliefs sought to be advanced by association pertain to political, economic, religious or cultural matters, and state action which may have the effect of curtailing the freedom to association is subject to the closest scrutiny."[3]

While *NAACP v. Alabama* was working its way to the United States Supreme Court, the city councils of Little Rock and North Little Rock, Arkansas, passed an ordinance that required, among other things, that any organization operating within the municipality provide the city clerk with "a financial statement of such organization, including dues, fees, assessments and/or contributions paid, by whom paid, and the date thereof, to whom and when paid, together with the total net income of such organization." Further, "All information obtained pursuant to this ordinance shall be deemed public and subject to the inspection of any interested party at all reasonable business hours."[4] Daisy Bates and Birdie Williams, custodians of the NAACP branch records, provided all of the requested information except the names and addresses of NAACP members and contributors. Williams said in a letter to the city council, "We cannot give you any information with respect to the names and addresses of our members and contributors or any information with respect to the names and addresses of our members and contributors or any information which may lead to the ascertainment of such information. We base this refusal on the anti-NAACP climate in this state. It is our good faith and belief that the public disclosure of the names of our members and contributors might lead to their harassment, economic reprisals, and even bodily harm."[5]

As a result of their refusal to comply entirely with the ordinance, Bates and Williams were tried, convicted, and fined; the Arkansas Supreme Court upheld their convictions. However, on February 23, 1960, a unanimous United States Supreme Court reversed it, relying heavily on *NAACP v. Alabama.* Justice Stewart, delivering the opinion of the Court, cited *NAACP v. Alabama* six times, at one point reiterating the concerns the earlier Court had expressed: "On this record it sufficiently appears that compulsory disclosure of the membership lists of the local branches of the National Association for the Advancement of Colored People would work a significant interference with the freedom of association of their members. There was substantial uncontroverted evidence that public identification of persons in the community as members of the organizations had been followed by harassment and threats of bodily harm."[6]

In a short concurring opinion, Justices Black and Douglas took a more expansive view of the Court's opinion: "Moreover, we believe . . . that First Amendment rights are beyond abridgment either by legislation that directly restrains their exercise or by suppression or impairment through harassment, humiliation, or exposure by government. One of those rights, freedom of assembly, includes of course freedom of association; and it is entitled to no less protection than any other First Amendment right. . . . These are principles applicable to all people under our Constitution irrespective of their race, color, politics, or religion. That is, for us, the essence of the present opinion of the Court."[7]

Ten months after the Court decided *Bates,* it declared invalid an Arkansas statute that compelled "every teacher, as a condition of employment in a state-supported school or college, to file annually an affidavit listing without limitation every organization to which he has belonged or regularly contributed within the preceeding five years."[8] As Thomas I. Emerson has indicated, the statute "was aimed primarily at uncovering and exposing members of the N.A.A.C.P."[9] In deciding against the state of Arkansas, the High Court did distinguish this case from *NAACP v. Alabama* and *Bates v. Little Rock,* arguing, "Here, by contrast, there can be no question of the relevance of a State's inquiry into the fitness and competence of its teachers." That said, however, the Court stated: "It is not disputed that to compel a teacher to disclose his every associational tie is to impair that teacher's right of free association, a right closely allied to freedom of speech and a right which, like free speech, lies at the foundation of a free society."[10]

Noting that the statute did not "provide that the information it requires be kept confidential," the Court declared: "The record contains evidence to indicate that fear of public disclosure is neither theoretical nor groundless."[11] The scope of the state's inquiry, said the Court, "is completely unlimited. The statute requires a teacher to reveal the church to which he belongs, or to which he has given financial support. It requires him to disclose his political party, and every political organization to which he may have contributed over a five-year period. It requires him to list, without number, every conceivable kind of associational tie— social, professional, political, avocational, or religious. Many such relationships could have no possible bearing upon the teacher's occupational competence or fitness."[12]

In all three cases, *NAACP v. Alabama, Bates v. Little Rock*, and *Shelton v. Tucker*, the High Court recognized the harmful and dangerous repercussions of state-compelled disclosure of one's associational ties; it referred to "economic reprisal, loss of employment, threat of physical coercion, and other manifestations of public hostility" and "harassment and threats of bodily harm." "The fear of public disclosure is neither theoretical nor groundless," said the *Shelton* Court.

Yet these concerns—economic reprisals, loss of employment, public hostility—were not expressed or considered by the High Court when HUAC-type committees demanded public disclosure of the political beliefs and associational ties of those appearing before the committees and invoking the First Amendment. One looks in vain in *Barenblatt, Uphaus, Anastaplo, Konigsberg, Braden*, and *Wilkinson* for any Court concerns related to the reprisals, hostilities, and humiliations experienced by these Americans who, like the NAACP, refused to divulge associational ties.

In 1963, the United States Supreme Court had to decide whether to uphold the contempt citation of the president of the Miami branch of the NAACP, who had refused to produce NAACP membership lists when he appeared before the Florida Legislative Investigation Committee, which had demanded the list. His refusal was based "on the ground that to bring the lists to the hearing to utilize them as the basis of his testimony would interfere with the free exercise of Fourteenth Amendment associational rights of members and prospective members of the N.A.A.C.P."[13] In a 5–4 decision for the NAACP, the United States Supreme Court majority relied heavily on *NAACP v. Alabama, Bates v. Little Rock*, and *Shelton v. Tucker*. Justice Goldberg, delivering the opinion of the Court, wrote: "[A]s declared in *NAACP v. Alabama.* . . . 'It is hardly a novel perception that compelled disclosure of affiliation with groups engaged in advocacy may constitute [an] . . . effective . . . restraint on freedom of association. . . . This Court has recognized the vital relationship between freedom to associate and privacy of one's associations. . . . Inviolability of privacy in group association may in many circumstances be indispensable to preservation of freedom of association, particularly where a group espouses dissident beliefs.' So it is here."[14]

Since the state of Florida had reminded the Court, the Court could not ignore that it had upheld the contempt citations against Uphaus, Barenblatt, Wilkinson, and Braden; hence Justice Goldberg, referring to the NAACP as "a concededly legitimate and nonsubversive organization," wrote: "Compelling such an organization, engaged in the exercise of First and Fourteenth Amendment rights, to disclose its membership presents, under our cases, a question wholly different from compelling the Communist Party to disclose its membership. . . . The fact that governmental interest was deemed compelling in *Barenblatt, Wilkinson*, and *Braden* and held to support the inquiries there made into membership in the Communist Party does not resolve the issues here, where the challenged questions go to membership in an admittedly lawful organization."[15]

Further, distinguishing *Gibson* from *Uphaus*, Goldberg argued: "In *Uphaus* this Court found that there was demonstrated a sufficient connection between subversive activity—held there to be a proper subject of governmental concern—and the World Fellowship, itself, to justify discovery of the guest list; no semblance of such a nexus between the N.A.A.C.P. and subversive *activities* has been shown here."[16]

Justice Douglas, who had dissented in *Uphaus, Barenblatt, Wilkinson*, and *Braden*, wrote a concurring opinion in *Gibson* in which he expressed concern about the erosion of privacy: "The right of association has become a part of the bundle of rights protected by the First Amendment (see, e.g., *NAACP v. Alabama, supra*), and the need for a pervasive right of privacy against government intrusion has been recognized, though not always given the recognition it deserves." At this point in his opinion, Douglas inserted a footnote quoting from the famous Warren and Brandeis *Harvard Law Review* article, "The Right to Privacy":

> The intensity and complexity of life, attendant upon advancing civiliza-
> tion, have rendered necessary some retreat from the world, and man, un-
> der the refining influence of culture, has become more essential to the
> individual; but modern enterprise and invention have, through invasions
> upon his privacy, subjected him to mental pain and distress, far greater
> than could be inflicted by mere bodily injury.[17]

After declaring that "whether a group is popular or unpopular, the right
of privacy implicit in the First Amendment creates an area into which
the Government may not enter," Douglas quotes form his 1952 dissenting opinion in *Public Utilities Comm'n v. Pollak*: "The First Amendment
in its respect for the conscience of the individual honors the sanctity of
thought and belief. To think as one chooses, to believe what one wishes
are important aspects of the constitutional right to be let alone."[18]

In his concurring opinion, Douglas referred to *Talley v. California*,
which involved a different type of freedom-not-to-speak question, but
which he found relevant to *Gibson*. On March 7, 1960, the United
States, Supreme Court held unconstitutional a Los Angeles ordinance
that required distributed handbills to have printed on the cover or face
the name and address of "the person who printed, wrote, compiled or
manufactured" and distributed them.[19] Justice Black, delivering the opinion of the Court, contended that "anonymous pamphlets, leaflets, bro-
chures and even books have played an important role in the progress of
mankind."[20] After referring to John Lilburne, who in the seventeenth
century "was whipped, pilloried and fined for refusing to answer questions designed to get evidence to convict him or someone else for the
secret distribution of books in England," as well as to the anonymously
published *Letters of Junius* and the *Federalist Papers*, Black concluded:
"It is plain that anonymity has sometimes been assumed for the most
constructive purposes."[21]

Black then turned to *Bates v. Little Rock* and *NAACP v. Alabama* to
support the Court's position that the Los Angeles ordinance was "void
on its face": "We have recently had occasion to hold in two cases that
there are times and circumstances when States may not compel members
of groups engaged in the dissemination of ideas to be publicly identified.
Bates v. Little Rock . . . ; *N.A.A.C.P. v. Alabama*. . . . The reason for
those holdings was that identification and fear of reprisal might deter
perfectly peaceful discussions of public matters of importance. This
broad Los Angeles ordinance is subject to the same infirmity."[22]

Talley was decided March 7, 1960. One year earlier, on June 8, 1959, the High Court had decided against Lloyd Barenblatt, who had refused to disclose to HUAC his past and present political affiliations. As we have noted, in *Barenblatt* the Court expressed little concern for the "fear of reprisal" awaiting Barenblatt as a result of HUAC's compelling him to publicly identify his political associations. Where in the NAACP cases the Supreme Court saw compelled disclosure of political affiliations as leading to reprisals of various kinds and constituting an "effective restraint on freedom of association," there was little application of these concerns in the cases involving the "unfriendly" HUAC witnesses.

One year after *Talley*, on February 27, 1961, the Supreme Court decided against Frank Wilkinson, who claimed that HUAC's interrogation constituted "unauthorized harassment and exposure."[23] The Court asserted that it could "find nothing to indicate that it was the intent of Congress [in passage of Rule XI] to immunize from interrogation all those (and there are many) who are opposed to the existence of the Un-American Activities Committee."[24] Similarly, in *Braden v. United States*, decided the same day, the Court expressed no concern for the exposure and reprisals that would be experienced by Braden, who had also refused to answer HUAC questions related to his political affiliations.

Yet at the same time as the United States Supreme Court decided in 1961 against Anastaplo, Braden, Konigsberg, and Wilkinson, it decided for Roy Torcaso, who had refused, upon being appointed to the office of notary public in Maryland, to assert a belief in the existence of God as required by the state of Maryland.[25] Delivering the opinion of the Court in *Torcaso v. Watkins*, Justice Black declared: "We repeat and again reaffirm that neither a State nor the Federal Government can constitutionally force a person 'to profess a belief or disbelief in any religion.' "[26] In 1961, the state could not compel an American citizen to profess a belief or disbelief in the existence of God, but it could compel that same citizen to profess other beliefs or disbeliefs.

Sixteen years later, the High Court went further in proscribing governmentally forced expression, but again the case revolved around religion. Jehovah's Witnesses George and Maxine Maynard considered New Hampshire's auto license carrying the message LIVE FREE OR DIE to be "repugnant to their moral, religious, and political beliefs" and therefore taped over the state's motto on the license plates of their car. After being found guilty three times for violating the New Hampshire statute that made it a misdemeanor "knowingly [to obscure] . . . the figures or letters on any number plate," the Maynards sought injunctive and declaratory relief against enforcement of the statute. The United States district court entered an order enjoining the state "from arresting and prosecuting [the Maynards] at any time in the future for covering over that portion of their license plates that contains the motto 'Live Free or Die.' "[27]

When the case reached the United States Supreme Court, Chief Justice Burger, delivering the opinion of the Court in *Wooley v. Maynard* (1977), went beyond prohibiting the state from forcing a person to profess a belief or disbelief in God: "We begin with the proposition that the right of freedom of thought protected by the First Amendment against state action includes both the right to speak and the right to refrain from speaking at all. . . . A system which secures the right to proselytize religious, political, and ideological causes must also guarantee the concomitant right to decline to foster such concepts. The right to speak and the right to refrain from speaking are complementary components of the broader concept of 'individual freedom of mind.' " [28] Burger did not limit the right to refrain from speaking to religious matters; that right also applies to "political and ideological causes," he wrote.

When the next American inquisition occurs, will the right to remain silent promised in *Barnette, Torcaso,* and *Wooley* be available to the "heretics" who refuse to reveal their political beliefs and associations to governmental authorities, whether in relation to loyalty oaths or un-American investigating committees? It can easily be argued that these three cases deal with religious beliefs and hence are not applicable to compelled political speech. *Barnette* was not helpful at all in protecting Barsky, Braden, Barenblatt, Konigsberg, Josephson, Uphaus, Wilkinson, and others punished for refusing to speak what the state or federal government demanded.

Torcaso was handed down too late in 1961 to be applied to the earlier 1961 decisions of *Anastaplo, Braden, Konigsberg,* and *Wilkinson,* and in all likelihood *Torcaso's* principle that government cannot "force a person 'to profess a belief or disbelief in any religion' " would have been held inapplicable to situations in which individuals were forced to profess a belief or disbelief in political or ideological matters. If Justice Jackson's opinion in *Barnette*—"If there is any fixed star in our constitutional constellation, it is that no official, high or petty, can prescribe what shall be orthodox in politics, nationalism, religion, or other matters of opinion or force citizens to confess by word or act their faith therein"—did not provide constitutional protection for those who refused to sign the loyalty oaths and to answer HUAC inquiries into personal beliefs, there is little reason to conclude that the opinion in *Torcaso* that "government cannot force a person to profess a belief or disbelief in any religion" would provide such protection.

Wooley v. Maynard (1977), of course, came too late to be of any use to victims of the mid-twentieth-century American inquisition. But even if *Wooley* had been decided a quarter-century earlier, would it have provided protection to the political "heretics" of the 1950s and 1960s? On the surface it appears that Burger is promulgating a freedom not to speak; however, since *Wooley* was a case involving religious objections to New Hampshire's compelled expression, it could be argued that the facts in *Wooley* are too far removed from the facts of *Barenblatt, Braden, Anastaplo, et al.* to be applicable to the latter. Further, Burger writes of the "concomitant right to decline to foster such concepts [religious, political, and ideological]." Maynard, it could be argued, was being forced to foster, through the LIVE FREE OR DIE motto on his auto license plates, a political or religious concept.

One is left wondering about Burger's assertion that "the right to speak and the right to refrain from speaking are complementary components of the broader concept of 'individual freedom of the mind.' " To whom does this freedom of the mind apply? Apparently it did not apply to those who refused to sign the loyalty oaths. *Wooley v. Maynard* was a 7–2 decision. The seven justices in the majority were the Chief Justice Burger and Justices Harlan, Stewart, Blackmun, Powell, and Douglas. Five years earlier, Justices Burger, Stewart, White, and Blackmun had declared in *Cole v. Richardson*, in a 4–3 decision, that the state could require a loyalty oath from Mrs. Richardson, who had refused to sign the following oath required of all public employees in Massachusetts: "I do solemnly swear (or affirm) that I will uphold and defend the Constitution of the United States of America and the Constitution of the Commonwealth of Massachusetts and that I will oppose the overthrow of the government of the United States of America or of this Commonwealth by force, violence or by any illegal or unconstitutional method."[29]

In 1977, Burger, Stewart, and Blackmun were all part of the majority in *Wooley*, an opinion containing references to freedom of thought, freedom of the mind, and the right to refrain from speaking. These same justices, in 1972, had nothing to say about these freedoms when they refused to give constitutional protection to Mrs. Richardson. It was the dissenters in *Cole v. Richardson* who spoke of forced expression and freedom of the mind. Justice Douglas stated in his dissenting opinion: "Test oaths are notorious tools of tyranny. When used to shackle the mind they are, or at least they should be, unspeakably odious to a free people."[30] Justice Marshall also wrote a dissenting opinion (joined by Brennan) in which he condemned governmentally forced expression: "The Constitution severely circumscribes the power of government to force its citizens to perform symbolic gestures of loyalty."[31]

Where in *Wooley* the Court wrote of the "right to refrain from speaking" when it gave constitutional protection to the Maynards, in *Cole* the Court did not apply this right to provide protection for Richardson. Similarly, the right was never applied by the Court majority in *Anastaplo, Braden, Uphaus, Wilkinson, et al.* The right to remain silent appeared to be applicable only in cases (such as *Barnette, Torcaso*, and *Wooley*) that involved religious objection to the compelled expression demanded by the state.

However, in the 1970s, some lower courts did give constitutional protection to students and teachers who refused to salute the flag because, they contended, there was not "liberty and justice for all" in the United States and because it was hypocritical to recite "with liberty and justice for all" when it was not true. Their refusals to speak were not based on religious objections.

In 1970, a United States district court decided for a student who had refused to participate in the flag-salute ritual because such participation was counter to his religious *and* political beliefs: "He testified that he is a Unitarian, that he believes a 'Uni-world' government is necessary to world peace, and further that his refusal to stand was a simple protest against black repression in the United States."[32] Relying heavily on *Barnette*, the district court concluded that "the First Amendment guarantees to the plaintiff [student] the right to claim that his objection to standing during the ceremony is based upon religious and political beliefs."[33]

In 1971, the court of appeals of Maryland decided for a social science teacher who "claimed that he would refuse to engage in a mandatory flag salute ceremony, not for religious reasons but because he could not 'in good conscience' force patriotism upon his class. . . . He indicated . . . that his son [a student] shared these views and would similarly refuse to engage in the flag salute."[34] In striking down the flag-salute requirement as unconstitutional, the Maryland court concluded: "Entertaining no doubt that there is ample authority to punish students and teachers who materially disrupt proper school activities, including voluntary patriotic programs, we are far from convinced that the mere refusal to participate in any phase of the pledge of allegiance ritual is punishable. To reach a contrary conclusion would allow the schools to discipline such refusal as 'an act of disrespect,' even though they may not compel this ceremony in the first place."[35]

In 1972, the United States Court of Appeals decided for high-school art teacher Susan Russo, who refused to participate in her school's flag-salute ceremony in the classroom. Russo's belief, said the court, was that "the phrase 'liberty and justice for all' appearing in the pledge, which to most of us represents the spirit and abiding genius of our institutions, in her mind simply did not reflect the quality of life in America today. For this reason, she felt it to be an act of hypocrisy on her part to mouth the words of the pledge when she lacked a belief in either their accuracy or efficacy."[36] Referring to *Barnette*, the court concluded with a strong defense of the right to remain silent:

> It is our conclusion that the right to remain silent in the face of an illegitimate demand for speech is as much a part of First Amendment protections as the right to speak out in the face of an illegitimate demand for silence. . . . Beliefs, particularly when they touch on sensitive questions of faith, when they involve not easily articulated intuitions concerning religion, nation, flag, liberty and justice, are most at home in a realm of privacy, and are happiest in that safe and secluded harbour of the mind that protects our innermost thoughts. To compel a person to speak what is not in his mind offends the very principles of tolerance and understanding which for so long have been the foundation of our great land.[37]

One year later, the same United States Court of Appeals decided for a student who refused to participate in the flag-salute ceremony because he believed that "there [isn't] liberty and justice for all in the United States."[38] Theodore Goetz, a senior and an honor student, refused to stand during the pledge of allegiance and refused to leave the classroom during the ceremony. In deciding for Goetz, the court of appeals argued: "Defendants [school officials] point out . . . that plaintiff has the option of leaving the classroom; he is not, as in *Barnette*, excluded from the school. While we agree that the effect upon plaintiff of adhering to his convictions is far less drastic than in *Barnette*, we do not believe that this disposes of the case. If the state cannot compel participation in the pledge, it cannot punish non-participation. And being required to leave the classroom during the pledge may reasonably be viewed by some as having that effect, however benign defendants' motives may be."[39]

In 1978, another United States Court of Appeals declared unconstitutional that part of the New Jersey statutory provision that required students to stand at attention during the pledge of allegiance. Deborah Lipp, a sixteen-year-old student who had challenged the constitutionality of the statute, "emphasized that in her belief, the words of the pledge were not true and she stood only because she had been threatened if she did not do so."[40] In deciding for Lipp, the court of appeals cited not only *Barnette* and lower court flag-salute cases, but also *Wooley v. Maynard*: "*Banks* and *Goetz* are precisely on point. They interdict the state from requiring a student to engage in what amounts to implicit expression by standing at respectful attention while the flag salute is being administered and being participated in by other students. *Cf. Wooley v. Maynard.* . . ."[41]

When Burger stated in *Wooley*, "We begin with the proposition that the right of freedom of thought protected by the First Amendment against state action includes both the right to speak freely and the right to refrain from speaking at all," he directed the reader: "See *Board of Education v. Barnette*, 319 U.S. 624, 633–634 (1943); *id.*, at 645 (Murphy, J., concurring)."[42] What is especially interesting about Burger's reference to those pages of *Barnette* is that Justice Jackson had applied the clear and present danger test to protect the students' silence, but the same test was not applied when the Court upheld the convictions of citizens who remained silent when confronted with HUAC inquiries and loyalty oaths. Delivering the opinion of the Court, Jackson declared:

> It is now a commonplace that censorship or suppression of opinion is tolerated by our Constitution only when the expression presents a clear and present danger of action of a kind the State is empowered to prevent and punish. . . . To sustain the compulsory flag salute we are required to say that a Bill of Rights which guards the individual's right to speak his mind, left it open to public authorities to compel him to utter what is not in his mind.[43]

This clear and present danger test was not used to provide Anastaplo, Barenblatt, Braden, Wilkinson, et al. with a "right to refrain from speaking."

Burger refers the *Wooley* reader also to "*id.*, at 645 (Murphy, J., concurring)," at which point Justice Murphy wrote: "The right of freedom of thought and of religion as guaranteed by the Constitution against State action includes both the right to speak freely and the right to refrain from speaking at all, except insofar as essential operations of government may require it for the preservation of an orderly society—as in the case of compulsion to give evidence in court." Murphy concluded that the flag-salute requirement "is not essential in the maintenance of effective government and orderly society."[44]

Following these references to *Barnette,* Burger presented *Miami Herald Publishing Co. v. Tornillo* (1974) to indicate that "the right to speak and the right to refrain from speaking are complementary components of the broader concept of 'individual freedom of mind' ": "This is illustrated by the recent case of *Miami Herald Publishing Co.* . . . , where we held unconstitutional a Florida statute placing an affirmative duty upon newspapers to publish the replies of political candidates whom they had criticized."[45] Concluding that the *Miami Herald* could not be compelled to publish a reply from Tornillo, who had been criticized by the newspaper, the United States Supreme Court declared: "Compelling editors or publishers to publish that which ' "reason" tells them should not be published' is what is at issue in this case."[46] The freedom to refrain from speaking, the freedom of the mind, the freedom of thought—all referred to in *Wooley*—were freedoms not available to the victims of the mid-twentieth-century inquisition when they refused to sign the mandatory loyalty oaths and to submit to HUAC inquiries into political beliefs and associations.

After *Wooley* (1977), the United States Supreme Court began applying the right to refrain from speaking to a variety of situations, including those involving union monies, shopping centers, advertising by attorneys, professional fundraisers, and a St. Patrick's Day parade.

On May 23, 1977, one month after *Wooley* was decided, the Supreme Court decided for non-union members of an "agency shop" who had objected to their fees being used for political and ideological purposes unrelated to collective bargaining. In so deciding, the High Court declared that "in a free society one's beliefs should be shaped by his mind and his conscience rather than by the State. . . . And the freedom of belief is no incidental or secondary aspect of the First Amendment's protections. . . ."[47]

In 1980, when the United States Supreme Court decided against a shopping center that had ordered students to leave when they began distributing pamphlets and securing petition signatures, the Court summarized the shopping center's argument, which relied on *Wooley*: "Appellants finally contend that a private property owner has a First Amendment right not to be forced by the State to use his property as a forum for the speech of others. They state that in *Wooley v. Maynard*. . . . , this Court concluded that a State may not constitutionally require an individual to participate in the dissemination of an ideological message by displaying it on his private property in a manner and for the express purpose that it be observed and read by the public. This rationale applies here, they argue, because the message of *Wooley* is that the State may not force an individual to display any message at all."[48]

Justice Rehnquist, delivering the opinion of the Court, rejected the comparison to *Wooley* and pointed out the differences: "Most important, the shopping center by choice of its owner is not limited to the personal use of appellants. It is instead a business establishment that is open to the public to come and go as they please. The views expressed by members of the public passing out pamphlets or seeking signatures for a petition thus will not likely be identified with those of the owner. Second, no specific message is dictated by the State to be displayed on appellant's property. . . . Finally, as far as appears here appellants can expressly disavow any connection with the message by simply posting signs in the area where the speakers or handbillers stand."[49]

Rehnquist also argued that the shopping center's reliance on *Barnette* and *Miami Herald Publishing Co.* was misplaced: "*Barnette* is inapposite because it involved the compelled recitation of a message containing an affirmation of belief. . . . Appellants are not similarly being compelled to affirm their belief in any governmentally prescribed position or view, and they are free to publicly dissociate themselves from the views of the speakers or handbillers."[50]

When in 1985 the United States Supreme Court in *Wallace v. Jaffree* declared unconstitutional Alabama's statute authorizing a period of silence "for meditation or voluntary prayer" in the public schools, Justice Stevens, in delivering the opinion of the Court, quoted at length from *Wooley* and concluded: "Just as the right to speak and the right to refrain from speaking are complementary components of a broader concept of individual freedom of mind, so also the individual's freedom to choose his own creed is the counterpart of his right to refrain from accepting the creed established by the majority."[51] Then, after citing Justice Jackson's classic line, "If there is any fixed star in our constitutional constellation, it is that no official, high or petty, can prescribe what shall be orthodox in politics, nationalism, religion, or other matters of opinion or force citizens to confess by word or act their faith therein," Stevens declared: "The State of Alabama, no less than the Congress of the United States, must respect that basic truth."[52]

While *Wooley* was helpful in protecting Jaffree's freedom not to speak, it did not help an attorney who had been reprimanded for omission in a newspaper advertisement of information regarding clients' fees; in *Zauderer v. Office of Disciplinary Counsel* (1985), the Supreme Court upheld the right of the state to discipline attorneys for misleading omissions in advertisements. Justice White, delivering the opinion of the Court, recognized that the Court had in the past "held that in some instances compulsion to speak may be as violative of the First Amendment as prohibitions on speech," and cited *Wooley, Miami Herald Publishing Co.*, and *Barnette.* "But the interests at stake in this case," argued White, "are not of the same order as those discussed in *Wooley, Tornillo*, and *Barnette*. Ohio has not attempted to 'prescribe what shall be orthodox in politics, nationalism, religion, or other matters of opinion or force citizens to confess by word or act their faith therein. . . . ' The State has attempted only to prescribe what shall be orthodox in commercial advertising, and its prescription has taken the form of a requirement that appellant include in his advertising purely factual and uncontroversial information about the terms under which his services will be available."[53]

In 1986 the United States Supreme Court decided in *Pacific Gas & Electric Co. v. Public Util. Comm'n* that Pacific Gas & Electric Company could not be required by the California Utilities Commission to include in its monthly billing envelopes materials by Toward Utility Rate Normalization (TURN), with which PG & E disagreed. PG & E argued that "it has a First Amendment right not to help spread a message with which it disagrees, see *Wooley v. Maynard*. . . . , and that the Commission's order infringes that right."[54] Justice Powell, announcing the judgment of the Court, referred several times to *Wooley* and described the requirement to include TURN materials in the PG & E billing envelopes as a kind of "forced response" which "is antithetical to the free discussion that the First Amendment seeks to foster."[55] Citing *Wooley*, Powell went on to state: "For corporations as for individuals, the choice to speak includes within it the choice of what not to say. *Tornillo*. . . ."[56]

In his dissenting opinion, Justice Rehnquist argued that protections of "the sphere of intellect and spirit" referred to in *Barnette*, the individual interest in "freedom of the mind" referred to in *Wooley*, and the "constitutional interest of natural persons in freedom of conscience" were not relevant to this case: "Extension of the individual freedom of conscience decisions to business corporations strains the rationale of those cases beyond the breaking point. To ascribe to such artificial entities as an 'intellect' or 'mind' for freedom of conscience purposes is to confuse metaphor with reality."[57]

State-compelled speech became an issue in *Riley v. National Federation of Blind* (1988), in which the United States Supreme Court dealt with a North Carolina requirement that "professional fundraisers disclose to potential donors, before an appeal for funds, the percentage of charitable contributions collected during the previous 12 months that were actually turned over to charity."[58] In deciding that this North Carolina requirement was unconstitutional, the Court emphasized the "right to refrain from speaking." Justice Brennan, delivering the opinion of the Court, wrote: "There is certainly some difference between compelled speech and compelled silence, but in the context of protected speech, the difference is without constitutional significance, for the First Amendment guarantees 'freedom of speech,' a term necessarily comprising the decision of both what to say and what *not* to say."[59] After citing *Barnette, Wooley, Pacific Gas & Electric Co.*, and other precedents, Brennan declared: "These cases cannot be distinguished simply because they involved compelled statements of opinion while here we deal with compelled statements of 'fact': either form of compulsion burdens protected speech."[60]

While coerced expression was an important factor in the Supreme Court's 1992 decision *Lee v. Weisman*, which addressed invocations and benedictions at graduation exercises, the justices did not make any references to *Barnette, Torcaso, Wooley*, or other precedents involving the freedom to refrain from speaking. In its 5–4 decision declaring unconstitutional the inclusion of invocations and benedictions in the form of prayers led by clergy at public-school graduation ceremonies, the High Court expressed concern about the coercion imposed on students: "The undeniable fact is that the school district's supervision and control of a high school graduation ceremony places public pressure, as well as peer pressure, on attending students to stand as a group or, at least, maintain respectful silence during the Invocation and Benediction. This pressure, though subtle and indirect, can be as real as any overt compulsion."[61] Justice Kennedy, delivering the opinion of the Court, argued: "It is the tenet of the First Amendment that the State cannot require one of its citizens to forfeit his or her rights and benefits as the price of resisting conformance to state-sponsored religious practice. To say that a student must remain apart from the ceremony at the opening invocation and closing benediction is to risk compelling conformity in an environment analogous to the classroom setting, where we have said the risk of compulsion is especially high."[62]

Kennedy concluded: "No holding by this Court suggests that a school can persuade or compel a student to participate in a religious exercise. That is being done here, and it is forbidden by the Establishment Clause of the First Amendment."[63]

Justice Souter, delivering the opinion of the Court in *Hurley v. Irish-American Gay, Lesbian and Bisexual Group of Boston, Inc.* (1995), stated at the outset just what the issue was in this case: "[W]hether Massachusetts may require private citizens who organize a parade to include among the marchers a group imparting a message the organizers do not wish to convey. We hold that such a mandate violates the First Amendment."[64] In 1993, the organizers of Boston's St. Patrick's Day Parade, who had received a city permit for the parade, denied GLIB (an organization composed of gay, lesbian, and bisexual descendants of Irish immigrants) permission to march in the parade as a unit carrying its own banner. In deciding that the organizers of the parade could not be compelled to permit the GLIB unit to march in the parade, the High Court, quoting from *Pacific Gas & Electric Co.*, stated: " 'Since *all* speech inherently involves choices of what to say and what to leave unsaid,' *Pacific Gas & Electric Co.* . . . , one important manifestation of the principle of free speech is that one who chooses to speak may also decide 'what not to say,' *id.*, at 16. Although the State may at times 'prescribe what shall be orthodox in commercial advertising' by requiring the dissemination of 'purely factual and uncontroversial information' . . . , outside that context it may not compel affirmance of a belief with which the speaker disagrees, see *Barnette.* . . ."[65]

The last quarter of the twentieth century saw the United States Supreme Court deciding that the Jehovah's Witnesses in *Wooley* could not be compelled to display the LIVE FREE OR DIE motto on their auto license plates; that the Pruneyard Shopping Center could be compelled to allow handbillers and petition-gatherers in its center; that Alabama could not provide "a moment of silence for meditation and prayer" in its public schools; that Ohio could reprimand attorneys for misleading omissions in their advertisements; that California could not require PG & E to include materials with which it disagreed in its billing envelopes;

and that Boston parade organizers could deny parade participation to a gay, lesbian, and bisexual unit in the St. Patrick's Day Parade.

Because the United States Supreme Court has decided that newspapers cannot be compelled to speak (*Miami Herald Publishing Co.*), that electric companies cannot be compelled to speak (*Pacific Gas & Electric Co.*), that Jehovah's Witnesses cannot be compelled to speak (*Wooley*), and that students cannot be compelled to speak (*Barnette, Jaffree, Lee*), can we conclude that American citizens cannot be compelled to speak when they refuse to reveal, through loyalty oaths and disclaimer affidavits and HUAC-type inquiries, their political beliefs and associations? It must be recognized that the later twentieth-century decisions described above did not repudiate or reject the arguments and decisions that led to the punishments imposed on Anastaplo, Barenblatt, Braden, Konigsberg, Uphaus, *et al.* Nowhere has the United States Supreme Court said that the coerced speech demanded of these individuals by the state is no longer constitutionally tolerable.

If the arguments and principles articulated in *Barnette* did not help save the mid-twentieth-century "heretics" who refused to sign oaths and answer HUAC-type inquiries, there is little reason to believe that those same and similar arguments and principles, articulated in 1987 in *Wooley* and in later decisions such as *Pacific Gas & Electric Co.*, *Riley*, and *Hurley*, will be there to help when the next American inquisition occurs.

HUAC-ism and McCarthyism, with all the coerced speech that came with them, have long since been discredited and condemned. The term "McCarthyism" has found its way into our vocabulary and our dictionaries, the term conveying unfairness, foul play, intimidation, and deception. The definition of McCarthyism in *The American Heritage Dictionary of the American Language* reads: "1. The practice of publicizing accusations of political disloyalty or subversion with insufficient regard to evidence. 2. The use of unfair investigatory or accusatory methods in order to suppress opposition."[66] Yet it is difficult to identify any constitutional law in place to assure us that it all cannot happen again, that HUAC-and McCarthy-type methods and inquiries will not occur again in the search for new "heretics."

There are, of course, those Supreme Court decisions that provided constitutional protection to Watkins, Sweezy, and Keyishian, who refused to speak when commanded to do so by the state. In these cases the Court found the coerced speech unacceptable, sometimes because such compelled expression could have a chilling effect on the freedoms of speech and association or violate academic freedom. Oaths and disclaimer affidavits might be found unacceptable for being too vague or too broad; HUAC's inquiries could be found impermissible because they were not "pertinent."

When in 1958 the United States Supreme Court decided in *NAACP v. Alabama* that the state could not require the NAACP to turn over its membership list to the state, the High Court concluded that to force the organization to reveal the list to the state might act as a "restraint on freedom of association." Sweezy received constitutional protection, in part, because to compel him to speak would constitute a violation of academic freedom. Keyishian received protection because the loyalty oath was an intrusion on academic freedom, which is "a special concern of the First Amendment, which does not tolerate laws that cast a pall of orthodoxy over the classroom." Torcaso received protection because requiring him to assert a belief in God violated the citizen's "freedom of belief and religion." Maynard received protection because the right to refrain from speaking is a component of the broader concept of "individual freedom of mind." But none of these concepts—"freedom of association," "freedom of belief," "academic freedom," or "freedom of the mind"—provided protection for Barsky, Josephson, Anastaplo, Barenblatt, Braden, Wilkinson, Uphaus, *et al.*

While the above freedoms are crucial to a free society, there is much more than freedom involved when church and state coerce speech. If it could be shown that Roman demands that Christians "sacrifice" to the gods did not interfere with freedom of belief; that King Henry's demand that Thomas More sign the loyalty oath did not have a chilling effect on speech; that the church's demand that Galileo recant his heretical views did not have any effect on freedom of inquiry; that HUAC's citing noncooperative witnesses for contempt of Congress and subjecting them to imprisonment or blacklisting did not have any effect on freedom of association—if all these efforts at coerced speech could be said to have had little or no effect on these crucial freedoms, would the coercion be any less evil?

Recant or be sent to the stake; inform and names names or be blacklisted; reveal your past political associations or be jailed; sign the loyalty oath or lose your job; repent or be labelled a heretic, an un-American. We are dealing here with more than interferences with the freedoms of speech, association, and academic freedom. We are dealing with human dignity, self-worth, personal autonomy, and integrity. We are dealing with church- and state-imposed degradation and humiliation. And as Avishai Margalit has observed, "It is clear that the spirit of a just society cannot tolerate systematic humiliation by its basic institutions. This is especially true since the good to be distributed, in the form of social conditions that enable people to have self-respect, is at the top of the just society's priority list. If humiliation means damaging people's self-respect, then it is clear that a necessary condition for the just society is that it should be a society that does not humiliate its members."[67]

Yet a review of some of the cases we have addressed reveals that degradation of the individual is a distinct aspect of these instances of compelled speech. The punishment of heretic William Sawtre in 1401 involved a ritual of degradation that preceded his being "committed to the fire." After the "Sentence of Degradation Pronounced on Sir William Sawtre" was read, it was ordered that "in some public and open place" Sawtre be burned for "detestation of his crime, and the manifest example of other Christians."[68]

When in 1535 Thomas More refused to take the oath demanded of him by Henry VIII, there was more at issue than freedom of association and freedom of speech. The evil of the oath requirement was that it required More to declare what he did not believe; it was a matter of conscience. Defending his right to remain silent, More declared: "Ye must understand that, in things touching conscience, every true and good subject is more bound to have respect to his conscience and to his soul than to any other thing in all the world beside; namely when his conscience is in such sort as mine is, that is to say, where the person giveth no occasion of slander, of tumult and sedition against his prince, as it is with me; for I assure you that I have not hitherto to this hour disclosed and opened my conscience and mind to any person living in all the world."[69]

As for being punished for his silence, More asserted: "Your statute cannot condemn me to death for such silence, for neither your statute nor any laws in the world punish people except for words or deeds, surely not for keeping silence."[70] Thomas More was sentenced to death and executed on July 6, 1535.

One century later, on June 21, 1633, Galileo Galilei was coerced into signing a recantation of the theory that the earth moves around the sun. Where English authorities had been unsuccessful in persuading More to speak, to take the oath, church authorities were successful in persuading

Galileo, with the threat of torture if he refused to speak, to declare what he did not believe. As in the case of Thomas More, the evil of the authorities' efforts at coerced speech, the demand that Galileo deny what he believed to be true, lay not so much in the fact that the coercion would negatively affect freedom of learning and inquiry (which it did), but in the fact that it was an attack on his dignity. Referring to Galileo's degradation, Giorgio de Santillana has stated: "It is as though the Pope had decided that what he really wanted was not simply repression but humiliation. It was his enemy's mind that had to be shamed, and his name dragged in the mud."[71]

Others have also recognized the role of humiliation in Galileo's "trial." Andrew White has written: "The world knows now that Galileo was subjected certainly to indignity, to imprisonment, and to threats equivalent to torture, and was at last forced to pronounce publicly, and on his knees his recantation. . . . To complete his dishonor, he was obliged to swear that he would denounce to the Inquisition any other man of science whom he should discover to be supporting the 'heresy of the motion of the earth.' "[72] The church's intent to humiliate Galileo has been recognized by F. Sherwood Tayler: "In university towns the mathematicians and philosophers were called together and the sentence read to them—a measure designed at once to humiliate Galileo and to discourage other followers of the new theories from giving expression to their views."[73] Karl von Gebler has written that after the sentence was decided by the church, "Galileo was compelled immediately after hearing it to make the following degrading recantation, humbly kneeling, before the whole assembly [the Holy Tribunal]."[74] Through the centuries, the degradations continued as the power of church and state was imposed on those who refused to speak what the authorities ordered.

The humiliation that came with naming names and signing loyalty oaths in the United States were recognized in the 1950s by journalist Alan Barth. At an American Association of University Professors (AAUP) annual dinner in March 1951, Barth said: "[T]he protestations extorted by loyalty oaths and inquiries are humiliating—senselessly humiliating." Further, he asserted that "these oaths and inquiries invade long-recognized rights of privacy" and "imply presumption of guilt instead of the presumption of innocence that has traditionally protected individuals under American law."[75] Two years later, at another AAUP meeting, Barth spoke of the degradation that came with HUAC-type inquiries: "When a committee of Congress hales a man before it and asks him if he has ever been a Communist, it impales him on one or another of the prongs of a trident. If the witness answers 'yes' to this question, the committee is all too likely to insist that he identify individuals who were in the party with him—a kind of degradation which any sensitive man might understandably desire to escape."[76]

When actor Larry Parks appeared before HUAC, as noted earlier, he begged the committee twice not to force him to "crawl through the mud" when it demanded that he name names.[77] Sterling Hayden, another Hollywood star, appeared before HUAC in 1951, was "cooperative," and named names. Hayden wrote in his 1963 autobiography of his regrets at having cooperated with the committee. He said to his psychoanalyst: "I'll say this too, that if it hadn't been for you I wouldn't have turned into a stoolie for J. Edgar Hoover. I don't think you have the foggiest notion of the contempt I have had for myself since the day I did that thing. . . . Fuck it! Fuck you too!"[78] He writes later in his autobiography: "These were the dismal years of the blacklist. These were the years of excommunication, when thirty or forty hostile witness writers were sent into exile, only to find that producers were willing to—very discreetly, of course—buy more than a hundred scripts underneath the table. Not often does a man find himself eulogized [as a "one-shot stoolie"] for having behaved in a manner that he himself despises."[79]

Using the power of the state to undermine the dignity of the individual, to humiliate and stigmatize, becomes especially vile when the political inquisition has an impact on religious beliefs and principles. Just as Zero Mostel as a Jew could not become an informer,[80] neither could Willard Uphaus, as a Christian theologian. Uphaus wrote in his 1963 autobiography: "The attempt of the attorney general of New Hampshire to use the State Subversive Activities Act of 1951 to harass and intimidate me and to destroy the work of the World Fellowship of Faiths by demanding the names and addresses of our 1954 guests, the identity of our employees, and the correspondence with speakers, is utterly contrary to the cherished tradition of religious freedom and peaceable assembly enshrined in the First Amendment to the Constitution of the United States. This action is a direct invasion of Christian conscience. . . ."[81]

An important part of the public intimidation and degradation imposed on those who defied the HUAC-type committees was a public mea culpa utterance. Blacklisted director Jules Dassin, who as director of the film *Rififi* received an award from the Cannes Film Festival in 1955, was told that a mea culpa from him was necessary if his film was to get wide distribution in America. Actress Marsha Hunt, who was blacklisted for criticizing HUAC, has spoken of attempts to persuade her to "swear to my non-Communism, past or present, and vow my fervent anti-communist efforts from then on." As she put it, "It was full of mea culpa. . . ."[82]

Linus Pauling, who had spoken out against the Cold War arms race and circulated peace petitions among world scientists, refused to answer when he was asked, "Are you a Communist?" Pauling explained in an interview:

> I was never a part of the University of California system, so I didn't have to deal with the loyalty oath. But I sent a letter to the governor protesting it, and was hauled before the California Committee on Education in Los Angeles. They asked me, "Are you a Communist? Did you send a protest letter to the governor?" "Yes, surely I did. I don't think an oath is a proper criterion. I don't think people should be required to sign them." Then again, "Are you a Communist?" "I refuse to answer."
>
> Then I had to reappear before this committee. The Chairman said, "Now I ask you again the question: Are you a Communist?" "I refuse to answer that question—not on the grounds of the Fifth Amendment or the First Amendment—I'm just not willing to answer the question about my beliefs.[83]

As noted in chapter 4, when playwright Arthur Miller refused to name names when he appeared before HUAC, he told the committee: "[M]y conscience will not permit me to use the name of another person."[84] While recognizing that Miller was not a Communist, a New York City official still wanted to hear Miller's repentance: "I'm not calling him a Communist. . . . [M]y objection is he refused to repent."[85]

The requirement that one go through a public recantation was an important element in the degradation ceremonies participated in by ex-Communists who appeared before the un-American activities committees as "friendly" witnesses. As John Cogley has explained in his *Report on Blacklisting*: "When a former member of the Party came to Brewer [friendly witness] for help, Brewer usually turned him over to Costigan [part of Brewer's staff]. The first thing Costigan insisted on was that the ex-Communist go to the FBI with all the information he had." However, providing information to the FBI was not enough: "Then the ex-Communist was put in touch with the House Committee and some kind of public repentance was worked out. The ex-Communist was expected to testify (which meant naming names in public session), denounce the Party at union meetings and, if he was prominent enough, make some kind of statement for the press, express his new feelings about the Party. Some converts refused to be 'rehabilitated' on these terms. They objected especially to the requirement that they name names."[86] While the "unfriendly" witnesses almost always lost their jobs as actors, screenwriters, directors, teachers, and state employees, the "friendly" witnesses who publicly demonstrated that they had been "rehabilitated" and had repented went back to work after they testified.

On October 30, 1947, screenwriter Ring Lardner, Jr., was escorted out of the HUAC hearings after he persisted in refusing to answer questions related to membership in the Screen Writers Guild and the Communist Party. HUAC chairman J. Parnell Thomas informed Lardner that "any real American would be proud to answer the question," "Are you or have you ever been a member of the Communist Party?" Lardner responded by stating that he could answer the question, "but if I did, I would hate myself in the morning." Lardner was cited for contempt, found guilty, and imprisoned for one year in the Federal Correctional Institution in Danbury, Connecticut, where J. Parnell Thomas was also imprisoned after being convicted of misusing government funds.

Fourteen years later, Lardner wrote the following in "My Life on the Blacklist": "When Arthur Miller admitted attending a single meeting under Communist auspices as an invited guest, but refused as a matter of conscience to say who else had been present, he was brought to trial and convicted of contempt. It was made clear beyond misunderstanding that there was no proper penance for past political misconduct except the naming of names; big names, little names, token names, names the Committee already had. It was a ritual, but not a meaningless one. To the unordained confessors in Washington and Hollywood, it was an act of perfect contrition."[87]

In a 1956 letter, Dalton Trumbo devoted a long passage to the informer and HUAC's ritual of coercing witnesses to name names: "The more I think on it the more it appears to me that the curse upon the informer which characterizes all religions and all philosophies lies at the very heart of the social compact: that without it there can be no decent relationship anywhere for anybody: that informing as a crime is worse than murder or rape, since the murderer and the rapist harm only specific victims while the informer poisons and destroys the spiritual life of whole peoples."[88] As to the ritual of naming names, Trumbo wrote:

"Indeed, the ritual often becomes more meaningful than the idea or act it symbolically recreates. If informing were a small ritual, the committee would place little emphasis upon it. Since the committee places it in a position of first importance, I'm obliged to give it that position also. The committee does not view it as a ritual; it views it as an act—an act of such urgent importance that if men refuse to perform it altogether the committee must cease to function."[89]

All through history, inquisitors have been interested in having the "heretic" publicly repent and name names. As Henry Lea has pointed out in *The Inquisition of the Middle Ages*, the heretic's "refusal to betray his friends and kindred was proof that he was unrepentant, and he was forthwith handed over to the secular arm" to be punished. During the inquisitions of the Middle Ages, "confession of heresy thus became a matter of vital importance, and no effort was deemed too great, no means too repulsive, to secure it."[90] The punishments imposed by the church on heretics were of varying grades, one of those being the *"poenae confusibiles"*—"the humiliating and degrading penances, of which the most important was the wearing of yellow crosses sewed upon the garments; and finally, the severest punishment among those strictly within the competence of the Holy Office, the 'murus,' or prison."[91] This penalty, of course, acted as a public sign of the heretic's wrong thinking, sin, and repentance. And, as Lea has observed, "the unfortunate penitent was exposed to the ridicule and derision of all whom he met, and was heavily handicapped in every effort to earn a livelihood."[92]

Commenting on the state's coerced loyalty oaths and the individual's "sacrifice of dignity," Harry M. Beggs wrote in 1964 in the *Arizona Law Review* of the "unfair choice" forced upon those of "unquestionable loyalty, but firm in their convictions and beliefs against oathtaking": "They may test their rights through costly litigation, abandoning their means of livelihood and becoming unemployed. They may abandon their life's vocation and procure employment in foreign fields. Or they may abandon adherence to their convictions and sign the oath. If they yield to the latter, the sacrifice of dignity subtracts from the very nature of man that which made us a free nation to begin with: the will to fight for what we cherish and believe. If the law destroys this shield of our freedom it is only a matter of biding time until our downfall."[93]

In his criticism of the *Barenblatt* decision that sent Lloyd Barenblatt to prison for refusing to answer HUAC questions related to his political associations, Alexander Meiklejohn expressed concern about preserving the "dignity of the free man": "There are nations which, to our horror, give to national self-preservation priority over the political freedom and the dignity of the individual person. But there are other nations which establish the freedom and consequent dignity of the individual as higher in status than the security, either of the individual himself or of the state of which he is a member. As between those two systems we have proudly chosen the latter. We believe, as we say, in the dignity of the free man."[94] That dignity was not accorded Barenblatt. He stated the following ten years after his imprisonment, as we saw in chapter 5: "The treatment of the witnesses by the committee was, without any exaggeration, inquisitional. . . . It was an act of contrition to inform on others."[95]

When in 1951 Justice Frankfurter agreed with the Court majority in *Garner* that the city of Los Angeles could impose a loyalty oath inquiring about Communist affiliations of city employees, he expressed concern at the same time about protecting "individual integrity": "The vice of this oath is that it is not limited to affiliation with organizations known at the time to have advocated overthrow of government. . . . I do not think it is consonant with the Due Process Clause for men to be asked, on pain of giving up public employment, to swear to something they cannot be expected to know. Such a demand is at war with individual integrity; it can no more be justified than the inquiry into belief which Mr. Justice Black, Mr. Justice Jackson and I deemed invalid in *American Communications Assn. v. Douds.* . . ."[96] Yet in deciding against the city employees who had challenged the constitutionality of the Los Angeles loyalty-oath requirement, the High Court did not opt for protecting individual integrity.

As noted in chapter 4, after author Lillian Hellman was subpoenaed to appear before HUAC on May 21, 1952, she sent a letter to HUAC Chairman John S. Wood. She explained that to "save herself" by naming names would be "inhuman and indecent and dishonorable." She told the chairman of HUAC that she had been taught "to try to tell the truth, not to bear false witness, not to harm my neighbor, to be loyal to my country, and so on. In general, I respected these ideals of Christian honor and did as well with them as I knew how. It is my belief that you will agree with these simple rules of human decency and will not expect me to violate the good American tradition from which they spring. I would, therefore, like to come before you and speak of myself."[97] Representative Wood replied: "[P]lease be advised that the Committee cannot permit witnesses to set forth the terms under which they will testify."[98] When she appeared before HUAC, Hellman refused to answer questions about membership in the Communist Party and to name names, basing her refusal on the Fifth Amendment.

Various jurists, philosophers, and scholars have argued that the dignity and integrity of the individual need to be protected in a free society. The nexus between dignity and human rights is explicated in a series of essays in *The Constitution of Rights: Human Dignity and American Values*; Alan Gewirth states at the outset of his essay: "The relations between human dignity and human rights are many and complex, but one relation is primary: human rights are based upon or derivative from human dignity. It is because humans have dignity that they have human rights."[99]

Again and again in his 1997 essay "My life on the Court," Justice Brennan comes back to the importance of preserving the dignity of the individual: "As I have said many times and in many ways, our Constitution is a charter of human rights and human dignity. It is a bold commitment by a people to the ideal of dignity protected through law."[100] After referring to several individual cases involving "everyday human dramas" (the police breaking down a citizen's door and "handcuffing her because she dared to examine their phony warrant," the cutting off of welfare payments leading a woman and her four nieces to eat out of garbage cans, sexual discrimination, and reapportionment), Brennan stated: "At the heart of each drama was a person who cried out for nothing more than common human dignity. In each case, our Constitution intervened to provide the cloak of dignity."[101]

At the end of his essay, Justice Brennan reiterated his strong commitment to the law's protection of human dignity: "If our free society is to endure, and I know it will, those who govern must recognize that the Framers of the Constitution limited their power in order to preserve human dignity and the air of freedom which is our proudest heritage. . . ."[102] Yet for a quarter of a century, those who governed mid-twentieth-century America did not limit their power to preserve human dignity; the power of the state was used to coerce speech, to compel the individual to participate in the degradation ceremonies requiring informing, recanting, and repenting.

Brennan's concern for preserving the dignity of the individual was reflected in several of his judicial opinions. In *Furman v. Georgia* (1972), in which the United States Supreme Court held that the imposition and carrying out of the death penalty in the cases involved in *Furman* constituted cruel and unusual punishment, Brennan wrote in his concurring opinion: "[T]he Cruel and unusual Punishments Clause prohibits the infliction of uncivilized and inhuman punishments. The State, even as it punishes, must treat its members with respect for their intrinsic worth as human beings. A punishment is 'cruel and unusual,' therefore, if it does not comport with human dignity."[103] Later, in the same opinion, Brennan wrote: "The primary principle is that a punishment must not be so severe as to be degrading to the dignity of human beings."[104]

Referring to "barbaric punishments" such as the rack, the thumbscrew, the iron boot, and the stretching of limbs, Brennan added: "When we consider why they have been condemned . . . we realize that the pain involved is not the only reason. The true significance of these punishments is that they treat members of the human race as nonhumans, as objects to be toyed with and discarded. They are thus inconsistent with the fundamental premise of the Clause that even the vilest criminal remains a human being possessed of common human dignity."[105]

All through his *Furman* opinion Brennan argues against "degrading" punishment and for punishment that "comports with human dignity"; he concludes his opinion by asserting: "In sum, the punishment of death is inconsistent with all four principles: Death is an unusually severe and degrading punishment; there is a strong probability that it is inflicted arbitrarily; its rejection by contemporary society is virtually total; and there is no reason to believe that it serves any penal purpose more effectively than the less severe punishment of imprisonment. The function of these principles is to enable a court to determine whether a punishment comports with human dignity. Death, quite simply, does not."[106]

Preserving the dignity of the individual was also of concern to Brennan in *Goldberg v. Kelly* (1970), which dealt with the question of "whether a State that terminates public assistance payments to a particular recipient without affording him the opportunity for an evidentiary hearing prior to termination denies the recipient procedural due process in violation of the Due Process Clause of the Fourteenth Amendment."[107] Delivering the opinion of the Court in favor of those seeking welfare benefits, Brennan straightaway declared: "From its founding the Nation's basic commitment has been to foster the dignity and well-being of all persons within its borders."[108]

The notion of the centrality of protecting the dignity of the individual appears in still another context when Ronald Dworkin discusses abortion rights and euthanasia; Dworkin writes:

The right of procreative autonomy has an important place not only in the structure of the American Constitution but in Western political culture more generally. The most important feature of that culture is a belief in individual human dignity: that people have the moral right—and the moral responsibility—to confront the most fundamental questions about the meaning and value of their own conscience and convictions. The most powerful arguments against slavery before the Civil War, and for equal protection after it, were framed in the language of dignity. . . . [109]

The importance of human dignity and self-respect also enter Dworkin's discussion of euthanasia: "Because we honor dignity, we demand democracy, and we define it so that a constitution that permits a majority to deny freedom of conscience is democracy's enemy, not its author."[110]

Protecting human dignity was important to Chief Justice Warren when he delivered the opinion of the Court in *Miranda v. Arizona* (1965): "It is obvious that such an interrogation environment is created for no purpose other than to subjugate the individual to the will of his examiner. This atmosphere carries its own badge of intimidation. To be sure, this is not physical intimidation, but it is equally destructive to human dignity. The current practice of incommunicado interrogation is at odds with one of our Nation's most cherished principles—that the individual may not be compelled to incriminate himself."[111]

Protecting the dignity of the individual is at the center of our judicial system. To repeat the words of Alan Gewirth: "[H]uman rights are based upon or derivative from human dignity. It is because humans have dignity that they have human rights." Drawing a relationship between freedom of expression and dignity, Thomas I. Emerson wrote in his classic work, *The System of Freedom of expression*, that "the system of freedom of expression in a democratic society rests on four premises." The first premise is that "freedom of expression is essential as a means of assuring individual self-fulfillment. The proper end of man is the realization of his character and potentialities as a human being. Hence suppression of belief, opinion or other expression is an affront to the dignity of man, a negation of man's essential nature."[112]

My primary argument here is that just as the suppression of expression of belief is "an affront to the dignity of man, a negation of man's essential nature," so too is compelled political and religious speech. Denying the freedom not to speak, like denying the freedom to speak, is a serious hindrance to "assuring individual self-fulfillment." Or, to look again at how Konvitz has put it, ordering one to profess "beliefs that one does not maintain may do more violence to the conscience than the failure to express the beliefs that one does maintain."[113]

What is it about coerced expression demanded by church and state that makes it degrading, shameful, abhorrent, and disrespectful? Speak or be punished! Coercion of this kind is an intrusion into our personal thoughts. The privacy of one's mind is essential to a free individual. In some ways, being denied the freedom not to speak is more of an attack on the dignity of the individual than being denied the freedom to speak. To prohibit a person from expressing a political or religious thought or belief is one thing; someone else might express the thought or belief at another time, in another place, or in another manner. If one is denied the freedom to speak, at least he or she has not been compelled to publicly reveal something private or forced into a position of lying, recanting, or informing on friends and associates. It is something else to coerce a person to deny what he knows is true, to express a belief she does not hold, to participate in a ritual that is personally repugnant. Under threat of punishment, what is private becomes public. It is not a proper function of the church or state to do violence to the citizen's conscience, to force participation in degradation ceremonies and humiliating rituals. One's thoughts, as various philosophers and others have told us, are not to be ordered to be expressed by the sovereign, the state, or any other authority.

Coerced expression was condemned by John Locke several times in his now-famous *A Letter Concerning Toleration*, published in 1689. Early in the *Letter* Locke writes:

> If anyone maintain that men ought to be compelled by fire and sword to profess certain doctrines, and form to this or that exterior worship, without regard had unto their morals; if any one endeavour to convert those that are erroneous unto the faith, by forcing them to profess things that they do not believe, and allowing them to practice things that the Gospel does not permit, it cannot be doubted indeed but such a one is desirous to have numerous assembly joined in the same profession with himself; but that he principally intends by those means to compose a truly Christian church, is altogether incredible.[114]

Locke's condemnations of coerced expression reappeared a century later in Thomas Jefferson's *Notes on Virginia*. Locke had written: "If a Roman Catholic believe that to be really the body of Christ, which another calls bread, he does no injury thereby to his neighbor. If a Jew do not believe the New Testament to be the word of God, he does not thereby alter anything in men's civil rights. If a heathen doubt of both Testaments, he is not therefore to be punished as a pernicious citizen."[115] In 1785, Jefferson expressed in his *Notes on Virginia* arguments against coerced speech very similar to those presented by Locke; Jefferson wrote:

> The error seems not sufficiently eradicated that the operations of the mind, as well as the acts of the body, are subject to the coercion of the laws. But our rulers can have authority over such natural rights, only as we have submitted to them. The rights of conscience we never submitted, we could not submit. We are answerable for them to our God. The legitimate power of government extend to such acts only as are injurious to others. But it does me no injury for my neighbor to say there are twenty gods, or no God. It neither picks my pocket nor breaks my leg.[116]

After a reference to Galileo's coerced abjuration, Jefferson wrote: "Subject opinion to coercion: whom will you make your inquisitors? Fallible men; men governed by bad passions, by private as well as public reasons. And why subject it to coercion? To produce uniformity. But is uniformity of opinion desirable? No more than of face and stature."[117]

Philosopher Avishai Margalit has asserted that the decent society is "one whose institutions do not humiliate people." Distinguishing between a civilized society and a decent society, he writes: "A civilized society is whose members do not humiliate one another, while a decent society is one in which the institutions do not humiliate people."[118] As to the relevance of integrity to a decent society, Margalit states: "Another claim might be that a humiliating society is one whose institutions cause people to compromise their integrity. This is a society that subjects people of integrity to blackmail and forces them to make despicable compromises. For example, only if you join the Party will your children be eligible to go to a 'proper' school; only if you sign a petition against your colleague will you be able to keep your job."[119]

To apply Margalit's observations to the coerced speech imposed on Americans in the middle of the twentieth century, only if you sign the loyalty oath and the disclaimer affidavit and only if you inform on colleagues when appearing before the various un-American activities committees will you be able to avoid punishment in the form of imprisonment, loss of job, or blacklisting. In a decent society there is no place for the degradation ceremonies of the HUAC hearings; in a decent society an actor like Larry Parks should not be forced to "crawl through the mud"; in a decent society an Arthur Miller should not be required to "repent"; in a decent society, requiring the citizen to sign loyalty oaths and disclaimer affidavits is a "diminution to his credit."

Unfortunately, when the courts in the United States have decided cases involving individuals who refused to divulge their political beliefs and associations when commanded to do so by the state, their arguments have not been based on premises of dignity, integrity, degradation, humiliation, or the "negation of man's essential nature." More often than not, these decisions have been based on whether the coerced speech constituted intrusions on freedom of speech, freedom of association, and academic freedom. While these freedoms did save Sweezy, Keyishian and Shelton, they did not save Braden, Barenblatt, and Uphaus.

What was lacking was a clearly defined freedom not to speak that was not premised on the freedom of speech and association, even though the rationale behind the freedom not to speak is partly to be found in the speech and association guarantees. There is much more at stake than these freedoms when the citizen is compelled to participate in church and state symbolic rituals, required to sign loyalty oaths and disclaimer affidavits, forced to reveal beliefs, thoughts, and associations to HUAC-type committees.

Even if forcing an individual to name names to these committees would not have any effect on academic freedom, or even if forcing a teacher to sign a loyalty oath would not cast a pall of orthodoxy over the classroom, or even if forcing a person to divulge his or her political and religious associations would not have any effect on freedom of association, the coerced speech must still be condemned, because it is an affront to the dignity of the human being, an attack on his or her integrity. The evil of church-and state-coerced speech, whether in the form of forced recanting, repentance, naming names, flag salutes, or loyalty oaths, lies in the coercion itself, not in its impact on other constitutional freedoms.

When in the second century the Roman governor demanded of Christian martyr Polycarp, "Take the oath and I will let you go; revile Christ," Polycarp refused the oath and refused to "revile Christ." While the punishment of the stake imposed on those who refused to take the Roman oath and to "revile Christ" may have had negative, chilling effects on speech and association, the greater evil lay in the state's demand that one utter what in good conscience one could not speak.

While the church's demand that Galileo recant, that he utter what he did not believe and inform on other heretics, did have the undesirable effect of discouraging further scientific learning in the Mediterranean, the greater evil of the of the church's coercion lay in its humiliating attack on Galileo's dignity, integrity, and personal autonomy. While HUAC's demand that Zero Mostel name names may have had a negative, chilling effect on speech and association, the greater evil of the state's coercion lay in requiring Mostel to became an informer who, as such, could not be buried in sacred ground.

Willard Uphaus declared that he could not become a "contemptible informer" because of his "inner conscience."[120] George Anastaplo told the committee that refused to certify him for admission to the Illinois bar, "I think fundamentally it is a facet of a certain feeling about human dignity, rights of man, which demands that we abstain from inquiring of an individual what his affiliations are, what his personal beliefs are."[121] Frank Wilkinson, in refusing to answer HUAC questions, told the committee: "As a matter of conscience and personal responsibility, I refuse to answer any questions by this Committee."[122] As we have seen, Arthur Miller refused to name names, telling HUAC that "my conscience will not permit me to use the name of another person."[123] Thomas More, in refusing to take King Henry's oath, explained that his silence was a matter of conscience: "In my conscience this was one of the cases in which I would bounden that I should not obey my prince . . . in my conscience the truth seemed to be on the other side . . . wherein I had not informed my conscience neither suddenly or lightly but by long leisure and diligent search for the matter. I leave everyman in his conscience and methinketh that in good faith so were it good conscience every man should leave me to mine."[124]

When in 1963 the Arizona Supreme Court decided against Barbara Elfbrandt, who had refused to sign the loyalty oath as a condition for teaching, Chief Justice Bernstein, while agreeing with the Court's decision, wrote a concurring opinion in which he expressed concern about protecting individuals who on the basis of conscience could not sign the oath: "Most Americans take a loyalty oath with a feeling of patriotic pride and satisfaction. Nevertheless, there are those whose loyalty is unquestioned who, in sincere conscientious conviction refuse to subscribe to such oaths. For some, the objection is grounded in religious beliefs, for others upon the concepts of academic or intellectual freedom. There are undoubtedly other reasons for refusal to take the oath. However much we may disagree with the logic or reasonableness of these objections, we must admit that they do not prove disloyalty."[125]

But in the end, when the United States Supreme Court declared most of the loyalty oaths unconstitutional, the oaths were struck down because of their vagueness, because of their chilling effects on the freedoms of speech and association and on academic freedom, not because the state had invaded the domain of the individual's conscience. However, when in 1943 the Supreme Court decided that the Barnette children could not be required to salute the flag, Justice Murphy wrote a concurring opinion in which he recognized the importance of "preserving freedom of conscience."

> I am unable to agree that the benefits that may accrue to society from the compulsory flag salute are sufficiently definite and tangible to justify the invasion of freedom and privacy that is entailed or to compensate for a restraint on the freedom of the individual to be vocal or silent according to his conscience or personal inclination. The trenchant words in the preamble to the Virginia Statute for Religious Freedom remain unanswerable: " . . . all attempts to influence [the mind] by temporal punishments, or burdens, or by civil incapacitations, tend only to beget habits of hypocrisy and meanness, . . . " Any spark of love for country which may be generated in a child or his associates by forcing him to make what is to him an empty gesture and recite words wrung from him contrary to his religious beliefs is overshadowed by the desirability of preserving freedom of conscience to the full. It is in that freedom and the example of persuasion, not in force and compulsion, that the real unity of America lies.[126]

While the citizens who refused to sign the oaths and to answer HUAC's inquiries into their political and religious beliefs did so on the basis of conscience, the courts failed to apply any freedom of conscience to protect them. The state's probing into the minds of its citizens through coerced speech was never seriously attacked by the courts as an intrusion into or a violation of conscience and privacy.

However, the United States Supreme Court did argue in 1969 in *Stanley v. Georgia* that the state was prohibited from invading one's home to inquire into the contents of his or her library. Delivering the Court's opinion, Justice Marshall wrote of the right to be free from "unwanted governmental intrusions into one's privacy": "Whatever may be the justifications for other statutes regulating obscenity, we do not think they reach into the privacy of one's own home. If the First Amendment means anything, it means that a State has no business telling a man, sitting alone in his own house, what books he may read or what films he may watch. Our whole constitutional heritage rebels at the thought of giving government the power to control men's minds."[127] Marshall cited a passage from Justice Brandeis's *Olmstead v. United States* dissenting opinion: "They [the makers of our Constitution] sought to protect Americans in their beliefs, their thoughts, their emotions and their sensations. They conferred, as against the Government, the right to be let alone—the most comprehensive of rights and the right most valued by civilized man."[128]

While Marshall relied on this "right to be let alone" to protect citizens from the state entering their homes to inquire into the contents of their libraries, it was never relied upon by the Court to protect us from the state entering our minds to inquire into thoughts and beliefs. The privacy of one's home may be protected by the Fourth Amendment; the privacy of one's mind received no such protection when the power of the state was used to coerce HUAC witnesses to reveal thoughts, beliefs, and associations. The Fourth Amendment in the Bill of Rights provides for "[t]he right of the people to be secure in their persons, houses, papers, and effects, against unreasonable searches and seizures . . ." One crucial rationale for such an amendment is that it protects the privacy and dignity of the individual. The state cannot willy-nilly invade the citizen's home and privacy; individual autonomy, individual dignity must be protected.

Yet in mid-twentieth-century America, while houses, papers, and effects may have been protected against unreasonable searches and seizures, the dignity of HUAC witnesses and of those who refused to sign the loyalty oaths received no protection when the power of the state was used to invade their minds. It is not unreasonable to argue that the privacy of our minds needed to be protected from state intrusions as much as, if not more than, our houses, papers, and effects. Protecting the contents of one's home library cannot be significantly more important than protecting the contents of one's mind when the state comes searching for political beliefs and thoughts.

In the second century A.D., the Greek philosopher Epictetus, critical of state inquiries into people's thoughts, wrote:

"Tell your secrets." I say not a word; for this is under my control. "But I will fetter you." What is that you say, man? Fetter me? My leg you will fetter, but my moral purpose not even Zeus himself has power to overcome. "I will throw you into prison." My paltry body, rather! "I will behead you." Well, when did I ever tell you that mine was the only neck that could not be severed?[129]

Nineteen centuries later, Louis Brandeis and Samuel Warren recognized the evils of coerced speech and its effects on freedom of thought; they wrote the following in their now-famous 1890 *Harvard Law Review* article, "The Right of Privacy": "The common law secures to each individual the right of determining, ordinarily, to what extent his thoughts, sentiments, and emotions shall be communicated to others. . . . Under our system of government, he can never be compelled to express them (except when upon the witness-stand); and even if he has chosen to give them expression, he generally retains the power to fix the limits of the publicity which shall be given them."[130] In a footnote relating to the above passage, Brandeis and Warren cite English jurist Yates, who had written in 1769: "It is certain every man has a right to keep his own sentiments, if he pleases. He has certainly a right to judge whether he will make them public, or commit them only to the sight of his friends."[131]

But in mid-twentieth-century America, citizens were coerced by the state to "tell their secrets," compelled to express their thoughts, beliefs, and sentiments. As we have noted previously, while academic freedom and freedom of association may have provided constitutional protection to some who refused to answer un-American activities committee inquiries (e.g., Sweezy) and who refused to take the loyalty oaths (e.g., Keyishian), those freedoms did not protect many others, who were either sentenced to jail or blacklisted. Freedom of speech did not protect the Hollywood Ten or Professor Horace Davis or Dr. Edward Barsky. Freedom of association did not protect attorney Raphael Konigsberg or college instructor Lloyd Barenblatt or clergyman Willard Uphaus. There was no freedom not to speak to protect Carl Braden, George Anastaplo, Frank Wilkinson, Pete Seeger, Lester Cole, Ring Lardner, Jr., Dalton Trumbo, Alvah Bessie, John Howard Lawson, Edward Dmytryk, Robert Adrian Scott, Herbert Biberman, Albert Malz, Samuel Ornitz, and Dashiell Hammett. To increase the likelihood that a freedom not to speak will be available when the next inquisition comes, and come it will, some changes have to take place in our thinking about why and how this freedom needs to be protected.

The courts must more seriously take into consideration the protection of the individual forced to participate in state-sponsored degradation ceremonies and humiliation rituals and acts of contrition imposed on "unfriendly" witnesses appearing before local and federal inquisitional committees. As Justice Brennan has argued, the Constitution is there to protect human dignity. It was Martin Luther King, Jr., who validly argued in his *Letter from Birmingham Jail:* "Any law that degrades human personality is unjust. All segregation statutes are unjust because segregation distorts the soul and damages the personality."[132] The conclusion that "all segregation statutes are unjust" follows from the two premises. Similarly, all state-sponsored actions and rituals that deny the citizen's dignity are unjust. HUAC-type questions and mandatory loyalty oaths are state actions and rituals that deny human dignity. Therefore, the HUAC-type questions and the oaths are unjust.

The clear and present danger test, not the less-protective balancing of interests test, must be relied upon to determine whether a citizen is to be punished for refusing to answer HUAC-type questions and for refusing to sign state-imposed loyalty oaths and disclaimer affidavits. It is worth stating again what Justice Jackson stated in giving constitutional protection to the students of the Jehovah's Witness faith who refused to salute the flag: "It is now a commonplace that censorship or suppression of expression of opinion is tolerated by our Constitution only when the expression represents a clear and present danger of action of a kind the State is empowered to prevent and punish. It would seem that involuntary affirmation could be commanded only on even more immediate and urgent grounds than silence.... To sustain the compulsory flag salute we are required to say that a Bill of Rights which guards the individual's right to speak his own mind, left it open to public authorities to compel him to utter what is not in his mind."

The "freedom to refrain from speaking" advanced in *Barnette*, *Wooley*, and *Torcaso* and in the "commercial speech" cases of *Miami Herald Publishing Co.*, *Pacific Gas & Electric*, and *Riley* must be consistently applied to those who decide to refrain from speaking about their political beliefs and associations when commanded to speak by the state. In arguing that PG & E could not be required to include with its bills a message with which it disagreed, the United States Supreme Court, citing *Wooley*, declared: "For corporations as for individuals, the choice to speak includes within it the choice of what not to say." That choice of what not to say must also be made available to those who appear before the various governmental committees demanding revelations of political beliefs and associations. The person who refuses to speak when asked to name names, to reveal political and religious beliefs, to sign a loyalty and a disclaimer affidavit deserves as much constitutional protection as a corporation, or as an individual who refuses to salute the flag or declare a belief in God.

The First, Fourth, Fifth, and Ninth Amendments in the Bill of Rights must be considered as furnishing us with a freedom not to speak that protects us from state inquiries and intrusions into our minds, beliefs, and political and religious associations. A penumbral freedom not to speak to protect the citizen against such state intrusions is just as crucial in a free society as the right of privacy, which was defined as a penumbral right in *Griswold v. Connecticut* (1965). Reversing the convictions of the directors of the Planned Parenthood League of Connecticut, who had been convicted of violating a Connecticut statute that made it a crime to use "any drug, medicinal article or instrument" for birth control, Justice Douglas, delivering the opinion of the Court, argued for a right to privacy based on several amendments of the Bill of Rights:

> The foregoing cases [dealing with the right to educate one's children as one chooses and the right of association] suggest that specific guarantees in the Bill of Rights have penumbras, formed by emanations from those guarantees that help give them life and substance. Various guarantees create zones of privacy. The right of association contained in the penumbra of the First Amendment is one, as we have seen. The Third Amendment in its prohibition against quartering of soldiers "in any house" in time of peace without consent of the owner is another facet of that privacy. The Fourth Amendment explicitly affirms the "right of the people to be secure in their persons, houses, papers and effects, against unreasonable searches and seizures." The Fifth Amendment in its Self-Incrimination Clause enables the citizen to create a zone of privacy which government may not force him to surrender to his detriment. The Ninth Amendment provides: "The enumeration in the Constitution, of certain rights, shall not be construed to deny or disparage others retained by the people."[133]

Underlying the First, Fourth, and Fifth Amendments is the promise of preserving the dignity and integrity of the individual by prohibiting the state from compelling citizens to reveal what they wish to remain their own.

There was no freedom not to speak when Roman authorities demanded that Polycarp "revile Christ," or when King Henry VIII demanded that Sir Thomas More sign the loyalty oath, or when the church demanded that Galileo recant and name names, or when colonial authorities demanded rejection of the idea of transubstantiation, or when HUAC demanded that the Hollywood Ten name names and reveal political affiliations. The twenty-first century will bring its own inquisitions, whether political or religious. The question that remains is whether the future Polycarp, More, Galileo, or Hollywood Ten will have a freedom not to speak.

Notes

NOTES TO THE INTRODUCTION

1. *Barsky v. United States,* 167 F. 2d 241, 254 (1948).

2. *Barsky v. United States,* 334 U.S. 843 (1948).

3. *New York Times,* June 15, 1948 :1.

4. House of Representatives, Hearings Before the Committee on Un-American Activities, *Investigation of the Un-American Propaganda Activities in the United States,* 80th Cong., 1st sess., March 21, 1947, 31.

5. *New York Times,* October 16, 1947: 5.

6. *United States v. Josephson,* 165 F. 2d 82, 93 (1948).

7. *Ibid.*

8. Charles Curtis, "Wringing the Bill of Rights," *Pacific Spectator* 2 (Autumn 1948), 368–69.

9. Leo Pfeffer, *The Liberties of an American* (Boston: Beacon Press, 1957), 96.

10. Milton Konvitz, *Fundamental Liberties of a Free People* (Ithaca: Cornell University Press, 1957), 119.

11. *American Communications Ass'n v. Douds,* 339 U.S. 382, 446 (1950).

12. Lewis Asper, "The Long and Unhappy History of Loyalty Testing in Maryland," *American Journal of Legal History* (April 13, 1969), 109.

13. *Ibid.*

14. Bernard Weintraub, "The Blacklist Era Won't Fade to Black," *New York Times,* October 5, 1997: WK5.

15. F. Sherwood Taylor, *Galileo and the Freedom of Thought* (London: Watts and Co., 1938), 170–71.

16. Thomas I. Emerson, *The System of Freedom of Expression* (New York: Vintage Books, 1970), 30.

17. Alan Barth, *The Rights of Free Men* (New York: Alfred Knopf, 1984), 54, 63.

18. Eric Bentley, *Thirty Years of Treason* (New York: Viking Press, 1971), 333.

19. *Ibid.,* 337.

20. *Miller v. United States*, 259 F. 2d 187 (1948).

21. Bentley, 822.

22. Vern Countryman, *Un-American Activities in the State of Washington: The Work of the Canwell Committee* (Ithaca: Cornell University Press, 1951), 101–102.

23. *Ibid.*, 114.

24. Victor Navasky, *Naming Names* (New York: Viking Press, 1986), xii.

25. Albert Einstein, "Letter," *New York Times*, June 12, 1953: 9.

26. House of Representatives, Hearings Before the Committee on Un-American Activities, *Investigation of Communist Activities in the State of Michigan*, Part VI, 83d Cong., 2d Sess., May 10, 1954, 5349.

27. *Ibid.*, 5350.

28. Carl Beck, *Contempt of Congress* (New Orleans: Phauser Press, 1959), 225.

29. Navasky, 319.

30. Avishai Margalit, *The Decent Society* (Cambridge, Mass.: Harvard University Press, 1966), 1.

31. "Blacklist: Memories of a World That Marks an Era," *New York Times*, July 31, 1994: H3.

32. *New York Times*, September 16, 1995: 18.

33. Michael Munk, "Oregon Tests Academic Freedom in (Cold) Wartime: The Reed College Trustees versus Stanley Moore," *Oregon Historical Quarterly* 97 (Fall 1996), 284.

34. *Ibid.*, 343.

35. *The Chronicle of Higher Education*, May 9, 1997: B-10.

36. Melvin Rader, *False Witness* (Seattle: University of Washington Press, 1998), 216.

37. Charles E. Porter, *Days of Shame* (New York: Coward-McCann, 1965), 7.

38. Richard Fried, *Nightmare in Red* (New York: Oxford University Press, 1990), 202.

39. Patrick McGilligan and Paul Buhle, *Tender Comrades* (New York: St. Martin's Press, 1997), 564.

40. Ron Magden, "The Schuddakoff Case, 1954–1958," *Pacific Northwest Quarterly* 89 (Winter 1997/98), 10.

NOTES TO CHAPTER 1

1. John A. O'Brien, *The Inquisition* (New York: Macmillan, 1973), 68.

2. Harold O. J. Brown, *Heresies* (New York: Doubleday and Co., 1984), 277–78.

3. Henry Charles Lea, *A History of the Inquisition in the Middle Ages* (New York: Macmillan, 1911), iii, 338.

4. Pliny, *Letters and Panegyricus*, trans. Betty Radice (Cambridge: Harvard University Press, 1975), ii, 286–87.

5. *Ibid.*, 287.

6. *Ibid.*, 289.

7. *Ibid.*, 293.

8. J. Stevenson (ed.), *The New Eusebius* (London: S. P. C. K., 1957), 21–22.

9. *Ibid.*, 29–30.

10. Frank Magill (ed.), *Great Events from History: Ancient and Medieval Series* (Englewood Cliffs, N.J.: Salem Press, 1972), ii, 812.

11. Stevenson, 260–61.

12. *Ibid.*, 287.

13. Marta Sordi, *The Christians and the Roman Empire*, trans. Annabel Bedini (Norman, Okla.: University of Oklahoma Press, 1986), 128.

14. Sidney Ehler and John B. Morrall (trans. and eds.), *Church and State Through the Centuries* (Westminster, Md.: Newman Press, 1954), 5.

15. Edward Peters, *Heresy and Authority in Medieval Europe* (Philadelphia: University of Pennsylvania Press, 1980), 25.

16. Clyde Pharr (trans.), *The Theodosian Code* (Princeton: Princeton University Press, 1952), 440.

17. *Ibid.*, 457.

18. Virginia Burrus, *The Making of a Heretic* (Berkeley: University of California Press, 1995), 97.

19. Joseph Strayer (ed.), *Dictionary of the Middle Ages* (New York: Scribner, 1982–89), x, 129.

20. *Encyclopaedia Britannica* (Chicago: Encyclopaedia Britannica, 1968), xviii, 555.

21. Burrus, 2.

22. Burrus, 3.

23. Pharr, 462.

24. R. I. Moore, *The Birth of Popular Heresy* (New York: St. Martin's Press, 1975), 83.

25. Moore, 84. See also R. I. Moore, "Heresy as Disease," in W. Laurdaux and D. Verhelst (eds.), *The Concept of Heresy in the Middle Ages* (Leuven: Leuven University Press, 1976), 1–11.

26. Moore, 90.

27. Moore, 89.

28. Moore, 12.

29. Moore, 14–15.

30. Moore, 19.

31. Moore, 20–21.

32. Henry Charles Lea, *A History of the Inquisition of the Middle Ages* (New York: Harbor Press, 1955), 87–88.

33. Frederick II, *Liber Augustalis*, trans. James M. Powell (Syracuse, N.Y.: Syracuse University Press, 1971), 7–9.

34. Soe Oldenbourg, *Massacre at Montsegur*, trans. Peter Green (New York: Pantheon Books, 1961), 378.

35. *New Catholic Encyclopedia* (New York: McGraw-Hill Book Co., 1967), vii, 536.

36. Jean Plaidy, *The Spanish Inquisition* (New York: Citadel Press, 1969), 18.

37. *New Catholic Encyclopedia*, vii, 536.

38. G. G. Coulton, *Inquisition and Liberty* (London: William Heinemann, 1938), 113.

39. Malcolm Lambert, *Medieval Heresy*, 2nd ed. (Oxford: Blackwell, 1992), 100.

40. Henry Charles Lea, *The Inquisition of the Middle Ages* (New York: Citadel Press, 1954), 96.

41. Gordon Leff, *Heresy in the Later Middle Ages* (New York: Barnes and Noble, 1967), 1.

42. Edward Peters, *Inquisition* (New York: Free Press, 1988), 60.

43. Lea, *Inquisition of the Middle Ages*, 108–10.

44. A. L. Maycock, *The Inquisition* (New York: Harper and Brothers, 1927), 157.

45. A. R. Myers (ed.), *English Historical Documents: 1327–1485* (London: Eyre and Spottiswood, 1969), 851.

46. R. Trevor Davies, *Documents Illustrating the History of Civilization in Medieval England* (London: Methuen and Co., 1926), 266–67.

47. John Foxe, *The Church Historians of England* (London: Seeleys, 1853), Part 1, 228.

48. *Ibid.*, 235–38.

49. Lambert, 316.

50. David Christie-Murray, *A History of Heresy* (Oxford: Oxford University Press, 1991), 117.

51. Matthew Spinka, *John Hus: A Biography* (Princeton: Princeton University Press, 1968), 287.

52. Jasper Ridley, *Thomas Cranmer* (Oxford: Clarendon Press, 1962), 392.

53. G. W. Bromiley, *Thomas Cranmer: Archbishop and Martyr* (London: Church Book Room Press, 1956), 117.

54. Paul Henri Michel, *The Cosmology of Giordano Bruno*, trans. R. E. W. Maddison (Paris: Hermann, 1973), 19.

55. Arthur D. Imerti, *The Expulsion of the Triumphant Beast: Giordano Bruno* (New Brunswick, N.J.: Rutgers University Press, 1964), 63.

56. Karl von Gebler, *Galileo Galilei and the Roman Curia*, trans. Jane Sturge (London: C. Kegan Paul and Co., 1879), 233.

57. *Ibid.*, 243.

58. Henry C. Lucas, *The Renaissance and the Reformation* (New York: Harper and Brothers, 1934), 358.

59. Henry Charles Lea, *Materials Toward a History of Witchcraft*, ed. Arthur Howland (New York: Thomas Yoseloff, 1957), xxix.

60. Walter Wakefield and Austin Evans, *Heresies of the High Middle Ages* (New York: Columbia University Press, 1969), 250.

61. Alan Kors and Edward Peters, *Witchcraft in Europe: 1100–1700* (Philadelphia: University of Pennsylvania Press, 1972), 79.

62. Arthur C. Howland (ed.), *Materials Toward a History of Witchcraft* (New York: Thomas Yoseloff, 1957), i, 207.

63. Jeffrey B. Russell, *Witchcraft in the Middle Ages* (Ithaca: Cornell University Press, 1972), 174.

64. Kors and Peters, 105–10.

65. Russell, 232.

66. Russell, 114.

67. *Ibid.*

68. Kors and Peters, 120.

69. *Ibid.*, 120–21.

70. *Ibid.*

71. *Ibid.*, 123–24.

72. Lea, *Materials Toward a History of Witchcraft*, 981–82.

73. Joseph Klaits, *Servants of Satan* (Bloomington: Indiana University Press, 1985), 52.

74. John Demos, *Entertaining Satan* (Oxford: Oxford University Press, 1983), 62.

75. Lea, *Materials Toward a History of Witchcraft*, 310–11.

76. Wakefield and Evans, 250.

77. Charles A. Hoyt, *Witchcraft* (Carbondale, Ill.: Southern Illinois University Press, 1981), 56.

78. Brian Levack, *The Witch-Hunt in Early Modern Europe*, 2nd ed. (London: Longman, 1995), 1.

79. Lea, *Materials Toward a History of Witchcraft*, i, 330.

80. *Ibid.*, 410.

81. *Ibid.*, ii, 591.

82. *Ibid.*, 944.

83. Henry Boguet, *An Examen of Witches*, trans. E. Allen Ashwin (Suffolk: Richard Clay and Sons, 1929), 90.

84. John Foxe, *The Church Historians of England* (London: Seeleys, 1855), iii, Part 2, 591.

85. Carol F. Karlsen, *The Devil in the Shape of a Woman* (New York: W. W. Norton and Co., 1987), 47.

86. Moore, 10–11.

NOTES TO CHAPTER 2

1. *Everson v. Board of Education*, 330 U.S. 1, 9 (1947).

2. *Ibid.*, 10.

3. *Torcaso v. Watkins*, 367 U.S. 488, 490 (1961).

4. Leonard Levy, *The Establishment Clause: Religion and the First Amendment*, 2nd ed. (Chapel Hill: University of North Carolina Press, 1994), 5.

5. Sanford H. Cobb, *The Rise of Religious Liberty in America* (New York: Macmillan Co., 1902), 176.

6. H. Shelton Smith, Robert T. Handy, and Lefferts A. Loetscher, *American Christianity: An Historical Interpretation with Representative Documents* (New York: Charles Scribner's Sons, 1960), i, 42–43.

7. *Ibid.*, 43.

8. Gustavus Meyers, *History of Bigotry in the United States* (New York: Random House, 1943), 48.

9. *Ibid.*, 44.

10. Thomas Wertenbaker, *The Puritan Oligarchy* (New York: Charles Scribner's Sons, 1947), 217.

11. Smith, Handy, and Loetscher, 121.

12. *Ibid.*, 122.

13. *Ibid.*

14. Albert E. McKinley, *The Suffrage Franchise in the Thirteen English Colonies in America* (Philadelphia: Publications of University of Pennsylvania, 1905), 35.

15. *Ibid.*, 310.

16. *Ibid.*, 74.

17. Harold Hyman, *To Try Men's Souls* (Berkeley: University of California Press, 1959), 31.

18. Sanford H. Cobb, *The Rise of Religious Liberty in America* (New York: Macmillan Co., 1902), 216.

19. Wertenbacker, 213.

20. *Ibid.*, 213–14.

21. Quoted in Carolina Robbins, "Selden's Pills: State Oaths in England," *Huntington Library Quarterly* 35 (August 1972), 303.

22. Carl Stephenson and Frederick Marcham (eds.), *Sources of English Constitutional History* (New York: Harper and Brothers, 1937), 345.

23. G. W. Prothero, *Statutes and Constitutional Documents of Elizabeth and James I* (Oxford: Clarendon Press, 1898), 258.

24. Danby Pickering (ed.), *Statutes at Large from the Twelfth Year of Charles II to the Last Year of King James II* (London: Cambridge, 1763), 392.

25. *Ibid.*, 390.

26. Stephenson and Marcham, 545.

27. Pickering, 33.

28. Charles G. Robertson, *Select Statutes, Cases and Documents* (London: Methuen and Co., 1947), 87.

29. William Penn and Richard Richardson, *A Treatise on Oaths* (Ann Arbor: University Microfilms, 1977), 14.

30. *Ibid.*, 28.

31. *Ibid.*, 30.

32. *Ibid.*, 34.

33. *Ibid.*, 35.

34. *Ibid.*, 37.

35. *Ibid.*, 39.

36. *Ibid.*, 40.

37. *Ibid.*, 41.

38. *Ibid.*

39. *Ibid.*, 50.

40. William Penn, *Reasons Why the Oaths Should not be Made a Part of the Test to Protestant Dissenters* (Ann Arbor: University Microfilms, 1984), 13.

41. Hyman, 85.

42. Arthur Mekeel, *The Relation of the Quakers to the American Revolution* (Washington, D.C.: University Press of America, 1979), 247.

43. Hyman, 89.

44. *Ibid.*, 92.

45. *Ibid.*, 93–94.

46. Margaret Bacon, *The Quiet Rebels* (New York: Basic Books, 1969), 73.

47. Rufus M. Jones, *The Quakers in the American Colonies* (London: Macmillan and Co., 1911), 569.

48. Jonathan Eliot, *Debates* (Philadelphia :J. B. Lippincott Co.), ii, 148.

49. *Ibid.*, 118–119.

50. Edward F. Humphrey, *Nationalism and Religion in America* (New York: Russell and Russell, 1965), 463–65.

51. Eliot, v, 446.

52. *Ibid.*, 498.

53. Harold Hyman, *The Era of the Oath* (Philadelphia: University of Pennsylvania Press, 1954), Preface.

54. Lewis Asper, "The Long and Unhappy History of Loyalty Testing in Maryland," *American Journal of Legal History* 13 (April 1969), 102–103.

55. Hyman, *Era of the Oath*, 157–58.

56. *Ibid.*, 158.

57. *Ibid.*, 20.

58. *Ibid.*, 159.

59. *Cummings v. Missouri*, 71 U.S. 277, 279–80 (1867).

60. *Ibid.*, 280–81.

61. *Ibid.*, 281.

62. Thomas Marclay, "The Liberal Republican Movement in Missouri: 1865–1871" (Columbia, Missouri: State Historical Society of Missouri, 1926), 55.

63. *Ibid.*, 59.

64. *Cummings v. Missouri*, 317.

65. *Ibid.*, 318.

66. *Ibid.*, 320.

67. *Ibid.*, 327.

68. *Ibid.*, 328.

69. *Ibid.*, 330.

70. *Ex parte Garland*, 71 U.S. 333 (1867).

71. *Ibid.*, 335.

72. *Ibid.*, 375.

73. *Ibid.*

74. *Ibid.*, 376.

75. *Ibid.*, 376–77.

76. *Ibid.*, 377.

77. *Ibid.*

78. William Russ, "The Lawyer's Test Oath During Reconstruction," *Mississippi Law Journal* 10 (December 1937), 154.

79. *Ibid.*, 167.

80. Hyman, *Era of the Oath*, 151.

81. *Ibid.*, 156.

82. Asper, 109.

83. *Congressional Globe*, 38th Cong., 2d Sess., December 22, 1864, 109.

84. Ralph Brown, *Loyalty and Security* (New Haven: Yale University Press, 1958), 181.

NOTES TO CHAPTER 3

1. Ralph Brown, *Loyalty and Security* (New Haven: Yale University Press, 1958), 111.

2. Harold Hyman, *To Try Men's Souls* (Berkeley: University of California Press, 1959), 338.

3. William Prendegast, "State Legislatures and Communism: The Current Scene," *American Political Science Review* 44 (September 1950), 556.

4. Brown, 92.

5. *Ibid.*, 181.

6. Thomas I. Emerson, *The System of Freedom of Expression* (New York: Vintage Press, 1970), 206.

7. *Ibid.*, 207.

8. *Speiser v. Randall*, 357 U.S. 513, 531 (1958).

9. *American Communications Ass'n v. Douds*, 339 U.S. 382, 386 (1950).

10. *Garner v. Los Angeles Board.* 341 U.S. 716, 718–19 (1951).

11. *Ibid.*

12. See *Congressional Digest*, 39 (April 1960) for arguments pro and con.

13. *Cramp v. Board of Public Instruction*, 368 U.S. 278, 279 (1961).

14. *Ibid.*, 288.

15. *Garner v. Board of Public Works*, 220 P. 2d 958, 995 (1950).

16. *Lawson v. United States*, 176 F. 2d 49 (1949).

17. *Garner v. Board of Public Works*, 995.

18. *Garner v. Los Angeles Board*, 720.

19. *Ibid.*, 721.

20. *Ibid.*, 722.

21. *Ibid.*, 735.

22. *Ibid.*, 736.

23. *Wieman v. Updegraff*, 344 U.S. 183, 184 (1952).

24. *Board of Regents v. Updegraff*, 237 P. 2d 131, 137 (1951).

25. *Wieman v. Updegraff*, 188.

26. *Ibid.*, 190.

27. *Ibid.*

28. *Ibid.*, 191.

29. *Ibid.*, 193.

30. *Ibid.*, 195.

31. *Gerende v. Election Board*, 341 U.S. 56 (1951).

32. *Adler v. Board of Education*, 342 U.S. 485, 493 (1952).

33. *Ibid.*, 492.

34. *Ibid.*, 493.

35. *Ibid.*, 497.

36. *Ibid.*, 509.

37. *Ibid.*, 510.

38. *Keyishian v. Board of Regents*, 385 U.S. 589, 605 (1967).

39. *Ibid.*, 603.

40. *Lerner v. Casey*, 357 U.S. 468, 472 (1958).

41. *Beilan v. Board of Education*, 357 U.S. 399, 400–401 (1958).

42. *Ibid.*, 404.

43. *Ibid.*, 406.

44. *Ibid.*, 409.

45. *Ibid.*, 412–13.

46. *Ibid.*, 416.

47. *Ibid.*, 418.

48. *Speiser v. Randall,* 357 U.S. 513 (1958) and *First Unitarian Church v. County of Los Angeles,* 357 U.S. 545 (1958).

49. *Speiser v. Randall,* 515.

50. *Ibid.*, 518.

51. *Ibid.*, 528–29.

52. *Ibid.*, 529.

53. *Ibid.*, 532.

54. *Ibid.*, 534.

55. *Ibid.*, 536.

56. *First Unitarian Church v. County of Los Angeles,* 547.

57. *Ibid.*

58. *Ibid.*, 548.

59. *Shelton v. McKinley,* 174 F. Supp. 351, 353 (1959).

60. *Shelton v. Tucker,* 364 U.S. 479, 483 (1960).

61. *Shelton v. McKinley,* 356.

62. *Shelton v. Tucker,* 485.

63. *Ibid.*, 485–86.

64. *Ibid.*, 488.

65. *Ibid.*, 490.

66. *Cramp v. Board of Instruction,* 368 U.S. 278, 279 (1961).

67. *Cramp v. Board of Public Instruction of Orange Co.,* 125 So. 2d 554, 558 (1960).

68. *Cramp v. Board of Instruction,* 286.

69. *Ibid.*

70. *Ibid.*, 288.

71. *Torcaso v. Watkins,* 162 A. 2d 438, 440 (1960).

72. *Ibid.*, 442.

73. *Ibid.*, 443.

74. *Ibid.*

75. *Torcaso v. Watkins,* 367 U.S. 488, 495 (1961).

76. *Ibid.*, 495–96.

77. *Adler v. Board of Education,* 492.

78. *Baggett v. Bullitt,* 377 U.S. 360, 361–62 (1964).

79. *Ibid.*, 365.

80. *Ibid.*, 362.

81. *Baggett v. Bullitt,* 215 F. Supp. 439, 447 (1963).

82. *Ibid.*, 448.
83. *Ibid.*, 449.
84. *Baggett v. Bullitt*, 377 U.S. 360, 366 (1964).
85. *Ibid.*, 367.
86. *Ibid.*
87. *Ibid.*, 368.
88. *Ibid.*, 370.
89. *Ibid.*, 371.
90. *Ibid.*, 380.
91. *Elfbrandt v. Russell*, 384 U.S. 11, 12 (1966).
92. *Ibid.*, 13.
93. *Ibid.*
94. *Elfbrandt v. Russell*, 397 P. 2d 944, 948 (1964).
95. *Ibid.*, 949.
96. *Elfbrandt v. Russell*, 384 U.S. 11, 16 (1966).
97. *Ibid.*, 19.
98. *Keyishian v. Board of Regents*, 595.
99. *Ibid.*, 596.
100. *Ibid.*
101. *Ibid.*, 601.
102. *Ibid.*, 604.
103. *Ibid.*, 605.
104. *Ibid.*, 606.
105. *Ibid.*
106. *Ibid.*, 608–609.
107. *Ibid.* 620.
108. *Ibid.*, 622.
109. *Ibid.*, 625.
110. *Ibid.*, 628.
111. *Whitehill v. Elkins*, 389 U.S. 54, 55–56 (1967).
112. *Ibid.*, 56.
113. *Ibid.*, 57.
114. *Ibid.*, 59.
115. *Ibid.*, 59–60.
116. *Ibid.*, 62.
117. *Baird v. State Bar of Arizona*, 401 U.S. 1, 4 (1971).
118. *Ibid.*, 3.
119. See *Konigsberg v. State Bar of California*, 366 U.S. 36 (1961) and *In re Anastaplo*, 366 U.S. 82 (1961).
120. *Baird v. State Bar of Arizona*, 3.
121. *Ibid.*, 4.
122. *Ibid.*, 5.

123. *Ibid.*, 6–7.
124. *Ibid.*, 7.
125. *Ibid.*, 7–8.
126. *In re Stolar*, 401 U.S. 23, 27 (1971).
127. *Ibid.*, 26.
128. *Ibid.*, 29.
129. *Ibid.*, 30.
130. *Ibid.*, 31.
131. *Law Students Research Council v. Wadmond*, 401 U.S. 154, 164–65 (1971).
132. *Ibid.*, 165–66.
133. *Ibid.*, 166.
134. *Ibid.*, 174–75.
135. *Ibid.*, 181.
136. *Ibid.*, 198.
137. *Heckler v. Shepard*, 243 F. Supp. 841 (1965).
138. *Georgia Conf. Amer. Ass'n of Univ. Prof. v. Bd. of Regents*, 246 F. Supp. 553 (1965).
139. *Brush v. State Bd. of Higher Ed.*, 422 P. 2d 266 (1966).
140. *Gallagher v. Smiley*, 270 F. Supp. 86 (1967).
141. *Opinion of the Justices*, 228 A. 2d 165 (1967).
142. *Myers v. Freedom Newspapers, Inc.*, 274 F. Supp. 93 (1967).
143. *Ehrenreich v. Londerholm*, 273 F. Supp. 178 (1967).
144. *Haskett v. Washington*, 294 F. Supp. 912 (1968).
145. *Thalberg v. Bd. of Trustees of Univ. of Illinois*, 309 F. Supp. 630 (1969).
146. *Connell v. Higginbotham*, 305 F. Supp. 445 (1969).
147. *MacKay v. Rafferty*, 321 F. Supp. 1177 (1970).
148. *Haining v. Roberts*, 320 F. Supp. 1054 (1970).
149. *Pockman v. Leonard*, 240 P. 2d 267, 273 (1952).
150. *Ibid.*
151. *Vogel v. County of Los Angeles*, 434 P. 2d 961, 966 (1967).
152. *Knight v. Bd. of Regents of Univ. of State of N.Y.*, 269 F. Supp. 339, 340 (1967).
153. *Ibid.*
154. *Ibid.*, 341.
155. *Ibid.*
156. *Knight v. Bd. of Regents of Univ. of State of N.Y.*, 390 U.S. 36 (1968).
157. *Hosack v. Smiley*, 276 F. Supp. 876, 878 (1967).
158. *Ibid.*
159. *Ibid.*, 879.
160. *Ibid.*, 880.

161. *Hosack v. Smiley*, 390 U.S. 744 (1968).

162. *Ohlson v. Phillips*, 304 F. Supp. 1152, 1153 (1969).

163. *Ibid.*, 1154–55.

164. *Ohlson v. Phillips*, 397 U.S. 317 (1970).

165. *Biklen v. Board of Education*, 333 F. Supp. 902, 903–904 (1971).

166. *Ibid.*, 904.

167. *Ibid.*, 905.

168. *Ibid.*

169. *Ibid.*, 906.

170. *Ibid.*, 909.

171. *Biklen v. Board of Education*, 406 U.S. 95 (1972).

172. *Cole v. Richardson*, 405 U.S. 676, 677 (1972).

173. *Richardson v. Cole*, 300 F. Supp. 1321, 1322 (1969)

174. *Ibid.*

175. *Ibid.*, 1323.

176. *Cole v. Richardson*, 683.

177. *Ibid.*, 684.

178. *Ibid.*, 686.

179. *Ibid.*, 692–93.

180. *Ibid.*, 695.

181. *Ibid.*, 697.

182. Clark Byse, "A Report on the Pennsylvania Loyalty Act," *University of Pennsylvania Law Review* 101 (January 1953), 483.

183. Albert Einstein, "Letter," *New York Times*, June 12, 1953: 9.

184. Lionel S. Lewis, *Cold War on Campus* (New Brunswick: Transaction Books, 197, 1988).

185. Harry Kalven, Jr., *A Worthy Tradition* (New York: Harper and Row, 1988), 341.

186. *American Communications Ass'n v. Douds*, 434–35.

187. E. Joshua Rosenkranz and Bernard Schwartz, *Reason and Passion: Justice Brennan's Enduring Influence* (New York: W. W. Norton and Co., 1997), 18.

188. *Ibid.*

189. *Ibid.*, 19.

NOTES TO CHAPTER 4

1. David Manwaring, *Render Unto Caesar: The Flag Salute Controversy* (Chicago: University of Chicago Press, 1962), 3.

2. *Ibid.*

3. *Ibid.*

4. *Gobitis v. Minersville School Dist.*, 24 F. Supp. 271, 272 (1938).

5. *Gobitis v. Minersville School Dist.*, 21 F. Supp. 581, 583 (1937).
6. *Ibid.*, 587.
7. Manwaring, 98.
8. *Gobitis v. Minersville School Dist.*, 24 F. Supp. 271, 274 (1938).
9. *Ibid.*
10. Manwaring, 106.
11. *Minersville School Dist. v. Gobitis*, 108 F. 2d 683 (1939).
12. *Ibid.*
13. *Ibid.*, 689.
14. *Ibid.*, 692.
15. *Ibid.*
16. *Ibid.*, 693.
17. Manwaring, 164.
18. See Manwaring, Chapter 8.
19. *Gobitis v. Minersville School Dist.*, 310 U.S. 586, 694 (1940).
20. *Ibid.*, 595.
21. *Ibid.*, 600.
22. *Ibid.*, 603–604.
23. *Ibid.*, 607.
24. *Ibid.*, 591–92.
25. *Ibid.*, 596.
26. *Ibid.*, 600.
27. *Ibid.*, 604.
28. *Ibid.*, 606.
29. Robert Cushman, "Constitutional Law in 1939–1940," *American Political Science Review* 35 (April 1941), 271.
30. Manwaring, 187–88.
31. *Ibid.*, 187.
32. *Jones v. City of Opelika*, 316 U.S. 584, 624 (1942).
33. *State v. Smith*, 127 P. 2d 518, 520 (1942).
34. *Ibid.*, 521.
35. *West Virginia State Board of Ed. v. Barnette*, 319 U.S. 624, 626 (1943).
36. *Barnette v. West Virginia Board of Ed.*, 47 F. Supp. 251, 252 (1942).
37. *Ibid.*, 253.
38. *Ibid.*
39. *Ibid.*, 254.
40. *Ibid.*
41. *Ibid.*
42. *Ibid.*, 255.
43. *State ex rel. Bolling v. Superior Court*, 16 Wash. 2d 373 (1943).
44. *Ibid.*, 380.
45. *Ibid.*, 382.

46. *Ibid.*, 387.

47. *Ibid.*

48. *West Virginia State Board of Ed. v. Barnette*, 314 U.S. 624 (1943).

49. Peter Irons, *The Courage of Their Convictions* (New York: Penguin Books, 1990), 33.

50. See Manwaring, Chapter XI, for summary of reactions.

51. Thomas I. Emerson, *The System of Freedom of Expression* (New York: Vintage Books, 1970), 29.

52. *West Virginia State Board of Ed. v. Barnette*, 642.

53. *Ibid.*, 630.

54. *Ibid.*, 631.

55. *Ibid.*, 633.

56. *Ibid.*

57. *Ibid.*, 634.

58. *Ibid.*, 635.

59. *Ibid.*, 637.

60. *Ibid.*, 638.

61. *Ibid.*, 640.

62. *Ibid.*, 641.

63. Bruce Ackerman, "Liberating Abstraction," in Geoffrey Stone, Richard Epstein, and Cass Sustein (eds.), *The Bill of Rights in the Modern State* (Chicago: University of Chicago Press, 1992), 320.

64. Rodney A. Smolia, *Free Speech in an Open Society* (New York: Vintage Books, 1992), 76.

65. Henry J. Abraham, *Freedom and the Court* (New York: Oxford University Press, 1972), 232.

66. Henry J. Abraham, *Freedom and the Court*, 4th ed. (New York: Oxford University Press, 1982), 243–44.

67. Franklyn Haiman, *Speech and Law in a Free Society* (Chicago: University of Chicago Press, 1981), 346.

68. Emerson, 29.

69. Carl Beck, *Contempt of Congress* (New Orleans: Hauser Press, 1959), 41.

70. *Ibid.*, 14.

71. Ralph S. Brown, *Loyalty and Security* (New Haven: Yale University Press, 1958), 92.

72. *Ibid.*, 181.

73. *American Communications Ass'n v. Douds*, 339 U.S. 382, 397 (1950).

74. *Ibid.*, 394.

75. *Ibid.*, 445.

76. *Ibid.*, 438.

77. *Ibid.*, 443.

78. *Ibid.*, 446.

79. *Ibid.*, 447.

80. *Congressional Record*, 80th Cong., 1st sess., February 18, 1947, 1130.

81. *Ibid.*

82. Lawson's statement and other Hollywood Ten opening statements are reprinted in Robert Vaughn, *Only Victims* (New York: Limelight Editions, 1996), 327–46.

83. House of Representatives, Hearings Before the Committee on Un-American Activities, *Hearing Regarding the Communist Infiltration of the Motion-Picture Industry*, 80th Cong., 1st sess., 1947, 366.

84. Committee on Un-American Activities, U.S. House of Representatives, *100 Things You Should Know About Communism and Religion* (Washington, D.C., 1948).

85. *United States v. Josephson*, 165 F. 2d 82, 96 (1948).

86. Eleanor Bontecou, *The Federal Loyalty-Security Program* (Ithaca: Cornell University Press, 1963), 280.

87. Committee on Un-American Activities, House of Representatives, *Guide to Subversive Organizations and Publications*, revised (Washington, D.C., 1961), 10.

88. *Bailey v. Richardson*, 182 F. 2d 46, 66 (1950).

89. *Ibid.*, 72–73.

90. *Ibid.*, 74.

91. *Sweezy v. New Hampshire*, 354 U.S. 234, 243–44 (1957).

92. *Ibid.*, 250.

93. Eric Bentley, *Thirty Years of Treason* (New York: Viking Press, 1971), 855.

94. *Ibid.*

95. Adam Yarmolinsky, *Case Studies in Personnel Security* (Westport, Conn.: Greenwood Press, 1955), 85.

96. *Ibid.*, 91.

97. *Ibid.*

98. Bentley, 688–90.

99. *United States v. Seeger*, 303 F. 2d 478 (1962).

100. Bentley, 747.

101. *Ibid.*

102. *Ibid.*, 767.

103. *Ibid.*

104. Willard Uphaus, *Commitment* (New York: McGraw-Hill Book Co., 1963), 212.

105. *Ibid.*, 150.

106. Victor Navasky, *Naming Names* (New York: Viking Press, 1986), xii.

107. Bentley, 539.

108. Lillian Hellman, *Scoundrel Time* (Boston: Little, Brown and Co., 1976), 93.

109. *Ibid.*

110. Bentley, 822.

111. *Ibid.*

112. *Ibid.*

113. House of Representatives, Hearings Before the Committee on Un-American Activities, *Communist Infiltration of Hollywood Motion-Picture Industry*, 82d Cong., 1st sess., 1951, 107.

114. Griffin Fariello, *Red Scare* (New York: Avon Books, 1995), 270.

115. *New York Times*, June 12, 1953: 9.

116. Daniel H. Pollitt, "The Fifth Amendment Plea Before Congressional Committees Investigating Subversion: Motives and Justifiable Presumptions — A Survey of 120 Witnesses," *University of Pennsylvania Law Review* 106 (June 1958), 1119.

117. *Quinn v. United States*, 349 U.S. 155, 162 (1955).

118. *Ullmann v. United States*, 350 U.S. 422, 426 (1956).

119. *Slochower v. Board of Education*, 350 U.S. 551, 557 (1956).

120. *New York Times*, March 28, 1957: 15.

121. Hearings Before the Permanent Subcommittee on Investigations of the Committee on Government Operations, United States Senate, 83d Cong., 1st sess., 101–102.

122. *Ibid.*, 125.

123. *New York Times*, June 22, 1953: 8.

124. Lionel S. Lewis, *Cold War on Campus* (New Brunswick: Transaction Books, 1988), 2.

125. See Vern Countryman, *Un-American Activities in the State of Washington: The Work of the Canwell Committee* (Ithaca: Cornell University Press, 1951; Ellen W. Shrecker, *No Ivory Tower* (New York: Oxford University Press, 1986); Lionel Lewis; and Melvin Rader, *False Witness* (Seattle: University of Washington Press, 1998).

126. Lewis, 160–61.

127. Schrecker, 208.

128. *Ibid.*, 212.

129. *Ibid.*, 236.

130. Fariello, 284.

131. Bentley, 718–19.

132. Navasky, 178.

133. Larry Ceplair and Steven Englund, *The Inquisition in Hollywood* (Garden City, N.J.: Anchor Press/Doubleday, 1980), 411.

134. Leonard G. Ratner, "Consequences of Exercising the Privilege Against Self-Incrimination," *University of Chicago Law Review* 24 (Spring 1957), 495.

135. Lewis, 272.

136. Pollitt, 1132–33.

137. *Ibid.*, 1137.

138. *Ballentine's Law Dictionary*, ed. William S. Anderson, 3d ed. (San Francisco: Lawyers Co-operative Publishing Co., 1969), 605.

139. Henry C. Black, *Black's Law Dictionary* (St. Paul: West Publishing Co., 1951), 908.

140. *Griffin v. California*, 380 U.S. 609, 610 (1965).

141. *Ibid.*, 614.

142. Roland H. Bainton, *Hunted Heretic* (Boston: Beacon Press, 1953), 3.

143. *Ibid.*, 209.

144. Earl M. Wilbur, *A History of Unitarianism* (Boston: Beacon Press, 1945), 169.

145. Giordano Bruno, *The Expulsion of the Triumphant Beast*, trans. Arthur D. Imerti (New Brunswick: Rutgers University Press, 1964), 64.

146. Karl von Gebler, *Galileo Galilei and the Roman Curia*, trans. Jane Sturge (London: C. Kegan Paul and Co., 1879), 243.

NOTES TO CHAPTER 5

1. Carl Beck, *Contempt of Congress* (New Orleans: Hauser Press, 1959), 129.

2. *Ibid.*, 127.

3. *United States v. Josephson*, 165 F. 2d 82, 91 (1947).

4. *Ibid.*, 88.

5. *Ibid.*, 96.

6. *Ibid.*, 95.

7. *Ibid.*, 96.

8. *Ibid.*, 97.

9. *Barsky v. United States*, 167 F. 2d 241, 250 (1948).

10. *Ibid.*, 254.

11. *Ibid.*

12. *Ibid.*, 258–59.

13. *Ibid.*, 249.

14. *Ibid.*, 250.

15. *Lawson v. United States*, 176 F. 2d 49, 50–51 (1949).

16. *Ibid.*, 52.

17. Willard Uphaus, *Commitment* (New York: McGraw-Hill Book Co., 1963), 138–39.

18. *Uphaus v. Wyman*, 360 U.S. 72, 74 (1959).

19. *Ibid.*, 155.

20. *Ibid.*, 162.

21. *Wyman v. Uphaus*, 130 A. 2d 278, 287 (1957).

22. *Uphaus v. Wyman*, 81.

23. *Ibid.*, 107–108.

24. House of Representatives, Hearings before the Committee on Un-American Activities, *Communist Methods of Infiltration (Education — Part I)* 83d Cong., 2d sess., June 28, 1954, 5807.

25. *Ibid.*, 5803.

26. *Ibid.*, 5805.

27. *Barenblatt v. United States*, 360 U.S. 109 (1959).

28. *Ibid.*, 126.

29. *Ibid.*, 134.

30. *Ibid.*, 127–28.

31. *Ibid.*, 144.

32. *Ibid.*, 154.

33. Peter Irons, *The Courage of Their Convictions* (New York: Penguin Books, 1990), 103.

34. *Ibid.*

35. *Ibid.*, 104.

36. Committee on Un-American Activities, House of Representatives, *Guide to Subversive Organizations and Publications*, revised (Washington, D.C., 1961), 69–70.

37. House of Representatives, Hearings before the Committee on Un-American Activities, *Communist Infiltration and Activities in the South*, 85th Cong., 2d sess., July 30, 1958, 2670.

38. *Ibid.*, 2673–74.

39. *Ibid.*, 2674.

40. *Braden v. United States*, 272 F. 2d 653, 660 (1959).

41. *Ibid.*, 661.

42. *Ibid.*, 662.

43. *Braden v. United States*, 365 U.S. 431, 432–33 (1961).

44. *Ibid.*, 435.

45. *Ibid.*, 444.

46. *Communist Infiltration in the South*, 2681.

47. *Ibid.*, 2584.

48. *Wilkinson v. United States*, 272 F. 2d 783, 787 (1959).

49. *Ibid.*

50. *Wilkinson v. United States*, 365 U.S. 399, 409 (1961).

51. *Ibid.*, 413–14.

52. *Ibid.*, 415.

53. *Ibid.*, 419–20.

54. *Ibid.*, 420–21.

55. *Ibid.*, 423.

56. Thomas I. Emerson, *The System of Freedom of Expression* (New York: Vintage Books, 1970), 261.

57. Dean Alfange, Jr., "Congressional Investigations and the Fickle Court," *University of Cincinnati Law Review* 30 (Spring 1961), 114.

58. William O. Douglas, *The Court Years: 1939–1975* (New York: Random House, 1980), 99.

59. House of Representatives, Hearings before the Committee on Un-American Activities, *Investigation of Communist Activities in the Chicago Area—Part III*, 83d Cong., 2d sess., April 29, 1954, 4268.

60. *Ibid.*, 4274.

61. *Ibid.*, 4275.

62. *Watkins v. United States*, 354 U.S. 178, 214 (1957).

63. *Communist Infiltration and Activities in the South*, 2669.

64. *Ibid.*, 2670.

65. *Sweezy v. New Hampshire*, 354 U.S. 234, 235 (1957).

66. *Ibid.*, 243–44.

67. *Ibid.*, 244.

68. *Ibid.*, 244–45.

69. *Ibid.*, 246–47.

70. *Ibid.*, 250.

71. *Ibid.*

72. *Ibid.*, 265.

73. *Konigsberg v. State Bar*, 366 U.S. 36, 39 (1961).

74. *Ibid.*, 44.

75. *Ibid.*, 49.

76. *Ibid.*, 50–51.

77. *Ibid.*, 70–71.

78. *Ibid.*, 80.

79. *In re Anastaplo*, 366 U.S. 82, 86 (1961).

80. *Ibid.*, 94.

81. *Ibid.*, 85.

82. *Ibid.*, 97.

83. *Ibid.*, 98.

84. *Ibid.*, 104.

85. *Ibid.*, 114.

86. Irons, 100.

87. *The American Heritage Dictionary of the English Language* (Boston: Houghton Mifflin, 1992), 1339.

88. Edward Peters, *Heresy and Authority in Medieval Europe* (Philadelphia: University of Pennsylvania Press, 1980), 201.

89. *Ibid.*

90. Henry Charles Lea, *A History of the Inquisition in the Middle Ages* (New York: Harbor Press, 1955), i, 484.

NOTES TO CHAPTER 6

1. *National Association for the Advancement of Colored People v. Alabama*, 357 U.S. 449, 462 (1958).
2. *Ibid.*, 462.
3. *Ibid.*, 460–61.
4. *Bates v. City of Little Rock*, 361 U.S. 516, 519 (1960).
5. *Ibid.*, 520.
6. *Ibid.*, 523–24.
7. *Ibid.*, 528.
8. *Shelton v. Tucker*, 364 U.S. 479, 480 (1960).
9. Thomas I. Emerson, *The System of Freedom of Expression* (New York: Vintage Books, 1970), 233.
10. *Shelton v. Tucker* 364 U.S. 479, 485–86 (1960).
11. *Ibid.*, 486.
12. *Ibid.*, 488.
13. *Gibson v. Florida Legislative Comm.*, 372 U.S. 539, 543 (1963).
14. *Ibid.*, 544.
15. *Ibid.*, 549.
16. *Ibid.*, 550.
17. *Ibid.*, 569.
18. *Ibid.*, 570.
19. *Talley v. California*, 362 U.S. 60, 61 (1960).
20. *Ibid.*, 64.
21. *Ibid.*, 65.
22. *Ibid.*
23. *Wilkinson v. United States*, 365 U.S. 399, 409 (1961).
24. *Ibid.*, 409–10.
25. *Torcaso v. Watkins*, 367 U.S. 488 (1961).
26. *Ibid.*, 495.
27. *Maynard v. Wooley*, 406 F. Supp. 1381, 1389 (1976).
28. *Wooley v. Maynard*, 430 U.S. 705, 714 (1977).
29. *Cole v. Richardson*, 405 U.S. 676, 677 (1972).
30. *Ibid.*, 688.
31. *Ibid.*, 697.
32. *Banks v. Bd. of Public Instruction of Dade County*, 314 F. Supp. 285, 295 (1970).
33. *Ibid.*, 296.

34. *State v. Lundquist*, 278 A. 2d 263, 266 (1971).

35. *Ibid.*, 274.

36. *Russo v. Central School Dist. No. 1*, 469 F. 2d. 623, 626 (1972).

37. *Ibid.*, 634.

38. *Goetz v. Ansell*, 477 F. 2d 636 (1973).

39. *Ibid.*, 638.

40. *Lipp v. Morris*, 579 F. 2d 834, 835 (1978).

41. *Ibid.*, 836.

42. *Wooley v. Maynard*, 714.

43. *West Virginia State Board of Ed. v. Barnette*, 319 U.S. 624, 633–34 (1943).

44. *Ibid.*, 645.

45. *Wooley v. Maynard*, 714.

46. *Miami Herald Pub. Co. v. Tornillo*, 418 U.S. 241, 256 (1974).

47. *Abood v. Detroit Board of Ed.*, 431 U.S. 209, 235 (1977).

48. *Pruneyard Shopping Center v. Robins*, 447 U.S. 74, 85–87 (1980).

49. *Ibid.*, 87.

50. *Ibid.*, 88.

51. *Wallace v. Jaffree*, 472 U.S. 38, 52 (1985).

52. *Ibid.*, 55.

53. *Zauderer v. Office of Disciplinary Council*, 471 U.S. 626, 651 (1985).

54. *Pacific Gas & Electric Co. v. Public Util. Comm'n.*, 475 U.S. 1, 7 (1986).

55. *Ibid.*, 16.

56. *Ibid.*

57. *Ibid.*, 32–33.

58. *Riley v. National Federation of Blind*, 487 U.S. 781, 796 (1988).

59. *Ibid.*, 797.

60. *Ibid.*

61. *Lee v. Weisman*, 505 U.S. 577, 593 (1992).

62. *Ibid.*, 596.

63. *Ibid.*, 599.

64. *Hurley v. Irish-American Gay, Lesbian and Bisexual Group of Boston, Inc.*, 515 U.S. 557, 559 (1995).

65. *Ibid.*, 573.

66. *The American Heritage Dictionary of the American Language*, 3rd ed. (Boston: Houghton Mifflin, 1992), 1114.

67. Avishai Margalit, *The Decent Society* (Cambridge: Harvard University Press, 1966), 273.

68. John Foxe, *The Church Historians of England* (London, 1855), iii, Part I, 228.

69. R. W. Chambers, *Thomas More* (Ann Arbor: University of Michigan Press, 1958), 336–37.

70. Christopher Hollis, *Thomas More* (Milwaukee: Bruce Publishing Co., 1934), 232.

71. Giorgio de Santillana, *The Crime of Galileo* (Chicago: University of Chicago Press, 1955), 256.

72. Andrew White, "A History of the Warfare of Science and Theology in Christendom," in *The Achievement of Galileo*, eds. James Brophy and Henry Paolucci (New York: Twayne, 1962), 201.

73. F. Sherwood Taylor, *Galileo and the Freedom of Thought* (London: Watts and Co., 1938), 170–71.

74. Karl von Gebler, *Galileo Galilei and the Roman Curia*, trans. Mrs. George Sturge (London: C. Kegan Paul and Co., 1879), 343.

75. Alan Barth, *The Rights of Free Men* (New York: Alfred Knopf, 1984), 54.

76. *Ibid.*, 63.

77. Eric Bentley (ed.), *Thirty Years of Treason* (New York: Viking Press, 1971), 333, 337.

78. Sterling Hayden, *Wanderer* (New York: Alfred Knopf, 1963), 378.

79. *Ibid.*, 391.

80. Victor Navasky, *Naming Names* (New York: Viking Press, 1986), xii.

81. Willard Uphaus, *Commitment* (New York: McGraw-Hill Book Co., 1963), 150.

82. See Patrick McGilligan and Paul Buhle, *Tender Comrades* (New York: St. Martin's Press, 1997), 219, 319.

83. Griffin Fariello, *Red Scare* (New York: Avon Books, 1995), 426–27.

84. Bentley, 822.

85. *Ibid.*, 790.

86. John Cogley, *Report on Blacklisting* (Fund for the Republic, Inc., 1966), 84.

87. Ring Lardner, Jr., "My Life on the Blacklist," *Saturday Evening Post*, October 14, 1951, 41–42.

88. Dalton Trumbo, *Additional Dialogue: Letters of Dalton Trumbo, 1942–1962*, ed. Helen Manfull (New York: M. Evans and Co., 1970), 372.

89. *Ibid.*, 373.

90. Henry Charles Lea, *The Inquisition in the Middle Ages* (New York: Harbor Press, 1955), i, 409–10.

91. *Ibid.*, 462.

92. *Ibid.*, 469.

93. Harry Beggs, "Loyalty Oaths, Conscience, and the Constitution," *Arizona Law Review* 5 (Spring 1964), 262–63.

94. Alexander Meiklejohn, "The Balancing of Self-Preservation Against Political Freedom," *California Law Review* 49 (March 1961), 14.

95. Peter Irons, *The Courage of Their Convictions* (New York: Penguin Books, 1990), 100.

96. *Garner v. Los Angeles Board*, 341 U.S. 716, 726–28 (1951).

97. Lillian Hellman, *Scoundrel Time* (Boston: Little, Brown and Co., 1976), 93–94.

98. Bentley, 538.

99. Alan Gewirth, "Human Dignity as the Basis of Rights," in Michael Myer and William Parent (eds.) *The Constitution of Rights* (Ithaca: Cornell University Press, 1992), 10.

100. E. Joshua Rosenkranz and Bernard Schwartz, *Reason and Passion: Justice Brennan's Enduring Influence* (New York: Norton and Co., 1997), 18.

101. *Ibid.*, 19.

102. *Ibid.*, 20–21.

103. *Furman v. Georgia*, 408 U.S. 238, 271 (1972).

104. *Ibid.*

105. *Ibid.*, 273.

106. *Ibid.*, 305.

107. *Goldberg v. Kelly*, 397 U.S. 254, 255 (1970).

108. *Ibid.*, 265.

109. Ronald Dworkin, *Life's Dominion* (New York: Vintage Books, 1994), 166–67.

110. *Ibid.*, 139.

111. *Miranda v. Arizona*, 384 U.S. 436, 457 (1965).

112. Thomas I. Emerson, *The System of Freedom of Expression* (New York: Vintage Books, 1970), 6.

113. Konvitz, 119.

114. John Locke, *A Letter Concerning Toleration* (Indianapolis: Bobbs-Merrill, 1950), 15–16.

115. *Ibid.*, 45.

116. Thomas Jefferson, "Notes on Virginia," in Philip S. Foner, ed. *Basic Writings of Thomas Jefferson* (New York: Willey Book Co., 1944), 157–58.

117. *Ibid.*, 158.

118. Avishai Margalit, *The Decent Society*, trans. Naomi Goldblum (Cambridge: Harvard University Press, 1996), 1.

119. *Ibid.*, 48–49.

120. Uphaus, 150.

121. Ephraim S. London, "Heresy and the Illinois Bar: The Application of George Anastaplo for Admission," *Lawyers Guild Review* 12 (Fall 1952), 169.

122. *Wilkinson v. United States*, 272 F. 2d 783, 785 (1959).

123. Bentley, 822.

124. Gordon Rupp, *Thomas More* (London: Collins, 1978), 58.

125. *Elfbrandt v. Russell*, 381 P. 2d 554, 563 (1963).

126. *West Virginia State Board of Ed. v. Barnette*, 646.

127. *Stanley v. Georgia*, 394 U.S. 557, 565 (1969).

128. *Ibid.*, 564.

129. Epictetus, *Discourses and Enchiridion*, trans. Thomas W. Higginson (New York: Walter J. Black, 1944), 6.

130. Samuel D. Warren and Louis D. Brandeis, "The Right of Privacy," *Harvard Law Review* 4 (December 1890), 198.

131. *Ibid.*

132. Martin Luther King, Jr., "Letter from Birmingham Jail," in Martin Luther King, Jr., *Why We Can't Wait* (New York: Mentor, 1964), 82.

133. *Griswold v. Connecticut*, 381 U.S. 479, 484 (1965).

Index

About the Author

Haig Bosmajian is Professor in the Department of Speech Communication at the University of Washington, Seattle. Among his many books and publications are *Metaphor and Reason in Judicial Opinions* and *The Language of Oppression* for which he received the NCTE's George Orwell Award. In 1991, he was selected for the Western States Communication Association's Bicentennial of the Bill of Rights Award for "scholarship in the defense of freedom of speech and other rights."